Locating US Theological Education in a Global Context

Locating US Theological Education in a Global Context

Conversations with American Higher Education

Edited by
HENDRIK R. PIETERSE

☙PICKWICK *Publications* • Eugene, Oregon

LOCATING US THEOLOGICAL EDUCATION
IN A GLOBAL CONTEXT
Conversations with American Higher Education

Copyright © 2019 Wipf and Stock Publishers. All rights reserved. Except for brief quotations in critical publications or reviews, no part of this book may be reproduced in any manner without prior written permission from the publisher. Write: Permissions, Wipf and Stock Publishers, 199 W. 8th Ave., Suite 3, Eugene, OR 97401.

Pickwick Publications
An Imprint of Wipf and Stock Publishers
199 W. 8th Ave., Suite 3
Eugene, OR 97401

www.wipfandstock.com

PAPERBACK ISBN: 978-1-5326-1886-4
HARDCOVER ISBN: 978-1-4982-4470-1
EBOOK ISBN: 978-1-4982-4469-5

Cataloguing-in-Publication data:

Names: Pieterse, Hendrik R., editor.

Title: Locating US theological education in a global context : conversations with American higher education / edited by Hendrik R. Pieterse.

Description: Eugene, OR : Pickwick Publications, 2019 | Includes bibliographical references.

Identifiers: ISBN 978-1-5326-1886-4 (paperback) | ISBN 978-1-4982-4470-1 (hardcover) | ISBN 978-1-4982-4469-5 (ebook)

Subjects: LCSH: Theology—Study and teaching—United States. | Theology—Study and teaching. | Education and globalization. | Religion—Study and teaching.

Classification: BV4020 .L59 2019 (paperback) | BV4020 .L59 (ebook)

Manufactured in the USA.   07/18/19

Contents

Acknowledgments | vii
Contributors | ix
Introduction | xi
  —Hendrik R. Pieterse

1 Internationalizing Theological Education? Musings on a Neglected Concept | 1
  —Hendrik R. Pieterse

2 Global Politics of Knowledge and US Theological Education: From Globalization to Planetarization | 23
  —Namsoon Kang

3 Globalization and Global Theological Education: Learning to Navigate the World of Creative Destruction | 44
  —Brent Waters

4 Globalizing the Campus: Implications for Theological Schools | 57
  —Luis R. Rivera

5 Church Affiliation and Higher Education in a Secularizing World: Insights and Questions for Theological Education | 81
  —E. Byron Anderson

6 The Glocalization of Theological Education: A Roman Catholic Perspective | 107
  —Margaret Eletta Guider, OSF

7 "Made in the USA": A Chinese Perspective on US Theological Education in Light of the Chinese Context | 134
  —K. K. Yeo

8 From "Globalization" to "Global Awareness and Engagement": Perspectives, Challenges, Futures | 158
  —Lester Edwin J. Ruiz and David Esterline

Acknowledgments

A NUMBER OF PEOPLE deserve thanks for making this project possible. A first word of gratitude goes to the contributors to this volume. Their dedication, collegiality, and friendship made this project a joy. Their depth of knowledge and breadth of experience in theological and higher education made it stimulating and rewarding.

I thank Dr. Lallene Rector, President of Garrett-Evangelical Theological Seminary, for her keen interest in and gracious support throughout our work. A special word of gratitude to my colleague Brent Waters, Director of the Jerre L. and Mary Joy Stead Center for Ethics and Values at Garrett-Evangelical Theological Seminary, for providing the financial support for the project. Without the Center's generosity, our working sessions and the publication of this volume would not have happened.

Finally, a sincere word of thanks to Mr. Toar Hutagalung, PhD student in theology and ethics at the seminary, for preparing the manuscript for publication. I greatly appreciate his attention to detail, expert skill, good humor and, above all, patience with the editor.

Hendrik R. Pieterse

Contributors

E. Byron Anderson, Ernest and Bernice Styberg Professor of Worship, Garrett-Evangelical Theological Seminary, Evanston, Illinois.

David Esterline, President and Professor of Cross-Cultural Theological Education, Pittsburgh Theological Seminary, Pittsburgh, Pennsylvania.

Margaret Eletta Guider, Associate Professor of Missiology, Boston College School of Theology and Ministry, Brighton, Massachusetts.

Namsoon Kang, Professor of Theology and Religion, Brite Divinity School, Texas Christian University, Fort Worth, Texas.

Hendrik R. Pieterse, Associate Professor of Global Christianity and Intercultural Theology, Garrett-Evangelical Theological Seminary, Evanston, Illinois.

Luis R. Rivera, Vice President for Academic Affairs and Academic Dean, Garrett-Evangelical Theological Seminary, Evanston, Illinois.

Lester Edwin J. Ruiz, Director of Accreditation and Global Engagement, Association of Theological Schools in the United States and Canada, Pittsburgh, Pennsylvania.

Brent Waters, Jerre and Mary Joy Stead Professor of Christian Social Ethics, Garrett-Evangelical Theological Seminary, Evanston, Illinois.

K. K. Yeo, Harry R. Kendall Professor of New Testament, Garrett-Evangelical Theological Seminary, Evanston, Illinois.

Introduction

Hendrik R. Pieterse

It is safe to say that US theological education finds itself in untested circumstances today—a state of affairs Association of Theological Schools (ATS) past executive director Daniel Aleshire describes as a "wilderness" experience in which "old practices and ways have dissipated, and new ones have not yet emerged in a stable form."[1] Given a rapidly emerging multicultural and multiracial US context, not to mention the impress of a Christian church now truly global, theological schools, he says, will need to learn to "live with the gifts and complexities of multiracial and multiethnic Christianity instead of talking about it theoretically." Yet he worries that many theological schools lack the requisite interpretive skills to negotiate these sweeping changes effectively. Impeding this process of skill-building for creative adaptation to these external realities, laments Aleshire, are forces of resistance internal to theological schools (sizable endowments, tenured faculty, treasured institutional heritages or identities to protect, etc.). The result is often an incremental and gradualist approach to change ill-suited for a rapidly changing environment[2]—an environment, we would add, that is increasingly globally interconnected and configured.

In some respects, Aleshire's worries are surprising, given ATS's decades-long conversation about "globalization" of theological education, the challenges of ecumenical and religious pluralism, and race, ethnicity, and gender as factors shaping the nature, scope, and delivery of theological education. Indeed, one might plausibly read the ATS conversation as a

---

1. Aleshire, "Promise," 1.
2. Aleshire, "Future of Theological Education," 381–83.

treasure trove of insight, prescription, and practice into what is commonly known as "internationalization at home"—efforts to incorporate international, intercultural, and global perspectives and skills into every aspect of the institution's life, from mission statements to curriculum to cross-border partnerships to student and faculty diversity.[3]

Yet, one might also read Aleshire's concerns as gesturing toward a larger question: With the ecology of global theological education growing increasingly salient, in fact taking on features of something like an intertwined and multivalent shared educational space, how do US theological institutions "locate" themselves amid these changes so as to be both *responsible participants* and *creative shapers* within it? One way to interpret Aleshire's worries is that the earlier debates, wide-ranging and rich as they were, left lacunae, questions, and issues yet to be addressed fully, or at least demanding fresh inquiry in order to guide US theological institutions in discerning their proper place and role within this emerging global theological environment today.

It is precisely the nature, scope, and dynamics of this work of institutional discernment that this book seeks to explore. The contributions in this volume proceed on the assumption that, in this work of discerning their place within an emerging global ecology of theological education, US theological schools have much to gain from a sustained conversation with the substantial research on the internationalization of American higher education. As a species of higher education, theological education is subject to similar changes, pressures, pitfalls, and opportunities. Indeed, one might plausibly contend that the decades-long debates over internationalization of American higher education, and the trajectories, strategies, and activities American colleges and universities are pursuing in response, can be seen as efforts to "locate" American higher education in an increasingly global higher education space so as to be competitive and effective. Thus, we suggest, this robust body of higher education research can provide theological educators with crucial perspectives as well as conceptual, methodological, and practical resources in navigating the volatile twenty-first-century context of teaching and learning. To this end, the higher education literature functions as the conversational context within which the essays that follow explore pertinent themes, challenges, and trajectories confronting US theological seminaries in a globalizing context.

---

3. Altbach, et al., *Trends*, 2.

The literature exploring the internationalization of American higher education is immense (spanning decades of discourse and debate reaching back at least half a century), not to mention breathtakingly wide-reaching and comprehensive in topic and research. Our engagement with this corpus is thus necessarily selective (but, we trust, not tendentious), connecting with themes that can illuminate, expand, and even correct corresponding concerns in US theological education. We trust that our reflections will stimulate further research into related topics in the literature that our contributions note but do not develop. Some of these topics include: teaching for global citizenship, the economics/funding of global engagement, the complexities of cross-border education (twinning, branch campuses, for-profit providers), and more.

"LOCATING" US THEOLOGICAL EDUCATION

The concern with properly "locating" US theological education within a global theological education environment is a framing theme in the book. Directly or indirectly, explicitly or implicitly, all the essays address the question of the appropriate locus and rightful role of US theological institutions in a world church. "Locus" and "role" highlight two key meanings in our use of the term *locate*.

Locating as "Place"

The first meaning has to do with US theological education's *place* in the larger whole of global theological education—its geographical, political, theological, and moral location. As such, the term attends to the geopolitical forces past and present, the normative theological narratives, and the constitutive practices that occasioned and still undergird that location, while simultaneously registering the theological and moral contestation surrounding it. A key resource in these debates is the constellation of discourses associated with the term *globalization*. Indeed, as this book also attests, globalization has become as indispensable to locating US theological education as its meanings and application are contested.

All of the contributions to this volume engage the globalization literature in various ways and accents and to different ends, with the concept featuring prominently as an object of analysis in the essays by Hendrik

Pieterse, Namsoon Kang, Brent Waters, Margaret Guider, E. Byron Anderson, and Lester Ruiz and David Esterline.

Drawing on debates on *internationalization* in the higher education literature, Pieterse recommends a retrieval of the term as an analytic, methodological, and conceptual tool in thinking through the rationale, motives, and means of global engagement on the part of US theological institutions. Waters counsels US theological educators to welcome the "creative-destructive" forces of globalization as empirical context and catalyst for innovation. Fundamental redefinitions of individual identities prompted by the global market state ("chosen and shared" identities replacing "given" or "accidental" identities) and loyalties ("multiple and crisscrossing loyalties" displacing loyalties to nation and citizen) requires that US theological schools fundamentally rethink *what* and *how* they teach. For Kang, postcolonial discourse allows theological educators to understand both the "bright and dark" sides of globalization: the US-centrism of the global theological education structure (especially in the use of English), the dominance of Western epistemology in knowledge construction and dissemination, and uses of power that sublimate nondominant discourses. What is needed is a new "interiority"—a new way of seeing and reading the world that manifests in an ethic of planetary responsibility and planetary hospitality.

Guider uses the global-local dynamic in globalization to argue for the "glocalization" of US Catholic theological education in the service of Catholic identity, diversity, and internationalization. A glocalized theological education holds three processes in creative tension in student formation and moral disposition—commitment to ecclesial identity, honoring local needs, and fostering an ecumenical, world-church, consciousness—while maintaining the formative needs of students as a "non-negotiable priority."

Anderson addresses similar topics in his essay, but with Protestant universities and theological schools in mind. He provides an in-depth analysis of the ways in which church-related Protestant universities and colleges are renegotiating that relationship in face of growing national and global competition for students and resources, expanding cultural and religious campus diversity, and denominational decline. For Anderson, these higher education debates bear directly on discussions about globalization of theological education. He uses Robert Benne's taxonomy of church affiliation to argue this claim, detailing correlations, implications, and lines of inquiry crucial for the theological education conversation.

Ruiz and Esterline explain and interpret the significance of the shift from "globalization" to "global awareness and engagement" in more recent ATS discourse. Dissatisfaction with the concept of globalization stems from its attachment to Western universalizing knowledge regimes and subsequent devaluing of alternative ways of thinking and doing. A more fulsome definition is needed, which stresses "relational, dialogical, and personal sensibilities" and opens up the "less-visible, religio-moral character of global awareness and engagement." They then show how this richer definition can shape and support effective global partnerships among theological schools, centered in personal relationships, dialogue and conversation, mutuality, and reciprocity—modeled in the ATS-supported Global Forum of Theological Educators (GFTE).

Locating as "Role"

A second meaning of the term *locate* has to do with how US theological schools participate—how they perceive and practice their *role*—in the emerging global ecology of theological education. Understanding one's proper role within a system requires self-critical awareness of one's strengths and limitations, one's contributions and needs, and one's relative power and influence vis-à-vis others. And such critical awareness bears directly on the *means* one employs in fulfilling this role—the practices and patterns that structure relationships and engagement with others in the system. What practices and patterns regulate relationships and engagement between US theological institutions and their counterparts elsewhere? Do US theological institutions still practice one-way, "export" patterns of international engagement? Or are new, more reciprocal, modes emerging? How might efforts to incorporate global concerns into curriculum and campus life and to cultivate intercultural competence among faculty, students, and staff on US seminary campuses function as means toward greater openness and receptivity to contributions of the global church?

These concerns reverberate throughout the essays, and become the focus of K. K. Yeo's contribution. Drawing on his years-long involvement with theological education in both the US and China, Yeo confronts US theological education with a "Made in the USA" mentality that still persists in many US seminaries. This model, he says, encourages a one-way, "export" mode of engagement, when what is needed is a new model based in friendship, reciprocity, partnership, and mutual exchange of gifts. In such a model, US and Chinese theological institutions can serve as "midwives" and "surrogates" to one another.

As alluded to above, US theological schools locate themselves not only in understanding their role in the global church "out there" but also in the global church "right here," in their neighborhoods and on their campuses. Here, "role" is expanded and deepened. US theological institutions participate most fully when they not only *relate to* but *reflect* the struggles, concerns, and gifts of the global church in their mission, curriculum, faculty, student body, and institutional life. This is what we referred to earlier as "internationalization at home." The discipline of incorporating international, intercultural, and global perspectives and skills into every aspect of a seminary's life cultivates greater openness, hospitality, receptivity, and solidarity in relationship, collaboration, and learning. Even a cursory perusal will register these concerns as salient features of all the contributions in this volume. One thinks of the various analyses of ATS's shift from "globalization" to "global awareness and engagement" in the essays by Pieterse, Ruiz and Esterline, and Luis Rivera. While not using the language per se, these themes are pertinent in Yeo's and Anderson's contributions as well.

The special merit of Rivera's essay is that he connects the ATS commitment to "global awareness and engagement" with the extensive higher education discourse and initiatives in internationalizing the home campus, sometimes called "comprehensive internationalization." For him, these higher education debates and experiments offer theological institutions' own globalizing efforts a trove of insights and cautionary tales in crucial areas like the following: curriculum and program design, student assessment, faculty development, budget, and global learning as pedagogical and institutional priority. Drawing on three programs by the American Council of Education, Rivera unpacks in detail theoretical, administrative, pedagogical, and practical resources for US theological schools in their pursuit of "global awareness and engagement."

US theological schools, this book asserts, will be unable to participate fully in a global church if they do not attend self-critically to their "location"—their distinctive place and role—in this emerging ecology of teaching and learning. Transformative participation requires a role that *embodies*, *facilitates*, and *practices* openness, receptivity, mutual responsibility, and a giving and receiving of gifts. It is our hope that the essays below provide resources in navigating the complexities, demands, joys, and possibilities of this task.

BIBLIOGRAPHY

Aleshire, Daniel O. "The Future of Theological Education: A Speculative Glimpse at 2032." *Dialog: A Journal of Theology* 30.4 (2011) 381–83.
———. "Promise: A Faithful Future for Theological Education." Schaff Lectures, Pittsburgh Theological Seminary, March 17, 2010.
Altbach, Philip, et al. *Trends in Global Higher Education: Tracking an Academic Revolution*. Paris: UNESCO, 2009.

1

Internationalizing Theological Education?

Musings on a Neglected Concept

HENDRIK R. PIETERSE

OVER THE PAST TWO decades, the concept *internationalization* has become a central feature of debates over the purpose, place, and role of American higher education in an increasingly global higher education context. Indeed, concern with internationalization has moved from a marginal activity in most American universities to an institutional imperative, driving mission, strategic planning, and educational policy. In fact, the drive to internationalize has become a global phenomenon. Observes prominent scholar Philip Altbach: "The phenomenon [of internationalization] is apparent at all levels of the higher education enterprise around the world, affecting individual institutions, regions within countries, and national systems of higher education."[1]

---

1. Altbach et al., *Trends*, 27. For example, a recent survey of 1,336 higher education institutions in 131 countries, representing every region of the world, indicates that 53 percent of institutions report having an institutional policy or strategy in place, with a further 22 percent in the process of preparing such strategies or policies; and, significantly, 16 percent report that internationalization is integrated into the overall institutional strategy of the university. See Egron-Polak and Hudson, *Internationalization of Higher Education*, 8.

The salience of *internationalization* in higher education discourse stands in sharp contrast to the fate of the term in debates over globalization of US theological education during the same period. In the latter conversation, sponsored by the Association of Theological Schools (ATS), the term was jettisoned early in favor of the concept *globalization* to articulate the purpose, place, and role of US theological schools in a global church. This decision, I argue below, was unfortunate. As the higher education literature shows, *internationalization* has turned out to be an extraordinarily fecund concept in clarifying, correcting, and implementing institutional purpose, policy, and program in a globalizing education environment. This literature, I suggest, is more relevant than ever to the US theological education discussion today. As their engagement and commerce with theological institutions worldwide continue to grow more frequent and more fraught, US theological educators would do well to mine the higher education literature for insights, lessons, and cautionary tales. To make good on this assertion, I proceed as follows: I begin with a brief review of the ATS discussion on globalization of theological education, showing how the decision to abandon internationalization as a framework of analysis created methodological aporias and conceptual confusion that impaired mutual understanding and slowed progress. Then, turning to the higher education literature, I explore the benefits of a critical retrieval of the concept of *internationalization* for theological uses. The chief benefit, I suggest, is engagement with a mature conceptual and methodological repertoire for constructing, assessing, and implementing institutional rationale, strategy, and responsibility in international outreach. I illustrate this benefit by briefly exploring insights, lessons, and cautions relative to two dimensions of theological education: the relationship between the global and the local, and the question of motive, rationale, and value in "going global."[2] As I hope to show, in both cases, theological educators have much to gain from the longstanding, vigorous debates on the part of their higher education colleagues.

GLOBALIZING THEOLOGICAL EDUCATION: THE ATS CONVERSATION

I begin with an analysis of relevant themes in the ATS-sponsored conversation during the 1980s and 1990s on the globalization of US theological

---

2. I borrow this phrase from the title of the recent book by Stiasny and Gore, *Going Global*.

education. It is surely indisputable that this multi-year effort is the most sustained and representative conversation about US theological education in a global context yet undertaken.

The centrality of *internationalization* as a concern in American higher education contrasts sharply with its near-absence in the ATS discussion, where it was jettisoned early in favor, eventually, of the term *globalization*. The latter choice bespeaks perceptions among participants that nation states were increasingly unstable entities and that the term *internationalization* would mask these changing fortunes. Moreover, for some, "internationalization" provided implicit comfort to economic globalization as a hegemonic Western enterprise.[3] Ironically, as it turned out, the term *globalization*, a non-theological construct, was employed primarily to describe a *theological* undertaking—a set of convictions and activities preparing US theological schools to "be active partners, doing theology and preparing people for ministry in an awareness of the new global context."[4] This effort crystalized out in four distinct approaches, as Don Browning showed in his influential essay. For some, globalization meant evangelism; for others ecumenism; for yet others, it signified interreligious dialogue; while a fourth group pressed the term in service of themes central to liberation theology—poverty, social and political oppression, and economic injustice (the latter framing arguably the most salient in ATS circles at the time).[5]

The choice to cast globalization as a theological project had wide-reaching impact. I begin with some conceptual and methodological consequences. One unfortunate result of the conflation of globalization with theological initiative was that it obstructed explicit and systematic analysis of relevant globalizing political, economic, technological, and other forces *on their own terms*. This meant that participants' varied perceptions of and misgivings about these globalizing realities did their work under the surface of the theological debates, contributing perhaps unwittingly to the intensity of the fault lines between the four approaches. Largely missing was a conceptual mechanism for negotiating the important distinction between globalization as a social, political, economic, and political process,

---

3. Aleshire, "Words and Deeds," 28. Fumitaka Matsuoka suggests that "though not clearly articulated in the inception of the 'globalization' discussion among ATS schools, the uneasy feelings about the effects of the emerging globalized economic, military, and technological/communication forces existed as a powerful subcurrent beneath of conversations" (Matsuoka, "Changing Terrain," 21).

4. Lesher and Shriver, "Stumbling," 9.

5. Browning, "Globalization," 43–44.

on the one hand, and theological construction as interpretive appropriation of analyses of this process, on the other. Thus, consideration of the full force and implications of these non-theological factors for global theological education, considered on their own terms, remained aspiration more than reality. Examples are not hard to find. Daniel Aleshire observes that each of Browning's four definitions was not only theologically but also ideologically driven, resulting in "different, even opposing meanings."[6] By "ideological," I take him to refer to the implicit, perhaps in some cases, tacit, appropriation of globalization theories or aspects of them. He adds that while the motivation for globalizing US theological education was to "de-parochialize theological education . . . the trajectory of this de-parochializing was undefined, and schools did not agree on what was to replace the earlier Euro-American theological order."[7] Likewise, Fumitaka Matsuoka notes that "the emerging concerns of economic, military, and technological globalization" in fact functioned as a powerful "subcurrent" beneath the ATS debates, even as it failed to achieve clear conceptual articulation, at least early on.[8] Furthermore, when theories of globalization or elements of them did show up in ATS conversations, they did so in a piecemeal, ad hoc fashion, and then largely to support a particular perspective or to criticize another. The upshot was that while overall the conversation "stumbled in the right direction" (to use Lesher and Shriver's felicitous phrase), momentum was lost in articulating conceptual clarifications and methodological frameworks crucial to fulsome theological constructions of US theological education's concern for global engagement. It is remarkable to find that, a decade into the conversation, Mark Heim, while arguing persuasively for the importance of social analysis for theological reflection on globalization, acknowledged that a coherent process for such a systematic approach remains an aspiration.[9]

That said, during the 1990s, ATS participants did take a major step in separating secular globalization discourse and theological construction by dropping the use of *globalization* as a noun and instead referring to theological institutions' globalizing efforts as "responses to globalization"

6. Daniel Aleshire remarks: "Each [of Browning's four definitions] is theologically and ideologically driven. They are not different shades of meaning of a broad construct—they represent fundamentally different, even opposing meanings" (Aleshire, "Words and Deeds," 29).

7. Aleshire, "Words and Deeds," 28.

8. Matsuoka, "Changing Terrain," 20–21.

9. Heim, "Mapping Globalization," 7–34.

or "global activities." The revised accreditation standards and more recent documents employ the language of "global awareness and engagement."[10]

This distinction between globalization as *process* and educational innovations as *responses* is a welcome clarification. As I will argue later, in this respect theological educators have much to learn from their higher education colleagues, who have retained the term *internationalization* as a conceptual tool for clarifying this distinction and sorting out the relevant respects in which globalization impinges upon the nature, forms, and practices of higher education.

Clarifying such a conceptual and methodological infrastructure for US theological education is especially important today, as awareness and experience of "global" Christianity become more salient through increasing cross-border educational partnerships, growing international enrollment, student and faculty exchange, and the like, not to mention the urgent questions facing us all in training leaders in and for this global body—a reality given empirical grounding in the recent global survey on theological education, conducted by David Esterline and his colleagues.[11] How US theological educators respond to this intellectual task will surely affect how US theological education "locates" itself within this emerging global ecology of leadership formation.

The discussion thus far prompts a second theme, namely, the aims, rationale, and hoped-for outcomes of globalizing US theological education. The question "Why globalize?" invokes a cluster of related concepts, principally how "global" should be conceived and, consequently, how to understand the dynamic between the global and the local. Such considerations are critical in discerning the place, role, and responsibilities of US theological education in a global church.

As may already be clear, questions about rationale, the global and the local, and the meaning and nature of the global arose early in the ATS conversations. Indeed, the four approaches summarized in Browning's typology are instances of how these questions were negotiated and incorporated into various proposals early on. And, as the conversation progressed over the decades, one notices a deepening and sharpening of analysis, as scholars complexified their theological proposals with considerations of gospel and culture, mission, contextualization, and the ecumenical. Indeed, we witness thoughtful casting about for suitable theological constructions of "global,"

10. ATS, "Global Awareness."
11. Esterline et al., "Global Survey."

fresh considerations of the ecumenical and the universal, and creative efforts to rethink the global-local dynamic in the language of catholicity and context. One thinks here of seminal essays by scholars like Donald Shriver, Francis Cardinal Arinze, David Schuller, Robert Schreiter, Max Stackhouse, Fumitaka Matsuoka, and Mark Heim, and especially the important issue on the Bossey Institute.[12]

And yet, the theological fault lines, evidenced in Browning's typology, also created challenges for a fulsome engagement with these questions. So, for example, the term *ecumenism* was abandoned early on as a framing concept for the ATS discussion, a casualty of the "evangelical-liberal split" within the community, thus depriving the conversation of a fertile theological category. Reflecting on these early discussions, Lesher and Shriver observe wryly: "In turning to 'globalization,' we let the secular world economic system name the project and so gave witness to the unity-disunity that plagues churches and seminaries in the late twentieth century."[13] Lesher and Shriver's observation captures the ambivalence early on about employing a non-theological term (*globalization*) to do theological work, for which it appears ill suited. And the reduction of globalization to global economic modalities in these early debates perhaps also helps illuminate the checkered, uneven, at times even tendentious, engagement with globalization theories and constructs as the project wore on.

Our review thus far, I believe, illustrates the need for greater conceptual precision and dexterity in putting the wide-ranging and multidisciplinary discourses of globalization to use in theological education. To this end, theological educators have much to gain from the experience of their higher education colleagues. Their half-century of reflection has yielded concepts, definitions, and meanings of terms like *globalization, global*, and *local* that are finely honed and contextualized for precise application to the work of higher education in a global context. I offer a couple of examples later in the chapter.

Perhaps the principal way in which the ATS conversation engaged scholars outside the United States in their discussion of globalizing theological education was through the formation of the World Conference of Associations of Theological Schools (WOCATI) in 1989, undertaken in collaboration with the World Council of Churches (WCC), and including a wide variety of regional associations of theological schools from around the

---

12. ATS, *Theological Education* 34.s
13. Lesher and Shriver, "Stumbling," 3.

world. The intent was to construct a "global forum for discussion of issues related to worldwide theological education." Glenn Miller considers the establishment of WOCATI "as perhaps the most important consequence of the [ATS] globalization movement," while noting the limited engagement with the World Council of Churches up to that time, citing the theological fault lines we have discussed earlier.[14] Indeed, Miller sees the value of WOCATI as yet to be realized:

> WOCATI's greatest service to American theological education may lie in the future. American religion, especially American Mainstream Protestantism, is changing rapidly, and these changes may require substantial changes in how the United States educates its ministers.... Just as America provided much of the world with the model of the graduate theological seminary, so the rest of the world may provide American Christians with fresh understandings and strategies of how to train their ministry.[15]

Miller may well be prescient. He is surely right to envision a global system that eschews the center-periphery, one-way flow of theological education resources from the West to the Rest, customary for too long. His reference to "understandings" and "strategies" points to two challenges that need attention for this prognostication to find realization, however, namely, vision and infrastructure. What conceptual, theological, and methodological questions arise in contemplating a global vision for theological education? Is such a vision even feasible, let alone appropriate? And what kind of institutional infrastructure would be adequate for implementing such a vision? Do the requisite global institutions already exist? Would WOCATI be up to the task? What about national or regional institutions for curating the myriad conceptual and practical challenges between the "global" and the "local"? Could ATS serve this function for US theological education? As by far the largest and most representative entity for US theological educators and schools, ATS is certainly well positioned to do so. Yet, current realities about both WOCATI and ATS provide clues to some of the difficulties involved. One difficulty is structural. ATS admits that its engagement with WOCATI is changing, given the shifts in membership in the two organizations. To wit, ATS is now largely dominated by Evangelical and Roman Catholic schools, while WOCATI, given its close association with the World Council of Churches, remains tethered to Mainline Protestantism.

14. Miller, *Piety and Plurality*, 297.
15. Miller, *Piety and Plurality*, 298.

Moreover, according to ATS, its membership (largely Evangelical Protestant and Roman Catholic) mirrors theological education outside North America, with Evangelical Protestant schools "perhaps even constituting the majority of Protestant theological schools in the majority world."[16] Such perceptions likely don't bode well for close theological collaboration and exchange. A second difficulty relates to institutional mission. A recent document outlining ATS's plans for "global awareness and engagement" consists largely of strategic initiatives. This preoccupation with activity, strategy, and program is surely understandable, given ATS's fundamental role as an accreditation agency. At the same time, as higher education scholars have discovered, *instrumental* approaches risk mistaking *means* for *ends*, thus obscuring critical scrutiny of the motives, rationale, and values that drive institutional efforts to internationalize. Instead, as we will note, they are calling for a return to fundamental questions of "why" internationalization—questions of rationale, outcomes, values. Indeed, an important stimulus behind the steady call for renewed focus on motives, goals, and ends is alarm at the increasing instrumentalizing and commodification of knowledge under the pressures of a globalizing "knowledge economy." This trend, many higher education scholars worry, impairs proper cultivation of higher education's humanitarian and ethical goals.[17]

If US theological institutions are going to discern their proper place, role, and contribution in an emerging global church, then the substantive streams of reflection on global theological education (such as those of the WCC and WOCATI) must be linked *organically*. Episodic and ad hoc engagement, or settling for strategic initiatives or instrumental aims, is no longer adequate. What we need is the cultivation of a shared framework for debating the above-mentioned matters of vision and infrastructure in theological education as a global enterprise.[18] Just on this point, we might do well to pay attention to the higher education debate. Here one discovers a remarkable consensus, not in perspective or ideology *but rather in the subject matter, discourses, methods, and at times even definitions, that should frame the debate*. So, for example, terms like *internationalization* and

16. ATS, "Global Awareness."
17. IAU, "Affirming Values," 1–5.
18. The recently published Werner et al., *Handbook of Theological Education*, illustrates the scope of the challenge. On the one hand, it is an extraordinarily rich survey of the state and practice of ministerial formation around the world. On the other hand, one is hard pressed to find a common vocabulary or a set of shared framing convictions in interpreting global theological education.

globalization are taken-for-granted fare. And some definitions, such as Jane Knight and Philip Altbach's casting of the relationship between *internationalization* and *globalization*,[19] have become influential enough to serve as shared constructs within widely diverging perspectives. Indeed, it is just this shared conceptual and analytic repertoire that enables and sustains the robustness and creativity among our higher education colleagues. In the remainder of the chapter, I highlight insights from this hard-won dialogue I find particularly helpful for theological education.

INTERNATIONALIZATION AND GLOBALIZATION: CAUTIONARY TALES, INSIGHTS, AND RESOURCES

In this final section, then, I set our conversation thus far alongside the longstanding debates about internationalization of American higher education. As noted at the outset of the chapter, I focus on two themes I find particularly useful for fruitful exchange in our ongoing reflection on US theological education in a global context. These two themes center around the concept *internationalization* as interpretive construct in (1) illuminating the nature and meaning of *the local and the global* in internationalizing higher education, and (2) critiquing and reformulating *the rationale, aims, and values* in educating beyond borders—to wit, contextualization and mission, respectively. My intent is not to recommend direct correlations or ready-made prescriptions. Rather, I wish to highlight insights and cautionary tales that might assist a critical retrieval of the term *internationalization* and its supporting concepts for theological uses.

Internationalization and Globalization

The career of the concept *internationalization* in higher education debates over the course of the twentieth century is instructive. From the start, political motives and national security concerns were important drivers of US international education, reaching their apex during the Cold War. As Hans de Wit and Gilbert Merkx note, during this period "the international dimension of higher education moved from incidental and individual into organized activities, projects, and programs, based mainly on political rationales and driven more by national governments than by higher

---

19. Altbach and Knight, "Internationalization of Higher Education," 290–305.

education itself." Notable events include establishment of the Fulbright scholarship program, rapid increase in international student enrollment, and the growth of area studies.[20] Following the fall of the Soviet Union in 1989, and with the rise of a global knowledge economy, competitiveness became the chief rationale for internationalization, forcing higher education to navigate the perils and promise of an emerging market society.

This entanglement of American higher education with national interest, political motive, and economic competition may simply affirm the wisdom of discarding *internationalization* as a useful construct for theological education. However, I would argue that quite the reverse might be the case. Retrieving this term for our conversations about US theological education, especially at a juncture of increasing global engagement, can serve an important critical function. First, it stands as a steady reminder that efforts to globalize theological education, too, are always already entangled with disparate cultural, national, economic, and political interests. For this reason, analysis of these realities must be *constitutive* elements of any theological account of global theological education fit for our times. As such, scholars must be explicit about how and what kind of work discourses on globalization do in their theological education proposals. To this end, theological educators will encounter in the higher education literature an impressive body of critical and constructive resources. Higher education theorist Felix Maringe, for example, offers a penetrating analysis of the attitudes toward and the understanding and uses of "internationalization" and "globalization" in the 2009 World Survey of the Impact of Globalization in Universities Project. Employing world-systems, world polity, world culture, and neoliberal theories of globalization as explanatory categories, he demonstrates convincingly that "how globalization is understood will influence the nature of internationalization activity in different universities."[21] Maringe's project is instructive in showing the powerful shaping—and distorting—effects when assumptions about globalization are allowed to function as unexamined subcurrents in internationalization efforts. Might a similar project among theological educators (employing, say, the 2013 Global Survey on Theological Education) not only facilitate greater mutual understanding but also shed light on the tethering of the "conservative-liberal split" to differing evaluations of globalization?

---

20. de Wit and Merkx, "History of Internationalization," 49–50, 53.
21. Maringe, "Meanings of Globalization, 17–34.

Second, the history of internationalization cautions us against reductionist accounts of globalization, a matter I noticed in the early ATS discussion, where economic globalization of a certain stripe was foregrounded. Precisely given American higher education's overt if contentious participation in national, political, and security concerns, the term *internationalization* has served as a catalyst for intense and sustained critical scrutiny of the *panoply* of globalization theories on offer—from world culture to world systems to neoliberal to postcolonial to culturalist.[22] The result is a rich literature on globalization's ambiguous and asymmetric yield of benefits and risks and the differential access to and enjoyment of the benefits of internationalization. To wit, on the one hand, improved quality of teaching, learning, and governance, through international cross-pollination of research; intercultural contact; greater access to educational opportunities not available at home; sharing of expertise and knowledge through participation in international/global academic and research networks; and greater mutual accountability and expanding of educational best practices through clearer standards and quality assurance programs.[23] On the other hand, danger of cultural homogenization; the limits to access imposed by the dominance of English; unhealthy tradeoffs with international partners in the frenzy to become globally competitive, especially for resource-poor institutions in countries with fragile economic and educational infrastructures; increasing commodification and commercialization of higher education, the growing global uniformity in curriculum, instruction, and testing, especially with the entry of the World Bank, OECD, and WTO/GATS into the higher education sphere; and brain drain, which diminishes the pool of much-needed talent in developing countries for improving national educational capacity and international competitiveness.[24]

Several higher education theorists, such as Simon Marginson, Peter Scott, and Kumari Beck, have illuminated these differential benefits and risks within analytic frameworks that intentionally engage *multiple* discourses of globalization.[25] The result are much more nuanced and methodologically differentiated accounts, enabling better interdisciplinary reflection, more precise analysis, and improved concrete proposals. Beck, for example,

22. Spring, "Research," 330–63.
23. IAU, "Affirming Values," 2–3.
24. Spring, "Research," 330–63.
25. See, for example, Marginson, "Imagining the Global," 10–39; Scott, "International Higher Education," 16–17; Beck, "Globalization/s," 133–48.

drawing on the work of Arjun Appadurai, develops a notion of internationalization as an "eduscape," which presupposes a theory of globalization not as a singular process but rather as a "complex, multidimensional, and fluid" jostling of various kinds of global "flows." Casting internationalization as an eduscape, says Beck, allows us to analyze the complex, often unpredictable ways in which it intersects with other "scapes": "ethnoscapes," "mediascapes," "finanscapes," and "ideoscapes." Each of these global flows impacts internationalization differently, at different times, and with different results. Such a more complex understanding of globalization (or, better, globalizations), claims Beck, "situates the university in a larger flow of internationalizing forces and elements rather than seeing it as [the] point where activity begins and ends." As such, one is able to appreciate internationalization as itself plural, multiple, multidimensional, and contextual.[26]

As this brief analysis has confirmed, I trust, *internationalization* has proven itself a remarkably fertile concept for analysis and construction—and, as such, a concept worthy of recovery by theological educators. After all, in contemplating US theological institutions' global place and role, we confront the very same challenges as our higher education colleagues. This means, further, that we, too, would be wise to construct and evaluate our international aspirations and activities within accounts of globalization that are both explicit and nonreductionistic. However, theological schools and seminaries face an additional task, namely, to critically incorporate their assumptions about internationalization and globalization into a *theological* account of theological education. In this respect, the earlier ATS conversation was exactly right to raise questions of theological conviction and perspective from the start, even if in a manner that was problematic, as I sought to show. Missiologist Robert Schreiter offers a helpful way to approach this theological task. Providing a theologically appropriate account of globalization, he says, means "finding concepts in theology that globalization can inform but not determine. Theology must be able to interact with globalization theory out of its own internal history and resources and not be simply reactive to it."[27] In this respect, consider, for example, possible theological meanings of the concept *internationalization* in its many uses, as discussed above. As I argued, one strength of the term is that it prompts explicit attention to boundaries, primarily national and international. Crossing national boundaries, however, also involves simul-

---

26. Beck, "Globalization/s," 135, 142.
27. Schreiter, *New Catholicity*, 118.

taneously traversing several other kinds of boundaries—cultural, political, social, linguistic. The salience of such boundary-crossing in its complexity should resonate deeply with Christians. After all, Christian mission is fundamentally a boundary-crossing affair as the gospel finds embodiment in different contexts.[28] How might a missional perspective of this sort provide resources in making the concept *internationalization* fruitful for theological education? Some connections come to mind. Take the rich body of missiological reflection on mission's checkered entanglement with colonial power in its political, economic, and social manifestations. Or consider the profound scholarship in intercultural hermeneutics, seeking to understand the dynamics of meaning creation across cultural boundaries. The insights and cautionary tales emerging from this literature would stand theological educators in good stead as they appropriate the concept of *internationalization* in their work. Such themes were already present in the earlier ATS debates, albeit largely ad hoc and episodically, as we saw. Explicitly retrieving the concept for theological uses prompts sustained systematic reflection. To this end, I suggest, mission studies have much to offer.

The Global and the Local

An important reason for retrieving the concept *internationalization* for theological education is that it offers a useful heuristic in framing the relationship between the global and the local—a key modality in thinking and doing education in a global context. To this end, Philip Altbach has suggested that the terms *internationalization* and *globalization* not be conflated. While closely related, they nevertheless refer to distinct realities. Globalization names "the broad economic, technological, and scientific trends that directly affect higher education and are largely inevitable in the contemporary world." Internationalization, on the other hand, denotes "the specific policies and programs undertaken by governments, academic systems and institutions, and even individual departments to deal with globalization." In other words, internationalization is a *response* to globalization. This distinction, Altbach feels, allows much-needed clarity on the agency, possibilities, and limits of internationalization efforts. As a political, social, economic, and technological process, globalization is beyond the control of any one or even any set of higher education actors, be they institutions, governments, or individuals. However, construed as response,

---

28. For mission as cross-cultural process, see Walls, *Cross-Cultural Process*.

internationalization can denote a "*strategy* for societies and institutions to respond to the many demands placed upon them by globalization and as a way for higher education to prepare individuals for engagement with a globalized world."[29] More precisely, as a strategy, to use Jane Knight's influential definition, internationalization "is the process of integrating an international, intercultural, and global dimension into the purpose, functions (teaching, research, and service), and delivery of higher education at the institutional and national levels."[30] Altbach and Knight summarize this framing of the globalization-internationalization dynamic succinctly: "Globalization may be unalterable, but internationalization involves many choices."[31]

This distinction between globalization and internationalization, while surely in need of nuance and qualification, as we will see below, nevertheless opens a much-needed conceptual and analytical space for attending to the complex logic of global flow and local appropriation of knowledge systems, discourse, products, and programs. To wit, framing globalization as *context* and internationalization as *response* allows more penetrating accounts of institutional agency, namely, how, why, and under what constraints they engage global processes. As Maringe has pointed out, uneven experiences of the benefits and risks of globalization prompt widely diverging valuations of globalization, and thus rationales and strategies for internationalization. Even a cursory perusal of the recent *Handbook of Theological Education in World Christianity*,[32] or the 2013 global survey of theological education noted earlier, reveals similar trends among theological institutions around the world. As missiologist Robert Schreiter has pointed out, global flows always elicit a spectrum of responses he calls "cultural logics," running the gamut of full-scale resistance to uncritical accommodation.[33] For example, many higher education scholars and practitioners outside the West (and many inside) lament what they perceive as all-too-easy accommodation of English as global language of instruction and educational commerce, to the detriment of national and local languages. Alternatively, North-American universities tend to resist preoccupation with revenue generation from international students, while higher education institutions in Africa and

---

29. Altbach et al., *Trends*, 23–24 (emphasis added).
30. Knight, *Higher Education*, xi.
31. Altbach and Knight, "Internationalization of Higher Education," 291.
32. Werner et al., *Handbook of Theological Education*.
33. Schreiter, *New Catholicity*, 14–27.

the Middle East consider brain drain a more important risk.[34] The above-mentioned *Handbook* and global survey would suggest ready correlates for theological training institutions.

Overall, then, the internationalization-globalization dialectic offered above provides theological educators with a trove of conceptual and methodological resources for rethinking what was perhaps too blithe early conflations of globalization as process with theological response, and for constructing theological accounts more capable of capturing the cultural, economic, and political complexity and disparity of institutional response in the emerging global ecumene of theological education. That is, at the methodological level, the process-response dialectic can help secure the relative autonomy of globalization scholarship, on the one hand, and theological construction, on the other. As such, it encourages clearer articulation of why, how, and to what ends a particular globalization discourse is employed in arguments in theological education. Might such a mechanism not enable fresh conceptual resources for addressing the seemingly intractable conservative-liberal split in the theological education debates? Further, might such casting of the global-local dynamic not invite fresh reflection on the dynamics of contextualization of theological education in a global context?

That said, some scholars have critiqued the above distinction as simplistic and potentially distorting. Internationalization is more than a one-way process of incorporating international, intercultural, and global dimensions into a university's mission and practice. Rather, as we already saw in Beck's analysis above, internationalization involves complex engagements with multiple globalizing forces, in the process of which both "globalization" and "internationalization" undergo change. Internationalization and globalization are *mutually shaping* processes, not a one-way activity of causal process and institutional response. Maringe agrees: "Globalization and internationalization [are] mutually reinforcing ideas. . . . Globalization largely provides the external impetus for accelerated institutional internationalization. On the other hand, the intensification of university internationalization activity reinforces accelerated globalization."[35] While by no means invalidating the Albach-Knight distinction, this critique allows more complex descriptions of the dynamics framing the global-local

---

34. See Altbach, *International Imperative*, 1–6; Egron-Polak and Hudson, *Internationalization of Higher Education*, 10.

35. Maringe, "Meanings of Globalization," 17.

dynamic. Indeed, in a recent essay (co-authored with Laura Rumbley), Altbach referred to the global-local intersection as a "crucial nexus" for higher education and illuminated an interesting layer in its complexity. Often neglected in discussions of the global and the local, they aver, is attention to properly trained leadership for effectively negotiating this fraught terrain. Discourses about the "big issues" (national polity, global trends, etc.) and those dealing with "practicalities" (student mobility initiatives, internationalizing the curriculum, etc.) too often happen in isolation. The fact is those charged with connecting these discourses for purposes of institutional strategy, policy, and program need careful training and skill-building to make intelligent and prudent choices.[36] This insight adds an important layer to our discussion of agency. Precisely because "agency" is such a complex and multivalent affair do we need "agents" properly empowered and resourced. Altbach and Rumbley's insight is surely salutary for theological educators also, if we are going to be effective in locating US theological education responsibly and effectively in a global context.

Motives and Rationale for Internationalization

Finally, I note a more recent debate around the need for a global higher education "space" structured by shared commitments and values. A growing chorus of prominent higher education scholars is calling for a reconsideration of the rationale, values, and outcomes proper to internationalization. Noted higher education scholar Jane Knight laments the shift in the meaning and practice of internationalization from "what has traditionally been considered a process based on values of cooperation, partnership, exchange, mutual benefit, and capacity building to one that is increasingly characterized by competition, commercialization, self-interest, and status building." She wonders: "Is internationalization having an identity crisis as to its fundamental values and what drives the process and outcomes?"[37] Similarly, Hans de Wit has suggested that internationalization has been conflated with strategy, program, and activity, thus turning the means into the end.[38] What needs recovery is attention to ends—to "the norms, values, or ethics of internationalization practice."[39] In other words, these scholars insist on

36. Rumbley and Altbach, "Local and Global," 7–13.
37. Knight, "Internationalization," 1.
38. de Wit, "Internationalization of Higher Education," 1–6.
39. de Wit, "Rethinking Concept of Internationalization," 216.

fresh critical scrutiny of the various *motives, rationales, and purposes* higher education providers employ in their global outreach.[40]

Two interrelated aspects of current proposals for addressing internationalization's identity crisis are noteworthy. First, a call for a more critical approach to "ensure that [the process of internationalization] retains its positive and constructive character, especially when implemented across different and highly diverse contexts." A key stimulus for this concern is the consistent reports of unacceptable risk and deleterious impact of internationalization efforts especially on the higher education opportunities of developing nations. To address these disparities, "it is essential," says Eva Egron-Polak, for the global higher education community to "recall, agree upon, reaffirm and articulate the central values and purposes of internationalization of higher education."[41] To this end, the document "Affirming Academic Values in Internationalization of Higher Education: A Call to Action" is a crucial first step in the direction of a normative framework to guide higher education institutions in ensuring their internationalization efforts aim to enlarge the possible benefits and mitigate the potential adverse effects for all involved.[42]

An important backdrop for this debate is the multivalent historical—and, in many ways, continuing—financial, institutional, and curricular dominance of the West in internationalization. In this context, the call for fresh scrutiny of the motives and rationale for internationalizing is salutary. At the very least, it prompts renewed examination of the fraught issue of responsibility. Given their relative wealth and superior resources, do Western higher education institutions have a special responsibility for the global common good? If so, why? And in what should such responsibility consist? Alternatively, how do Western institutions share their considerable gifts without perpetuating paternalizing habits? Moreover, in a higher education environment in which internationalization is fast becoming a global enterprise—from everywhere to everywhere, to invoke a missional phrase—how should *mutual* responsibility be clarified and practiced? In this respect, the "values, principles, and goals" outlined in the document "Affirming Academic Values in Internationalization of Higher Education" offers valuable guidance. Importantly, the document is clear that these values and

---

40. For a fine analysis of the range of rationales for internationalization, see Altbach and Knight, "Internationalization of Higher Education," 290–305.

41. Egron-Polak, "Internationalization of Higher Education," 15.

42. IAU, "Affirming Values," 4.

principles are "neither slogans nor vague abstractions." On the contrary, they should do real work in concrete decision-making about policy and practice: "As institutions develop their internationalization strategies, they should be clear and transparent about why they are undertaking a particular initiative, how it relates to their academic mission and values, and what mechanisms can be put in place to avoid possible negative consequences."[43] Connecting values to specific internationalization rationales is an important step in making responsibility concrete. Responsibility is not all-encompassing or always the same. It is contextual, receiving form and force in specific goals, motives, and actions.

The implications of this discussion for theological education are not hard to find. For one thing, the values, principles, and guidelines for responsible international engagement evince remarkable agreement with those outlined in the recent directive to ATS member institutions, titled "Global Awareness and Engagement Initiative."[44] This guidance is especially important at a juncture when US theological institutions are experiencing increased international commerce in a global church of extraordinary disparity in educational capacity, need, and resources.[45] Like our higher education colleagues, we too confront the question of responsibility and sharing of gifts. How do US theological institutions "locate" themselves responsibly and with integrity in a global church that continues to bear the marks of our past mistakes, missteps, and shortsightedness? How do we participate with humility while avoiding the paralysis of a "Western guilt complex"?[46]

The second aspect of the higher education discussion flows directly from this call to renewed mutual responsibility. It involves calls for an "internationalized" internationalization or a "globalization of internationalization." The central idea is to invite institutions of higher education to envision themselves as part of "an emerging global system of higher education," whose health depends vitally on the responsible participation of each member. Such a systemic understanding would prompt universities and other providers of higher education "to consider whether or not their actions are shaping the kind of global educational system that will advance

---

43. IAU, "Affirming Values," 5.
44. ATS, "Global Awareness."
45. For statistics and analysis, see Esterline et al., "Global Survey."
46. The phrase comes from Lamin Sanneh. See his insightful essay Sanneh, "Christian Missions," 331–34.

and transform higher education as a whole." Indeed, as Susan Sutton and Darla Deardorff aver, an approach to internationalization as a global system would ultimately invite institutions of higher education to engage "as global citizens through partnerships in an authentic dialogue, measuring success in terms of mutual benefit and global action." From the global vantage point, internationalization "becomes a process of increasing synergies among scholars, deepening student and institutional engagement in the world, and creating ever larger networks of discovery, transforming the very nature of higher education itself."[47]

This call for a global system of higher education grounded in parity, partnership, and collaboration is surely a cautionary tale for US theological educators. As the higher education experience has shown, a rapidly expanding global educational "market place" tends to favor economic leverage and competitive advantage at the cost of equity, collaboration, and fair play. And US theological education today, looking increasingly outward for fresh student flows and new income streams, not to mention competitive edge in a shrinking educational market at home, is by no means exempt from this trap. The challenge of constructing the global educational space Sutton and Deardorff envision appears no less daunting for theological institutions.[48]

The higher education call for a vibrant, equitable global educational space, with its attendant challenges, perhaps increases the wisdom of retrieving another concept—the *ecumenical*—sublimated early the ATS conversation. The WCC's "Magna Charta on Ecumenical Formation in Theological Education" speaks eloquently of the need for an educational ecumene shaped by values and virtues genuinely reflective of a global Christian church in all its multicentered and multifaceted plurality of gift and need. This is nothing less than the search for a new ecumenism for theological education as global community of teaching and learning. Robert Schreiter's notion of a "new catholicity," while not directed to theological education per se, is redolent with resources for a new sense of the global for theological education as a global enterprise—a space "marked by a wholeness of inclusion and fullness of faith in a pattern of intercultural exchange

---

47. Sutton and Deardorff, "Internationalizing Internationalization," 17. See also Jones and de Wit, "Globalization of Internationalization," 35–54.

48. For helpful background on this challenge, see Werner, "Theological Education," 92–100; Scharen and Miller, *Bright Spots*.

and communication."[49] And while, as the WCC document reminds us, this educational ecumene remains an "unfinished theological and didactic process,"[50] US theological educators have a rich history to draw on—complete with its own cautionary tales, missteps, and successes—in pursuing this goal. And, as I sought to argue in this essay, in that process of discernment, our higher education colleagues can lend a powerful helping hand.

BIBLIOGRAPHY

Aleshire, Daniel O. "Words and Deeds: An Informal Assessment of Globalization in Theological Schools." *Theological Education* 35.2 (1999) 27–31.

Altbach, Philip G. *The International Imperative in Higher Education*. Rotterdam: Sense, 2013.

Altbach, Philip G., et al. *Trends in Global Higher Education: Tracking an Academic Revolution*. Report Prepared for the UNESCO 2009 Conference on Higher Education. Paris: UNESCO, 2009.

Altbach, Philip G., and Jane Knight. "The Internationalization of Higher Education: Motivations and Realities." *Journal of Studies in International Education* 11.3–4 (2007) 290–305.

Association of Theological Schools (ATS). "Global Awareness and Engagement Initiative." 2013. http://www.ats.edu/resources/current-initiatives/global-awareness-and-engagement-initiative.

———. *Theological Education* 34.s (1997).

Beck, Kumari. "Globalization/s: Reproduction and Resistance in the Internationalization of Higher Education." *Canadian Journal of Education* 35.3 (2012) 133–48.

Browning, Don S. "Globalization and the Task of Theological Education." *Theological Education* 23.1 (1986) 43–59.

de Wit, Hans. "Internationalization of Higher Education: Nine Misconceptions." *International Higher Education* 64 (2011) 9–12.

———. "Rethinking the Concept of Internationalization." In *Going Global: Identifying Trends and Drivers of International Education*, edited by Mary Stiasny and Tim Gore, 213–18. Bingley, UK: Emerald, 2013.

de Wit, Hans, and Gilbert Merkx. "The History of Internationalization of Higher Education." In *The SAGE Handbook of International Higher Education*, edited by Darla K. Deardorff, et al., 43–60. Los Angeles: SAGE, 2012.

Egron-Polak, Evan, and Ross Hudson. *Internationalization of Higher Education: Growing Expectations, Fundamental Values*. IAU 4th Global Survey. Paris: International Association of Universities, 2014.

Esterline, David, et al. "Global Survey on Theological Education 2011–2013: Summary of Main Findings." Presented to the World Council of Churches, tenth assembly, Busan, Korea, October 30–November 8, 2013.

---

49. Schreiter, *New Catholicity*, 132.
50. WCC, "Magna Charta," 5.

Heim, S. Mark. "Mapping Globalization for Theological Education." *Theological Education* 26.s (1990) 7–34.
International Association of Universities (IAU). "Affirming Academic Values in Internationalization of Higher Education: A Call to Action." April 2012. https://www.iau-aiu.net/IMG/pdf/affirming_academic_values_in_internationalization_of_higher_education-3.pdf.
Jones, Elspeth, and Hans de Wit. "Globalization of Internationalization: Thematic and Regional Reflections on a Traditional Concept." *AUDEM: The International Journal of Higher Education and Democracy* 3 (2012) 35–54.
Knight, Jane. *Higher Education in Turmoil: The Changing World of Internationalization.* Rotterdam: Sense, 2008.
———. "Is Internationalization Having an Identity Crisis?" *IMHE Info* 1 (2011) 1.
Lesher, William E., and Donald W. Shriver, Jr. "Stumbling in the Right Direction." *Theological Education* 32.5 (1999) 3–16.
Marginson, Simon. "Imagining the Global." In *Handbook on Globalization and Higher Education*, edited by Roger King, et al., 10–39. Cheltenham, UK: Elgar, 2011.
Maringe, Felix. "The Meanings of Globalization and Internationalization in HE: Findings from a World Survey." In *Globalization and Internationalization in Higher Education: Theoretical, Strategic, and Management Perspectives*, edited by Felix Maringe and Nick Foskett, 17–34. London: Bloomsbury, 2012.
Matsuoka, Fumitaka. "The Changing Terrain of 'Globalization' in ATS Conversations." *Theological Education* 35.2 (1999) 17–25.
Miller, Glenn T. *Piety and Plurality: Theological Education Since 1960.* Eugene, OR: Cascade, 2014.
Rumbley, Laura E., and Philip G. Altbach, "The Local and the Global in Higher Education Internationalization: A Crucial Nexus." In *Global and Local Internationalization*, edited by Elspeth Jones, et al., 7–13. Rotterdam: Sense, 2016.
Sanneh, Lamin. "Christian Missions and the Western Guilt Complex." *The Christian Century*, April 8, 1987, 331–34.
Scharen, Christian, and Sharon Miller. *Bright Spots in Theological Education: Hopeful Stories in a Time of Crisis and Change.* Auburn Studies 22. New York: Auburn Theological Seminary, 2016.
Schreiter, Robert J. *The New Catholicity: Theology between the Global and the Local.* Maryknoll, NY: Orbis, 1995.
Scott, Peter. "International Higher Education and the 'Neo-Liberal Turn.'" *International Higher Education* 84 (2016) 16–17.
Spring, Joel. "Research on Globalization and Education." *Review of Educational Research* 78 (2008) 330–63.
Stiasny, Mary, and Tim Gore, eds. *Going Global: Identifying Trends and Drivers of International Education.* Bingley, UK: Emerald Group, 2013.
Sutton, Susan Buck, and Darla K. Deardorff. "Internationalizing Internationalization: The Global Context." *IAU Horizons* 17.3/18.1 (2012) 16–17.
Walls, Andrew F. *The Cross-Cultural Process in Christian History: Studies in the Transmission and Appropriation of Faith.* Maryknoll, NY: Orbis, 2002.
World Council of Churches (WCC). "Magna Charta on Ecumenical Formation in Theological Education in the Twenty-First Century—10 Key Convictions." N.p.: WCC/ETE, 2008.

Werner, Dietrich. "Theological Education in the Changing Context of World Christianity—An Unfinished Agenda." *International Bulletin of Missionary Research* 35.2 (2011) 92–100.

Werner, Dietrich, et al., eds. *The Handbook of Theological Education in World Christianity: Theological Perspectives, Ecumenical Trends, Regional Surveys.* Oxford: Regnum International, 2010.

2

Global Politics of Knowledge and US Theological Education
From Globalization to Planetarization

Namsoon Kang

"There is no neutral or natural place in teaching."
—Jacques Derrida[1]

"I propose the planet to overwrite the globe. . . .
The globe is in our computers. No one lives there. . . .
The planet is in the species of alterity, belonging to another system;
and yet we inhabit it, on loan."
—Gayatri Chakravorty Spivak[2]

---

1. Derrida, "Where a Teaching Body Begins," 69.
2. Spivak, "Planetarity," 72.

GEOPOLITICAL IMPLICATIONS OF GLOBALIZATION FOR US HIGHER EDUCATION

IN THE TWENTY-FIRST CENTURY, the reality of globalization is unavoidable in terms of the world's economy and politics, not to mention current information and communications technologies. At the same time, the growing hegemonic role of the English language affects the nature, ethos, and climate of the academic institutions worldwide. Globalization has stimulated internationalization activities and programs in universities with its external pressure. The term *internationalization* in higher education became a buzzword, especially after the GATS (General Agreement on Trade in Services) conference in 2003, which seeks to liberalize trade in goods and services not only in industries but also in education. For GATS, higher education is "an international service industry to be regulated through the marketplace and through international trade agreements,"[3] signaling a new trend in higher education worldwide. In this context, "internationalization is changing the world of higher education, and globalization is changing the world of internationalization."[4]

The terms *globalization* and *internationalization* can mean different things in different contexts, and people have used them in different ways. Therefore, one may need to think about working definitions whenever one uses these terms. In addition to thinking about the specific meaning of the terms, one needs to critically reflect on the precise purpose of internationalization of higher education, the benefits one can expect from such internalization of higher education, whose interests it serves, the dark and bright sides of internationalization, and the geopolitical implications of internationalization of US higher education.

A large number of universities and theological schools in the United States are eager to internationalize by establishing academic programs abroad and setting up branch campuses overseas. In this context, globalization and internationalization in higher education reinforce each other in complex ways.[5] Globalization provides an external rationale for internationalization of higher education. The perception of internationalization may vary, but it would mean the process of integrating an international, intercultural, or global dimension into the purpose and functions of higher

---

3. Bassett, *WTO and University*, 4.
4. Knight, "Internationalization Remodeled," 5.
5. Maringe, "Meaning of Globalization," 17.

education.⁶ The desire for internationalization of schools reflects values of capitalism: competition and expansion. In this context, the crisis in higher education that I sense has resulted from the very ethos of education that becomes more and more capitalized, expansionist, and competitive. Universities are becoming business enterprises that try to maximize their visible and tangible profits through the process of internationalization of higher education. This process involves exchanging staff and students, creating joint programs with overseas institutions, developing international partnerships, and enhancing language programs, academic programs, and research initiatives.

Many theological schools seem to romanticize and idealize the internationalization of theological education primarily in terms of launching their extended programs overseas without looking at the negative consequences of internationalization: the expansion of west-centric values and the desire to control the world in the name of internalization. Theological educators need to de-romanticize the so-called internationalization of US theological education by examining both bright and dark sides of the internationalization, which requires a critical, sophisticated reexamination of the discourse and practice of internationalization. Teaching and learning are always already *political* acts, through which one both shapes and operates one's own interpretative lens and value system that affect one's way of thinking, judging, and acting, on both a personal and public level. In this sense, "there is no neutral or natural place in teaching. . . . *Here*, for example, is not an indifferent place."⁷

Theological education has two sites of construction: interiority and exteriority. In theological education, exteriority primarily concerns issues of educational programs, curriculum, and extracurricular activities, whereas interiority addresses the issues of shaping the value systems and ethos of both teachers and learners through the educational systems and processes. In my chapter, I attempt to focus more on the interiority than the exteriority of US theological education and its *glocal* implications, though I am mindful of possible entanglements of these two aspects in particular contexts.

---

6. Knight, "Internationalization Remodeled," 5–31.
7. Derrida, "Where a Teaching Body Begins," 69 (emphasis added).

US-CENTRISM AND LINGUISTIC IMPERIALISM: SITES OF WORLDING THE WORLD

Contemporary societies are becoming *knowledge societies*.[8] In this rapidly evolving knowledge-intensive context, theological educators should examine the production, distribution, and use of knowledge in theological education in a global context. My larger concern is to open the question of *US-centrism* of the knowledge structure we inhabit—a question of enormous significance facing theological education today and the need and possibilities of discovering ways of making US theological education respond more adequately to the hierarchical situation between the global north and the global south.

Nowadays, many higher education teachers speak of the so-called "academic revolution," denoting a series of transformations and changes that have impacted most aspects of higher education in an era of globalization. The nature of this academic revolution, however, is hard to pinpoint in simplistic ways. One of the critical aspects of such a "revolution" can be the "massification" of higher education,[9] which signifies "elite, mass, and universal access"[10] to higher education worldwide, expanding its impact from the global north to the global south, but not vice versa.

US-centric standardization of higher education through internationalization of curriculum constituted in English could have serious impacts. People have begun taking English, for instance, as the global standardized means in the emergence of a global knowledge system and research for production, dissemination, and archivization of such global knowledge through and within higher education. As Jean-Luc Nancy points out, the English term *globalization* "has already established itself in the areas of the world that use English for contemporary information exchange."[11] The English language has become the *universal* instrument of mediation between the construction of global knowledge of the world and of the people.

Promoting a homogenized, US-centric perspective amounts to *worlding*, an act of *othering the rest* of the world and remaking it along US-centric lines. It is also an act of making the world through US-centric views. *Worlding* denotes one of a number of processes of *othering* implemented through

---

8. Rubio and Baert, *Politics of Knowledge*, 1.
9. Altbach et al., *Trends*, 1.
10. Altbach et al., *Trends*, 1.
11. Nancy, *Creation of World*, 27.

colonial, hegemonic discourses. The act of *worlding*, a term coined by Gayatri Spivak, redefines colonized natives and territories in Eurocentric terms, translated through the colonial language and designated as subject to Eurocentric authority. As Spivak points out, "meaning/knowledge intersects power."[12] Language as the means of the construction of knowledge is a powerful site of power.

In an era of globalization, the English language has become a more and more powerful means for constructing the ethos and value systems of higher education through the process of internationalization. Scrutinizing the impact of the spread of English as a universal language in theological education in a global context is becoming more important than ever because the dominance of a particular language would mean the dominance of the values, worldviews, and powers of the very language in the rest of the world, which takes a form of *linguistic imperialism*.

Linguistic imperialism comprises "ideologies, structures, and practices which are used to legitimate, effectuate, and reproduce an unequal division of power and resources (both material and immaterial) between groups which are defined on the basis of language."[13] In this context, *English linguistic imperialism,* a sub-type of "linguicism," occurs when "the dominance of English is asserted and maintained by the establishment and continuous reconstitution of structural and cultural inequalities between English and other languages."[14] In this regard, the *English-holder* becomes *power-holder*, and the English language becomes a powerful means of imperialistic domination regardless of the intentionality of English language holders. Furthermore, the hegemony of English constitutes a form of *linguistic terrorism* of people whose primary language is other than English: "Because we speak with tongues of fire we are culturally *crucified*. Racially, culturally and linguistically . . . we speak an *orphan tongue* . . . as long as I have to accommodate the English speakers rather than having them accommodate me, my tongue will be illegitimate."[15]

Jacques Derrida delivered a lecture at an international conference organized by UNESCO (United Nations Educational, Scientific, and Cultural Organization) in Paris in May 1991. At a roundtable that focuses on Derrida's UNESCO presentation, titled "Of the Humanities and Philosophical

12. Spivak, "Rani of Sirmur," 255.
13. Phillipson, *Linguistic Imperialism*, 47.
14. Phillipson, *Linguistic Imperialism*, 47.
15. Anzaldúa, *Borderlands/La Frontera*, 58–59 (emphasis added).

Disciplines: The Right to Philosophy from the Cosmopolitical Point of View (The Example of an International Institution)," Derrida begins his remarks for the roundtable discussion with the following point:

> Should I apologize for having left my paper in French? I should, of course. But on the other hand, I think that seeing the problem of language, and especially of the dominant and excluded languages, is already alluded to by Kant and in the paper, in different ways. I wanted to effectively—performatively, let's say—ask the question, Why read my text in French? Now, if I do so, it's not a matter of . . . antagonism or anti-Americanism, or some well-known opposition to the current linguistic, political hegemony of English, American English. It's because, on the one hand, I think that our conference, our project, bears witness to [the fact] that the Anglo-American is and will remain our medium in our discussions. Why is it so? How can we account for that? Usually, although it's a well known phenomenon that today Anglo-American is the universal language—the only universal language, effectively—the reasons why it is so are not clear, not simply a question of political or economic power. We should account for that, and have responsible answers to this current hegemony.[16]

Here Derrida evokes a serious question of hegemonic language at an international conference. From my perspective, however, he has "public permission" to present his lecture in his own language, French. If his language were other than European (French, German, Spanish, etc.)—languages such as Korean, Chinese, Hindi, Arabic, or Bengali—would Derrida even have had "permission" to present his lecture in his heart language at such an international conference? I doubt it, because the *linguistic hierarchy* between former colonial languages and the languages of *the rest* still works in powerful ways, explicitly and implicitly, in academia and the public world. The linguistic hierarchy sets a hierarchy between languages worldwide, in which English occupies the position as the first language, the former colonial languages as the second ones, and finally the languages of *the rest* as having the lowest linguistic status.

One should note that "the present-day world status of English is primarily the result of two factors: the expansion of British colonial power . . . and the emergence of the United States as the leading economic power of the twentieth century" and that "the latter factor which continues to explain

---

16. Derrida, *Ethics*, 20.

the world position of the English language today."[17] Although only one quarter of the world population is able to use English to communicate,[18] scholars cannot become internationally known without handling English. Needless to say, the *language-holder* becomes *power-holder* in many ways. One's choice of language constitutes how one defines oneself in one's context, especially in relation to the world one engages. The academic hierarchy between English-speaking scholars/students and non-English-speaking scholars/students takes a form of *academic colonialism*. Language has been one of the significant sites of power, domination, and control. The colonial control over languages through *standardization* has remained the most potent instrument of control. In this sense, I would say that language is one of the most critical issues in the US-centric internationalization of theological education, and serves as a significant exemplar for the colonial residue in the US higher education.

Today, the United States is not just one of many nation-states in the world. The term *US-Empire* indicates that non-Western academics and universities do not have the luxury to ignore what is happening in US higher education because of its powerful influence on the global context in terms of the production, dissemination, standardization of global knowledge, and impact of academic discourse and disciplinary structure on the rest of the world.

Institutional practices in such standardized curricula often perpetuate US-centric scholarship. Furthermore, when schools base admission of students from overseas on language test scores, such as TOEFL or GRE, or ignore faculty members' scholarly achievements done in languages other than Euro-US languages, they are practicing a form of *linguistic imperialism*. United States higher education in general and theological education in particular need to pay attention to the geopolitical sensitive issues like *linguistic imperialism* or *academic colonialism*. Otherwise, US theological education may result in students who lack the deep philosophical and theological understanding of their purpose as Christians, ministers, theologians, citizens, or public intellectuals that theological educators envision to produce in this era of globalization. In this sense, a theological education relevant in the contemporary world can be possible only with the fundamental transformation of the very geopolitical consciousness of the theological educators and administrators themselves.

17. Crystal, *English*, 59.
18. Crystal, *English*, 69.

GLOBAL POLITICS OF KNOWLEDGE AND US THEOLOGICAL EDUCATION

What constitutes knowledge has become a challenging question in academia especially since the second half of the twentieth century. Many scholars have challenged the traditional concept of knowledge, pointing out a "deepening sense of crisis in the modern knowledge system,"[19] in which people understand knowledge as objective, value-neutral, and universal. In fact, knowledge is subjective, value-laden, and context-specific. The changes in the perception of knowledge as objective, value-neutral, and context-specific to knowledge as subjective, value-laden, and context-specific require the fundamental transformation of the epistemological foundations of understanding of theological knowledge, and of the ways in which educators assess different processes and institutional forms of knowledge production in global contexts.

Without the internal transformation of the consciousness and worldviews of theological educators, a mere external change of the curricula, the content of the learning objectives and goals, the learning outcomes, or international programs for faculty and students would bring only an *exterior fix*, but not the actual change of the nature and purpose of the theological education.

Postcolonial discourse, along with other power-sensitive discourses such as feminism and postmodernism, reminds us that theological education and its pedagogy are always already inextricably linked to *power*. Theological educators exercise power both institutionally and personally, locally and globally, whether they intend to or not. The question they must wrestle with is, however, not how to eradicate the power itself. Rather, they must consider *how* to bring about the enlargement of human liberation, equality, and justice in the world, regardless who/what one is, through the *right exercise* of institutional power in the world, especially in an era of globalization where the power disparity between the United States and *the rest* becomes wider than ever.

The concept *politics of knowledge* denotes that knowledge is constitutive of the world and therefore political; and, at the same time, that knowledge and power are inextricably intertwined. The traditional perception of knowledge as objective, value-neutral, and universal does not reveal the intimate linkages between the power and knowledge. One must critically ask

---

19. Kothari, "Humane Governance," 283.

a fundamental question: How do people in power produce, use, legitimate, disseminate, and preserve certain knowledge, whether political, economic, sociocultural, or religious, and how do they devalue, ignore, delegitimize, or eradicate the knowledge by the powerless?

By adding the adjective *global*, I attempt to examine how the knowledge production and dissemination of US theological education through internationalization have impacted the construction, production, dissemination, and archivization of theological knowledge and practice in the rest of the world. Arriving at a better understanding of this linkage between power and knowledge is crucial to any attempt to formulate a theory of theological knowledge and its production worldwide. Nowadays the West, i.e., the Euro-United States, is everywhere in the world. In this contemporary context, US theological education needs to explore the question of responsibility in research and knowledge production across a global North-South divide. In the postcolonial context, the Euro-US professional intellectual is positioned as "the one who diagnoses"[20] the world, and as those who are producing "world class" theories and practices. The Euro-United States has produced knowledge about the world and "spoken for" the world.

Michel Foucault points out the inextricable links between knowledge and power and takes up this issue with a critical sensitivity.[21] People use knowledge to legitimate power and, they also use power to legitimate knowledge. So, the center of power and the center of knowledge coincide. Knowledge is the site of legitimation of power. For example, politicians often justify, legitimate, even sanctify their political decisions by reference to particular forms of knowledge. This line of reasoning can have significant implications for the role of university and higher education:

> As more and more areas of life are 'scientized' and taken out of the reach of participatory politics to be handed over to experts, the universities as the final depository of expertise have become a major global political actor of our times. In addition to their other tasks, they legitimize the 'expertization' of public affairs and the reign of the professionals.[22]

Theological education, like education in general, has played two roles: a mere reproducer of existing reality and a visionary challenger of the *status quo* for an alternative reality and possibility that requires a *prophetic*

---

20. Spivak, *Critique of Postcolonial Reason*, 255.
21. Foucault, *Power/Knowledge*.
22. Nandy, "Recovery of Indigenous Knowledge," 116.

criticism of the world. Theological educators must revisit the roles of theological education that an individual theological school has played. To envision a transformative theological education requires one to seriously take up and challenge the issue of power/knowledge, the politics of knowledge, on the one hand, and to fundamentally seek to reconstruct and reimagine theological discourse, curriculum, pedagogy, or institutional systems from a perspective of the geopolitical context of human equality and plurality, on the other.

In an era of globalization, traditional theological education has encountered fundamental challenges through the emergence of new discursive and geopolitical trends. One of the challenges is a growing disjuncture between the *internationalization of knowledge* and the *knowledge of internationalization*. Economic globalization, as an uneven economic process, has created a fragmented and uneven distribution of resources of learning and teaching between the global North and the global South. Through globalization, the Westcentric education has become a more and more powerful channel through which it established the West as normative in the name of *universality*. In this way, the traditional theological education grounded in the perception of the West as the normative could perpetuate the Westcentric norms and perspectives not only in the global North but also in the global South, which has been a significant site of contestation from a postcolonial perspective.[23]

Most resources for theological education in the world, in terms of institutional, financial, and human resources with enormous means to research, archive, and disseminate knowledge, have resided in the global North, while the dire need for theological educational infrastructures and resources has drastically grown in the global South. Furthermore, neocolonialism and neoimperialism take new forms of political, cultural, and economic dependency on particular Western nations such as the United States. Now theological educators must ask critical questions with *postcolonial sensibility* such as "Who is speaking and from what location? Whose purpose does the discourse serve? What vision is produced through the practical possibilities? In what way is this vision one of great social, personal, and planetary flourishing?"[24]

In this context, I have a strong reservation about the way scholars use such rhetoric of a *shift of the center of Christianity from the North to*

23. Kang, "Envisioning Postcolonial Education."
24. Chopp, *Saving Work*, 93.

the South, primarily due to the absence of critical challenge in using the rhetoric of the *center-margin.* When we adopt the notion of power in terms of the production, geopolitics, economics, archives, and dissemination of knowledge, it becomes obvious that the *quantitative growth* of Christians in the global South does not necessarily bring to the disempowered the *power* of the center in geopolitics. At the same time, the quantitative decline of Christians in the global North does not automatically diminish the power of the global North as the center of the Christian geopolitics.

In this context, the frame of reference for a theory of knowledge is by no means confined to the institutional and the national levels. It would not be complete unless one takes the international dimension into account as well, especially in an era of globalization.[25] People describe such international dimension not only by a worldwide information flow that technology increasingly facilitates but also by its own kind of politics. For the supposed openness of the international knowledge system tends to hide extreme global disparities between the global North and the global South in access to the production, reproduction, dissemination, and preservation of knowledge. In this era of globalization and internationalization of higher education, one of the most prominent features of the global knowledge system is its particular division of labor between the global North and the global South, in which key academic tasks, such as setting theoretical agendas and methodological standards, are the prerogative of a relatively small number of societies and institutions that play a disproportionately important role in this knowledge system. These societies and educational institutions are almost without exception located in the socioeconomically, culturally, and politically privileged regions of the world—the Euro-United States.

This particular type of hierarchy in our contemporary global knowledge system is by no means concerned only with knowledge but reflects quite faithfully the international hierarchies of economic influence, and linguistic and political power with which the global knowledge system maintains a completely reciprocal relationship. This relationship in turn has parallels to the relationship of mutual legitimation between knowledge and power, as the concept of politics of knowledge illustrates. This paradigmatic hegemony of knowledge norms, which has its origins in Western societies and their scientific institutions, has, however, not gone unchallenged. Indeed, the increasingly intense controversy over a new international system

25. See Drori et al., *Science.*

of knowledge is one of the most interesting and significant political phenomena of recent years.

Nowadays, no one outside the United States has the luxury to ignore what is happening in the country. The United States will continue to remain the *sovereign, theoretical subject* of all knowledge in theological education, whereas *the rest* is and will be in a position of subalternity: "It [the West] is a name for a subject which gathers itself in discourse . . . a name always associating itself with those regions, communities, and peoples that appear politically or economically superior to other regions."[26] No one can deny that the United States has become the center of the West. Numerous postcolonial scholars have pointed out that scholars in the West have consistently excluded non-Western thought from the constitution of the knowledge system.[27] People have regarded the theological discourses from the West as *normative* theology, whereas they have labeled theologies from the non-West as *indigenous* or *contextual* theology. This perception and naming imply the very Westcentric idea that theologies from or by the non-Westerners are applicable only to a *particular* context and thereby lack a *universal* status, unlike theologies from the West.

Furthermore, the absence of reciprocity of knowledge between the *Euro-US* and the *Rest* seems the "natural" order of things. In this context, theologians and educators from the *Euro-US* have produced and reproduced *universal* theological knowledge and educational systems that "embrace the entirety of humanity" but "in relative, and sometimes absolute, ignorance of the majority of humankind—that is, those living in non-Western cultures."[28] The question as to how an "insurrection of subjugated knowledge" or a *return of knowledge*[29] is possible in theological education within the global context remains a shared task across regional boundaries of the world.

Here one should note that reclaiming *subalternized knowledge* does not mean to simply reverse the Western colonial universalizing gesture and replace the Western with the non-Western knowledge and perspective—which one could call "postcolonial revenge." The task of moving beyond the Euro-US-centrism in theological discourse, curriculum, or institutional

---

26. Sakai, *Translation and Subjectivity*, 154.
27. See Chakrabarty, *Provincializing Europe*.
28. Chakrabarty, *Provincializing Europe*, 29.
29. Foucault, *Power/Knowledge*, 81.

systems in a global context is far from exercising a *politics of reversal* or *postcolonial revenge* by the non-West.

RADICAL BORDER-TRAVERSING: TRANSFORMING US THEOLOGICAL EDUCATION

The rise of international higher education in a globalized society poses a serious challenge to US theological education, which has had serious impact all over the world. Is it possible to achieve a discourse of knowledge free from its imperialist, colonialist, and ethnocentric context, in which the structure of knowledge is deeply embedded? What would comprise the tools of so-called "global learning," and texts students and faculties would read about the global world? Through what channel would students and faculty gain knowledge about the non-Western world, as "translation" of non-Western languages is always already uneven? As Foucault has revealed, those who have the power and means of communication have created and perpetuated the discourse of knowledge—the English language as the absolute means of communication. In order to break this power structure within the discourse of knowledge, one of the urgent tasks for US theological educators is to critically examine and deconstruct the process of knowledge-making, knowledge-disseminating, and knowledge-archiving worldwide. Foucault points out:

> "Truth" is to be understood as a system of ordered procedures for the production, regulation, distribution, circulation, and operation of statements. "Truth" is linked in a circular relation with systems of power which produce and sustain it, and to effects of power which it induces and which extends it. A "regime" of truth. . . . It's not a matter of emancipating truth from every system of power (which would be a chimera, for truth is already power), but of detaching the power of truth from the forms of hegemony, social, economic, and cultural, within which it operates at the present time. The political question . . . is not error, illusion, alienated consciousness, or ideology; it is truth itself.[30]

Aiming to detach the power of truth from forms of hegemonic social institutions, such as the family, the church, or the educational institutions, can be one of the significant tasks of US theological education today. In a globalized world, the diversity of language and culture can not only constrain

30. Foucault, *Foucault Reader*, 74–75.

and dampen theological educators' desire to explore the lives and experiences of those marginalized but also force them to face the existing power structure in the production, reproduction, authentication, legitimation, and circulation of theological knowledge. Who has the privilege and power of producing knowledge? Does the dissemination of Western-produced theological knowledge silence the voices of those marginalized, instead of making them heard in a globalized world?

We are living in a world in which the issues of dislocation, migration, and cultural survival are becoming a daily struggle for many people throughout the world. Dislocation and/or relocation constantly alter one's sense of identity because migration, for instance, involves more than a physical crossing the national/regional/cultural borders. In this context, various movements people make today require totally different articulations about the meanings and socio-politico-cultural implications of people's identities, affiliations, or allegiances both as individuals and groups. Some scholars contend that we are experiencing the beginnings of the end of national belonging and that the context for a citizenship based on belonging to a single nation is being eroded, although the process and experience of erosion is not even.[31]

We are entering an era in which the number of people who carry multiple-belonging, multiple-identities, or diasporic subjectivity is ever growing, and the traditional way of boundary-drawing does not reflect the complexity of people's lives of *in-between*. In this sense, the either-or approach to the issue of Christianity in the global North versus the global South, the *local* versus the *global*, or the *particular* versus the *universal* is repeating and reproducing the dualistic mode of thinking that is fundamentally problematic. This binary approach also loses its discursive effectiveness due to the inextricable interconnectedness of those two poles. How to constantly move back and forth between the borders of these seemingly separate but inseparable aspects of reality is one of the significant issues with which theological educators should wrestle today.[32]

Internationalization of theological education does not happen just by expanding educational sites "out there," by exchanging faculty and students with schools outside one's region, or by designing international

---

31. See Tan, *Justice without Borders*.

32. For an exemplary attempt to connect the global North and the global South, and the local and the global among various theological institutions in the world, see Werner et al., *Handbook of Theological Education*.

travel courses, which pertain to the *exteriority* of theological education. An authentic meaning of the globalization/internationalization of theological education would be possible only when theological educators' mode of *seeing/reading* the world becomes transformed, not merely in the construction of new theological discourses but also in the radical transformation of the concrete implementation of the discourse in the praxis of an individual theological school—the interiority of theological education. The radical transformation has to do with the *interiority* of theological education. Here, the two sites of theological education, *exteriority* and *interiority*, are irreducible to one each other, but at the same time inextricably intertwined.

What theological educators in the world need to do in constructing new models for theological education and reconstituting the nature and praxis of theological education is to engage the *universals* of justice, equality, freedom, and human rights in an uneven world today, but without any colonial, imperial or Euro-US-centric implications through discourses and institutional practice. The recovery of its *universalizing* function without any *subalternizing* the others will be one of the most urgent tasks that theological education in the United States faces today.

FROM GLOBALIZATION TO PLANETARIZATION: THEOLOGICAL EDUCATION-TO-COME

One of the substantial dark sides of globalization that reinforces internationalization, especially in US higher education, is its tendency of homogenization and totality in terms of communication, practices, forms, and procedures of higher education. One cannot deny the sheer fact that the "'global' evokes the notion of a totality as a whole, in an indistinct integrality."[33] Globalization results in the homogenization, totalization, and unification of all parts of the world that is in fact enormously heterogeneous and diverse. Such a totalization produced by the economic, technological, cultural, and discursive logic of globalization perpetuates "a global injustice against the background of general equivalence"[34] that creates an inhabitable world that philosopher Jean-Luc Nancy terms "the un-world [*immonde*]."[35]

Nancy laments "the fact that the world is destroying itself is not a hypothesis: it is, in a sense, the fact from which any thinking of the world

33. Nancy, *Creation of World*, 27.
34. Nancy, *Creation of World*, 54.
35. Nancy, *Creation of World*, 34.

follows, to the point, however, that we do not exactly know what 'to destroy' means, nor which world is destroying itself."[36] Nancy points out as follows the aspects of the destruction of the world by globalization in creating the reality of "everywhere and anywhere" that sanctifies the disintegration of the world:

> This network cast upon the planet—and already around it, in the orbital band of satellites along with their debris—deforms the *orbis* as much as the *urbs*. The agglomeration invades and erodes what used to be thought of as *globe* and which is nothing more now than its double, *glomus*. In such a *glomus*, we see the conjunction of an indefinite growth of techno-science, of a correlative exponential growth of populations, of a worsening of inequalities of all sorts within these populations—economic, biological and cultural—and of a dissipation of the certainties, images and identities of what the world was with its parts and humanity with its characteristics.[37]

Here Nancy introduces a French term *mondialisation* (which, he argues, is untranslatable) in juxtaposition with *globalization* in its different ethos. Mondialisation is *world-forming* that emphasizes the singularity of creation, in opposition to globalization as *world-destroying*. Concentration of wealth and resources in globalization is hardly possible without the exclusion and exploitation of the powerless who are on the margin in the world. In a similar line of thinking, Gayatri Spivak proposes to replace *the globe* with *the planet*:

> I propose the planet to overwrite the globe. Globalization is the imposition of the same system of exchange everywhere. . . The globe is in our computer. No one lives there. It allows us to think that we can aim to control it. The planet is in the species of alterity, belonging to another system and yet we inhabit it, on loan.[38]

The shift from globalization to *planetarization* that one should make in theological education, I propose, is to adopt an *ethics of singularity*,[39] rather than ethics of uniformity as in the case of globalization. *Planetarization* of theological education grounds itself in the geopolitical sensitivity to the power differentials between different regions of the world and seeks radi-

---

36. Nancy, *Creation of World*, 35.
37. Nancy, *Creation of World*, 33–34.
38. Spivak, "Planetarity," 72.
39. Kang, *Cosmopolitan Theology*, 49.

cal hospitality, responsibility, and cosmopolitan justice for every singular person in the world regardless of one's gender, class, race and ethnicity, ability, sexuality, or religion in its pedagogical philosophy and practices.

As Emmanuel Levinas and Jacques Derrida define the term, *religion* is an ethical relation to the other, and "the ethical relation is a religious relation."[40] In this sense, I would argue, theological education today in its process of internationalization should be about teaching the *ethical relation* to the other in the world. In the process of internationalization of US theological education, we have to then *redeem* the interiority of US theological education by reconstituting the nature and contents of education to disseminate and embody the Christian and human universal values of *ethical singularity* that enhances justice, hospitality, compassion, solidarity, and peace for each and every individual human being that resides on the surface of the earth.

In this context, significant epistemological grounds for US theological education today are geopolitical sensitivity to the power disparity between the United States and the Rest and *planetary* responsibility toward the rest of the world, in which the United States has exercised its unchallenged powers over the Rest, politically, socioeconomically, culturally, religiously, and academically. Jacques Derrida portrays the university he envisages, a *university-to-come*, as follows:

> This university demands and ought to be granted in principle, besides what is called academic freedom, an *unconditional* freedom to question and to assert, or even, going still further, the right to say publicly all that is required by research, knowledge, and thought concerning the *truth*. . . . The university *professes* the truth, and that is its profession. It declares and promises an unlimited commitment to the truth.[41]

Derrida's "university without condition," the "unconditional university," or the "university-to-come" is "an ultimate place of critical resistance . . . to all the powers of dogmatic and unjust appropriation . . . to economic powers (to corporations and to national and international capital), to the powers of the media, ideological, religious and cultural powers, and so forth—in short, to all the powers that limit democracy to come."[42] The *university-to-come* in this sense should be cosmopolitan and universal, "extend-

---

40. Derrida, "Violence and Metaphysics," 96.
41. Derrida, "University Without Condition," 202.
42. Derrida, "University Without Condition," 204–5.

ing beyond worldwide citizenship and the nation-state in general."[43] The university without condition, the university-to-come, does not of course exist in reality but remains as a promise that we must work on tirelessly.

Here, I would like to propose the *theological education-to-come* that makes a decisive shift from the spirit of globalization to that of planetarization, of which the primary profession is to profess a *truth* that is fundamentally linked to an unlimited commitment to *planetary responsibility* for the singular persons, and to *planetary hospitality* beyond borders of citizenship, religion, race, gender, or sexuality, which is governed by an *ethics of singularity*, not of totality or uniformity as in the spirit of globalization. If the university, as Derrida envisions, should be an ultimate place of critical resistance to all the powers of unjust appropriation, theological education should be an act of teaching students how to profess *the truth* and to resist to all kinds of unjust powers that are dominating and subjugating the others.

In our contemporary world, one finds it hard to draw a sharp line between *the local* and *the global* due to the interconnectivity of our life in the world. What people used to perceive as *local* is now inevitably intertwined with what people traditionally considered *global*. Everything interrelates with everything else. In this rapidly changing contemporary world, where globalization and neo-imperialism impact the concrete reality of people, both within and outside Christianity, at home and abroad, learning how to understand/construct Christianity in terms of its theological education, discourse, and institutional practice in various part of the world and how to form a *worldly coalition and solidarity* have become more pressing issues than before.

Derrida describes ten plagues of the contemporary world that I believe US theological education needs to critically engage today in an era of globalization: unemployment; large-scale exclusion of homeless citizens; eviction or deportation of exiles, stateless individuals, and immigrants; unsparing global economic war; lack of capacity to grasp the contradictions inherent in the free market; the affliction of foreign debt on a global scale; the ubiquity of the arms industry; an out-of-control expansion of nuclear weapons; inter-ethnic wars; the global reach of powerful, wealthy drug cartels; and the present condition of international law and of its institutions.[44]

Just as the university should be a place of unconditional resistance to all the powers of domination and unjust appropriation in the world, as

---

43. Derrida, "University Without Condition," 204.
44. Derrida, *Specters of Marx*, 100–104.

Derrida illustrates, US theological education should promote discourses and practices of *radical resistance* to dogmatic, doctrinal, religious, theo-political, and ideological powers that relegate the non-Western, non-Christian, women, sexual minorities, undocumented workers and immigrants, and refugees to the inferior margin of the world. I believe that "religion is responsibility or it is nothing at all,"[45] and that US theological education in an era of globalization needs to reconstitute the nature, direction, discourse, and practice of education in ways that take planetary responsibility for the world, where issues of wars, conflicts, extreme poverty, exploitation and domination, ecological destruction, or all forms of hatred function as plagues that destroy countless lives of people in the world.

Today, US higher education in general and US theological education in particular could be complicit in Euro-US-centrism, English-centrism, White-Anglo-centrism, Christian-centrism, and phallogocentrism worldwide, relegating women, non-Christian, and non-US-European men to a primitive developmental position. *Planetarization* of US theological education is to reject any type of colonizing principle of unifying narratives. Essential to the colonial project is the attempt to bring all knowledge and knowing together under one meta-narrative that is always already the language of colonizing or hegemonic groups. To decolonize and to planetarize US theological education in an era of globalization would mean to reground it upon geopolitical sensitivity, radical responsibility, cosmopolitan justice, and hospitality, seeing individual humans in the world as singular beings, who are unique and irreplaceable, *regardless*.

BIBLIOGRAPHY

Altbach, Philip G., et al. *Trends in Global Higher Education: Tracking an Academic Revolution, Global Perspectives on Higher Education*. Paris: UNESCO, 2010.

Anzaldúa, Gloria. *Borderlands/La Frontera: The New Mestiza*. San Francisco: Spinsters/Aunt Lute, 1987.

Bassett, Roberta Malee. *The WTO and University: Globalization, GATS, and American Higher Education*. London: Routledge, 2006.

Chakrabarty, Dipesh. *Provincializing Europe: Postcolonial Thought and Historical Difference*. Princeton: Princeton University Press, 2000.

Chopp, Rebecca S. *Saving Work: Feminist Practices of Theological Education*. Louisville: Westminster John Knox, 1995.

Crystal, David. *English as a Global Language*. 2nd ed. Cambridge, UK: Cambridge University Press, 2003.

45. Derrida, *Gift of Death*, 2.

Derrida, Jacques. *Ethics, Institutions, and the Right to Philosophy*. Translated and edited by Peter Pericles Trifonas. New York: Rowman & Littlefield, 2002.

———. *The Gift of Death*. Translated by David Willis. Chicago: University of Chicago Press, 1995.

———. *Specters of Marx: The States of the Debt, the Work of Mourning, and the New International*. Translated by Peggy Kamuf. New York and London: Routledge, 1994.

———. "The University Without Condition." In *Without Alibi*, edited and translated by Peggy Kamuf, 202–37. Stanford: Stanford University Press, 2002.

———. "Violence and Metaphysics." In *Writing and Difference*, 79–153. Chicago: University of Chicago Press, 1978.

———. "Where a Teaching Body Begins and How It Ends." In *Who's Afraid of Philosophy?: Right to Philosophy* 1, 67–98. Translated by Jan Plug. Stanford: Stanford University Press, 2002.

Drori, Gili S., et al. *Science in the Modern World Polity: Institutionalization and Globalization*. Stanford, CA: Stanford University Press, 2003.

Foucault, Michel. *The Foucault Reader*. Edited by Paul Rabinow. New York: Pantheon, 1984.

———. *Power/Knowledge: Selected Interviews and Other Writings, 1972–1977*. Edited by Colin Gordon. New York: Pantheon, 1980.

Kang, Namsoon. *Cosmopolitan Theology: Reconstituting Planetary Hospitality, Neighbor-Love, and Solidarity in an Uneven World*. St. Louis: Chalice, 2013.

———. "Envisioning Postcolonial Education: Dilemmas and Possibilities." In *The Handbook of Theological Education in World Christianity: Theological Perspectives, Ecumenical Trends, Regional Surveys*, edited by Dietrich Werner, et al., 30–41. Oxford: Regnum International, 2010.

Knight, Jane. "Internationalization Remodeled: Definition, Approaches, and Rationales." *Journal of Studies in International Education* 8.1 (2004) 5–31.

Kothari, Rajni. "On Humane Governance." *Alternatives* 12.3 (1987) 277–90.

Maringe, Felix. "The Meaning of Globalization and Internationalization in HE: Findings from a World Survey." In *Globalization and Internationalization in Higher Education: Theoretical, Strategic, and Management Perspective*, edited by Felix Maringe and Nick Foskett, 17–34. New York: Continuum, 2010.

Nancy, Jean-Luc. *The Creation of the World or Globalization*. Translated by François Raffoul and David Pettigrew. Albany, NY: SUNY Press, 2007.

Nandy, Ashis. "Recovery of Indigenous Knowledge and Dissenting Futures of the University." In *The University in Transformation: Global Perspectives on the Future of the University*, edited by Sohail Inayatullah and Jennifer Gidley, 115–24. Westport, CT: Bergin & Garvey, 2000.

Phillipson, Robert. *Linguistic Imperialism*. Oxford: Oxford University Press, 1992.

Radhakrishnan, R. *Theory in an Uneven World*. Oxford: Blackwell, 2003.

Rubio, Fernando Dominguez, and Patrick Baert, eds. *The Politics of Knowledge*. London and New York: Routledge, 2012.

Sakai, Naoki. *Translation and Subjectivity: On "Japan" and Cultural Nationalism*. Minneapolis: University of Minnesota, 1997.

Spivak, Gayatri Chakravorty. *A Critique of Postcolonial Reason: Towards a History of Vanishing Present*. Cambridge, MA: Harvard University Press, 1999.

———. "Planetarity." In *Death of a Discipline*, by Gayatri Chakravorty Spivak, 71–102. New York: Columbia University Press, 2005.

———. "The Rani of Sirmur: An Essay in Reading the Archives." *History and Theory* 24.3 (1985) 247–72.

Tan, Kok-Chor. *Justice without Borders: Cosmopolitanism, Nationalism, and Patriotism.* Cambridge: Cambridge University Press, 2004.

Werner, Dietrich, et al., eds. *The Handbook of Theological Education in World Christianity: Theological Perspectives, Ecumenical Trends, Regional Surveys.* Oxford, UK: Regnum International, 2010.

3

Globalization and Global Theological Education

Learning to Navigate the World of Creative Destruction

Brent Waters

GLOBALIZATION IS A RECENT phenomenon that presents significant economic challenges and opportunities. Globalization is predicated upon the notion of "creative destruction," in which rapidly changing global markets are creating short-term winners and losers, while presumably benefitting nearly everyone on a long-term basis. Globalization also presents some important implications for higher education in general, and theological education in particular. This chapter examines some of these implications.

THE "CREATIVE DESTRUCTION" OF GLOBALIZATION

"Globalization" is an admittedly vague and inelegant word that refers to many things. But the images it most readily conjures are those of an increasingly globally integrated economy. Trade is the most obvious example—huge ships and lengthy trains transporting stacks of rectangular cargo containers. We think nothing of buying items made in virtually every corner of the world. Labor migration is another prominent feature of globalization. For many, it is commonplace to work with or for immigrants; and if potential workers are prevented from migrating, then jobs migrate to them through outsourcing and offshoring. Less obvious but perhaps more important is relatively free-flowing capital. Direct foreign investment, venture capital, pension, and retirement funds are diversified and invested in businesses, equities, and other financial instruments around the world.

If nothing else, globalization refers to a series of new and rapidly expanding global markets. And these markets are dynamic and fiercely competitive, replete with what Joseph Schumpeter calls their inherent creative destruction.[1] By their nature, markets are always churning and never stationary. Consequently, market leaders rise and fall with alarming alacrity. Ten years ago, for example, Nokia and Blackberry dominated the global mobile phone market, only to be quickly displaced by Apple and Samsung (provided their batteries stop exploding). Over the past two decades, the dynamism of these new and expanding markets have helped to produce new jobs, created unprecedented wealth, and benefitted consumers with a widening range of affordable and readily available goods and services. These same markets have also helped to displace workers and corrode communities. Further, a globally integrated economy is accompanied by risk and vulnerability—bad mortgages in the United States, for instance, damaged banks and pension funds in Europe.

Globalization has lost some of its luster, particularly in the aftermath of the recent great recession (2008–16). The ensuing anxiety, fear, and anger have prompted many politicians to appeal to protectionism, nationalism, and anti-immigration as solutions for easing this seething unrest. Globalization is not without its troubling issues that need to be addressed, such as providing reasonable safety-nets for displaced workers and helping them acquire competitive skills. However, many of the simplistic solutions now being proffered will not do the trick.

Although the palpable anxiety prompted by the creative destruction of competitive global markets is understandable, there is no turning back. There are two reasons why this is the case. First, it is not practical. Unraveling a globally integrated economy, diminishing trade, and greatly restricting labor migration would create greater unemployment and increase the cost of consumer goods and services, prompting even greater social anger

1. See Schumpeter, *Capitalism*, 82.

and political unrest. In short, trying to dismantle globalization would create more problems than solutions. To use a crude analogy, once the toothpaste is out of the tube you can't put it back in without resorting to a great deal of uncreative destruction.

The second reason is that any attempted retreat from globalization is undesirable. Despite its problems, globalization has been good news for the world's poor. With the liberalization of trade following the end of the Cold War, nearly a billion people have escaped dire poverty, and a nascent global middle class is emerging. It is important to keep in mind that over the long term and at a macro level, genuinely competitive markets tend to foster more creativity than destruction. This is why Martin Wolf insists that the "failure of our world is not that there is too much globalization, but that there is too little."[2] Additionally, as I argue below, globalization is helping to create a kind of world that is more congenial to the church's mission and its life of pilgrimage.

As noted, globalization generates many economic issues and challenges. Global markets create more opportunities, and greater risk; it is a package deal. But there is also a broader range of social and political implications to consider. Philip Bobbitt, for instance, contends that we are in the early stage of a transition from nation-state to what he calls the market-state.[3] Nation-states have often restricted trade, capital flows, and immigration to protect its citizens from some of the riskiest and unwanted outcomes of competition. Although such measures provide some protection and stability, as well as solidifying a shared national identity, it comes at a cost, namely, higher prices, limited opportunities, and constricted economic growth. In contrast, the market-state enables an expansive range of economic opportunities for its individual citizens, by easing or eliminating restrictions on trade, capital flow, and labor migration. Such a scheme enables greater economic growth and prosperity. Although most citizens enjoy long-term financial benefits from this market orientation, others are crushed in the short term due to their inability to compete in new and expanding global markets.

Bobbitt is clear that this transition from nation-state to market-state will be neither easy nor orderly, and it will transform how individuals conceive and express an expanding and overlapping series of identities and loyalties. According to Bobbitt, the "basis for the state's legitimacy" shifts,

---

2. Wolf, *Globalization*, 4.
3. See Bobbitt, *Shield of Achilles*; *Terror and Consent*.

in part, "away from assuring mass welfare and towards maximizing individual opportunity."[4] One result is that the "market state is classless and indifferent to race, ethnicity, and gender, but it is also heedless of the values of reverence, self-sacrifice, loyalty, and family."[5] In the emerging market-state, one's identity and interests as a consumer, for instance, may conflict with those of being a citizen.

Similarly, Hedley Bull wondered if a neo-medievalism was challenging or even beginning to supplant the hegemony of the modern nation-state.[6] By "neo-medievalism" he means a decentralized political order consisting of people with multiple and crisscrossing loyalties that are expressed and governed by a range public and private institutions and authorities. The reason why this is medieval is because, according to Sean McFate, "sovereignty was fragmented, as different political actors—church, emperor, king, princes, city-states, monasteries, and so on—made overlapping claims of authority over people, places, and things." In short, there is "no state monopoly of identity and loyalty."[7] Bull developed five criteria to test his hypothesis. Neo-medievalism may be said to exist when there is simultaneously regional integration of states, disintegration of states, restoration of private international violence, transnational organizations, and technological unification of the world.[8] Bull conceded that some of these elements were present, but they were nascent and weak, and there was no danger of the modern world being supplanted by a new medieval one.

Bull wrote his masterpiece in the early 1970s at the height of the Cold War, and there was no realistic alternative on offer to challenge the hegemony of the nation-state. But quite a bit has happened since then, and Bull's criteria now have a more prescient feel to them. There is greater regional integration of states—think European Union, NAFTA, ASEAN. Greater disintegration of states—think Soviet Union and Yugoslavia, and more recently, Somalia and Libya. The past few decades have witnessed a dramatic growth of private security firms and return of mercenaries, who now routinely fight alongside or against the armed forces of nation-states. There is now a long and growing list of transnational organizations such as the World Trade Organization (WTO), International Monetary Fund

---

4. Bobbitt, *Terror and Consent*, 87.
5. Bobbitt, *Terror and Consent*, 90.
6. Bull, *Anarchical Society*.
7. McFate, *Modern Mercenary*, 72.
8. See Bull, "Decline of States System," 248–71.

(IMF), International Court of Justice, and a burgeoning collection of global corporations and NGOs could be added to the list. Most prominently, communication, information, and transportation technologies have unified the world.

Virtually any political context or issue now involves a crowded arena of actors, promoting their respective, and often conflicting, interests. These actors certainly include nation-states, but they must contend with regional and global political alliances, corporations, NGOs, criminal and terrorist organizations, and consumers—many of which effectively regard the world as their shopping mall. In addressing various issues or undertaking assorted tasks, these actors often form temporary, shifting, and expedient relationships. A nation-state, for example, may adopt liberal trade policies to lower consumer costs, effectively creating cozy relationships with various global corporations, while at the same time working with NGOs to assert greater scrutiny and regulation over these same corporations. In conducting its humanitarian work, the United Nations turns to NGOs and corporations to deliver material goods and services. In turn, these corporations and NGOs contract private security firms to protect their employees working in dangerous locales. And the same technologies driving globalization are also a favorite means criminals and terrorists use to commit acts of crime and terror on a global scale.

Additionally, a transition to a market-state or neo-medievalism promotes the idea that an individual's identity is derived from and expressed through a variety of sources.[9] Which source may dominate can vary from one setting to another, and they often create tensions that cannot be easily reconciled. In the Westphalian system that has dominated political theory and practice for the past four centuries, nation-states tried to assert a monopoly over the identities of the people they governed. To what extent they ever achieved this goal is debatable, but this ideal is now clearly in decline. In addition to citizenship, individuals may appeal to race, ethnicity, gender, religion, career, and consumer interests as sources of identity that cut across or even challenge political loyalties in respect to particular circumstances. For instance, one's interest as a consumer may trump those of being a citizen in response to taxation policies. Or to what extent does one's citizenship, race, gender, or religion enable or impede one's pursuit of a chosen career? Moreover, the ordering or emphasis upon these multiple sources of identities may vary widely from setting to setting. My religious identity

9. See Taylor, *Sources of Self.*

may dominate my support of an NGO, while my career and consumerist interests may form my unfavorable reactions to governmental regulations.

I want to make two general observations in response to this transition to the market-state and rise of neo-medievalism that are pertinent to the theme of this book. First, what may be characterized as chosen and shared identities are displacing given or accidental sources of identity. If a person's identity is crafted and expressed primarily through career and consumer interests, for instance, then subsequent political convictions and actions are ordered accordingly. Moreover, the so-called "accidental" sources of identity—those we are born into rather than choose—are becoming more fluid and less definitive. We can change or radically redefine our meaning of citizenship, gender, and religion. For their part, race and ethnicity may diminish over time through intermarriage, or be dismissed as irrelevant for certain kinds of activities such as the anonymous exchanges conducted in global markets. Consequently, there is a pronounced and perhaps irreconcilable conflict between globalism and multiculturalism, because the former is dedicated to the primacy of individual identity, while the latter seeks to preserve group or collective identities.

Second, a preference for mobility, both physical and imaginatively, is displacing a proclivity for fixed locale. To take full advantage of globalization, one must or should be willing and able to live a nomadic life. One should be free not only to wander the world in search of economic opportunities but also agile to navigate the treacherous waters of creatively destructive global markets. To remain fixed in a globally integrated economy is almost a certain strategy for becoming materially impoverished. Consequently, temporary space, both physical and virtual, is increasingly privileged over physical place.[10] Human associations are becoming progressively short term and organized around shared interests and tasks in which close proximity is often a liability that is neither needed nor wanted. The neighbors our Lord commands us to love are increasingly faceless.

GLOBALIZATION AND THEOLOGICAL EDUCATION: WHAT AND HOW TO TEACH

What exactly does the transition to the market-state and the rise of neo-medievalism have to do with theological education? Quite a bit, I think. If

10. For a more detailed account of the privileging of space over place, see Waters, *Christian Moral Theology*.

the purpose of theological education is, in part, to help believers discern the signs of the times, then globalization cannot be ignored. It is a part of the world in which we live and should be seen as such. Additionally, if I am correct that there is no realistic prospect of turning back from globalization, then it needs to be understood rather than denounced or naively championed. I often tell my students that to be for or against globalization is tantamount to being for or against icebergs. The challenge is to neither condemn nor praise icebergs, but to learn how to navigate around them. I believe theological education has a duty to teach some navigational skills that are applicable to a contemporary life of faith. In trying to identify what such instruction might entail, two questions come readily to mind: what should be taught? and how might it be taught? Addressing these questions will take up the remainder of this chapter, and the answers I offer are suggestive rather than conclusive. Consonant with the aims of this volume, I will focus my remarks on US theological education.

What Should Be Taught?

At its most basic level, theological education should teach those skills that assist the church to pursue its mission and ministry and enable its members to live faithful lives as followers of Jesus Christ. Rather than concentrating on what these practical skills might entail, however, I want to focus on some theological themes that provide an interpretive lens of the world that in turn suggest what kinds of practices need to be developed and pursued.

One such theme is the *theology of the cross*. This doctrine means many things, but if nothing else, it requires that we must deal with the thing as it is and not how we might prefer it to be. The "thing" in question here is the world in which Christian faith is lived out, and globalization is a driving force that is shaping the contemporary world. It is a world of fiercely competitive markets in which there are both short-term winners and losers. It is a world in which political sovereignty, power, and authority are less centralized and more dispersed. The very notions of what constitutes stability and security are now in dispute. This is the way the world is, and there is no compelling reason why theological education should ignore or try to sugarcoat the inherent creative destruction of globalization. But neither is there any compelling reason to offer any sweeping condemnation, for this is the world in which the church pursues its mission and ministry. And the

Cross reminds us that suffering and redemption are both endemic to this and any age.

The creative destruction of globalization, however, is replete with generating welcome opportunities. To have lifted nearly a billion people out of dire poverty is no small accomplishment, and this was achieved primarily through liberalized trade and commerce, economic growth, and decentralized governments.[11] There is again no reason why theological education should ignore or denigrate the ends and means of the accomplishments accompanying globalization, nor any reason to fear or castigate the emerging market-state and rise of neo-medievalism. This is where *pneumatology* comes in. The Holy Spirit is rather unwieldly, like the wind blowing where it will (John 3:8), and refusing all efforts to be domesticated and subject to our beck and call. The Spirit, in short, often works in unexpected and surprising ways—ways that we would not choose. Is there any reason why this principle is not applicable to globalization? After all, the Spirit is presumably at work in destroying "stable" systems that enslave in order to liberate captives. I am not suggesting that creative destruction is the work of the Spirit, but can we not at least entertain the possibility that globalization creates opportunities for the Spirit to be at work that did not exist previously?[12] And are not these opportunities, however initially daunting, to be welcomed?

One such welcome opportunity involves *ecclesiology*. Given the diffusion of political actors, loyalties, and identities, the church has an opening to recover its catholicity and life as a pilgrim people. Christianity is not a territorial religion. Rather, it is a gathering church, drawn from every race and nation;[13] it exists wherever two or three are gathered in Christ's name. Those involved in shaping theological education should help students, and more broadly the church, understand and respond accordingly regarding how they order and express their multiple identities and loyalties. Or in other words, how can a shared, universal faith be practiced in pluriform ways? In this respect, breaking down the nation-state's attempted monopoly on identity is a welcome moment.

The mobility that globalization promotes is another welcome development. A gathering church is not a settled institution, and its members are a

---

11. See Wolf, *Globalization*.

12. For a more in-depth account of the relation between globalization and the work of the Holy Spirit, see Waters, "Creative Destruction," 60–79.

13. See O'Donovan, "Church," 158–92.

pilgrim rather than a settled people. As Saint Augustine recognized, Christians are always a bit restless,[14] for they know that they are never entirely at home in the world. Consequently, they belong in the world wherever God calls them to be for however short or long a period of time it proves to be. Presumably it will prove easier and more productive for a pilgrim people to engage nomads rather than settlers, for they understand that mobility is an asset rather than a liability—with an important caveat: mobility is not an end itself, but a means of expressing a restless hope for one's eventual settled and eternal home.

Additionally, being a pilgrim people requires reclaiming the secular callings and vocations of the laity. Particularly in the context of a neo-medieval market-state, the work and ministry of the church cannot be adequately performed by a small cadre of clergy and lay volunteers. Rather, in virtue of their baptism, all Christians are ministers of Jesus Christ; and, since there are no part-time Christians, there are also no part-time ministers. Through their work in the world they express their faith in and bear witness to Christ, and they need to be affirmed and empowered to do so. Through their participation in dynamic global markets they express, albeit obliquely, a love of neighbors, who are becoming increasingly anonymous, distant, and competitive.

How Might It Be Taught?

The advent of globalization has forced businesses to recognize that it is no longer business as usual. With new and expanding global markets, they face a new and expanding range of competitors, as well as global consumers with a larger range of idiosyncratic demands. Over the past few decades, firms have had to rethink how best to advertise, sell, and deliver their goods and services, particularly in response to the development of the Internet and rapid transport. To remain profitable, most businesses have also been forced to become leaner and more agile to respond to rapidly changing market conditions. This has often been accomplished by reducing labor costs, either through technological innovation, expanding the range of suppliers, or outsourcing and offshoring certain services such as accounting, legal services, and human resource management. This in turn has affected the workforce in which individuals must also respond rapidly to changing markets, so that many increasingly sell their skills and knowledge on

---

14. Augustine, "Book One," 3.

a contracted or piecemeal basis rather than seeking permanent employment that may not be on offer even if wanted. Both labor and management must be entrepreneurial to remain competitive. The phrase "change or die" captures the tone of the ubiquitous creative destruction of global markets. Yet despite this somber adage it is arguable that it is consumers who benefit most from globalization by having a greater range of affordable goods and services at their disposal.

This adage and its benefit are also apt for higher education. Universities and professional schools have had to adapt in developing and delivering their products within global markets of both competitors and clients. I do not think that theological education can or should be spared changing how it goes about doing its work. Theological schools and seminaries will also be competing in increasingly global markets, and they too must become leaner and nimbler in order not only to survive, but also to better match supply with demand. These changes carry many implications, but I want to mention four briefly: delivery, funding, accreditation, and workforce.

Delivery

I am particularly fond of lecture halls, the mustier the better. But I recognize that its appeal is rapidly declining as a principal mode of delivering theological education. The image of the lecture hall assumes that students must come to campus at prescribed times to learn the knowledge and acquire the skills they seek. But in a highly mobile and consumer-oriented age, this will not do. Schools will also need to go out to its students through online courses (in both real and virtual time), weekend or short-term seminars at various locales, and other forms of convenient instruction. This raises a question of perception: Should theological education conceive itself primarily as a campus-based activity or as a dispersed service in which the geographical proximity of students is often irrelevant? Or in crasser terms, should theological education look more like Walmart or Amazon?

Funding

Most churches have recognized that they should bear at least part of the cost of educating clergy and lay leaders. This has often been accomplished, albeit inadequately, by denominationally owned or partially funded seminaries and schools. But is the church best served by this model?[15] Such funding is often accompanied by policy requirements that may serve to constrain institutions, as well as produce a homogenous collection of schools. Within global markets institutional constraints and homogeneity are liabilities best avoided. Would churches be better served if instead of funding institutions they instead funded students? Perhaps they would, for it would presumably create a wider range of distinctive rather than similar institutions by appealing to a greater range of student demand. And, arguably, variety rather than homogeneity better meets the interests of those being served. Sweden, for example is generally regarded as having a first-rate primary and secondary educational system, and it is almost entirely funded through vouchers. There is stiff competition among state, nonprofit, and for-profit schools in which enrollment determines success.[16] Is it time for something equivalent, in part, to voucher funded theological education?

Accreditation

The professions and public have generally been well served by accrediting agencies. Experts in various fields vouchsafe the reliability of colleges, universities, and professional schools. But in the more consumerist-oriented environment that globalization promotes, the wisdom of the expert tends to be supplanted by the wisdom of consumers, who presumably know best about how to satisfy their needs and wants. Many consumers do not make their purchases based on accredited expertise; they are more interested getting what they want at the lowest cost possible. The religious bodies served by theological education may adopt a similar consumerist stance in respect to training their clergy and lay leaders. If so, I don't know what will become of traditional accreditation. It could evolve into a rating service like the Better Business Bureau. Alternatively, religious bodies could establish independent accreditation standards. Or, more extremely, accreditation could become effectively irrelevant, replaced by a buyer-beware approach. At the very least it might prove prudent if accrediting agencies start thinking and acting more in global rather than national or regional terms.

---

15. Funding models have come under increasing scrutiny in recent years, as US theological schools have struggled with declining revenue. See, for example, Ruger and Meinzer, *Through Toil*.

16. Micklethwait and Wooldridge, *Fourth Revolution*.

Workforce

Similar to what is already occurring in many business firms, theological seminaries and schools will probably utilize outsourcing and offshoring to reduce costs. This will include not only such administrative tasks as accounting, human resources, and custodial services but also instruction. Schools will need to respond quickly to the rapidly changing demands of expanding and competitive global markets. Providing the range of requisite expertise and delivery skills in responding to shifting market demands through a permanently employed faculty is probably neither an efficient nor affordable model. Alternatively, institutions may increasingly partner or collaborate with one another to offer an expanding range of instruction. In any case, a traditional faculty comprised of tenured members who pursue curriculum reform and governance at a glacial pace is a heavy liability in an age when institutions require flexibility and swiftness to compete and take advantage of new opportunities. Contracted instruction may, out of necessity, become the new norm. Teachers and scholars may need to become more pilgrim-like to better teach a pilgrim faith.

CONCLUSION

I have no idea what theological seminaries and schools might look like fifty or even twenty-five years from now, but I suspect they will be very different.[17] If the economic, social, and political forces driving globalization continue apace or grow more intense, then matching supply with demand will need to adapt accordingly, perhaps even radically. Let me illustrate with a scenario I do not think is inevitable or necessarily desirable, but surely possible. Increasingly, students may become less interested in being enrolled in a particular school. Why can't they pick and choose teachers and scholars scattered around the world with whom they wish to study for a while? Academics may also wonder why the students they teach are confined to those enrolled in institutions in which they happen to be employed. And churches may come to wonder if their needs would be better met by breaking out of these institutional constraints—perhaps what they need are faculties and not schools. If so, then what kinds of organizations will emerge to match supply with demand? At the very least, for those of

---

17. For an educated guess by a seasoned educator, see Aleshire, "Future of Theological Education," 380–85.

us involved in theological education, perhaps we should think more in terms of how the educational needs of the religious bodies we serve are best met, rather than concocting strategies of institutional survival. Or, to put it bluntly: Is theological education in need of some creative destruction?

I acknowledge that many people, perhaps especially theological educators, regard the prospect of greater globalization with fear and trembling. This is understandable, for the emerging market-state and rise of neo-medievalism will undoubtedly be accompanied by great uncertainty and instability—a world of unremitting flux and fluidity. But I think we should resist becoming dismayed. Rather, as theological educators we should welcome globalization. It is admittedly a destructive force but it is also creative, and I believe the opportunities it offers outweigh the challenges. Moreover, when did Christ ever promise his followers stability, at least this side of eternity?

BIBLIOGRAPHY

Aleshire, Daniel O. "The Future of Theological Education: A Speculative Glimpse at 2032." *Dialog: A Journal of Theology* 30.4 (2011) 380–85.

Augustine. "Book One: The First Fifteen Years." In *Confessions*, edited by Michael P. Foley, 3–21. Translated by F. J. Sheed. 2nd ed. Indianapolis: Hackett, 2006.

Bobbitt, Philip. *The Shield of Achilles: War, Peace, and the Course of History*. New York: Knopf, 2002.

———. *Terror and Consent: The Wars for the Twenty-First Century*. New York: Knopf, 2008.

Bull, Hedley. *The Anarchical Society: A Study of Order in World Politics*. 4th ed. New York: Columbia University Press, 2002.

McFate, Sean. *The Modern Mercenary: Private Armies and What They Mean for World Order*. Oxford: Oxford University Press, 2014.

Micklethwait, John, and Adrian Wooldridge. *The Fourth Revolution: The Global Race to Reinvent the State*. New York: Penguin, 2014.

O'Donovan, Oliver. "The Church." In *The Desire of the Nations: Rediscovering the Roots of Political Theology*, 158–92. Cambridge, UK: Cambridge University Press, 1996.

Ruger, Anthony, and Chris A. Meinzer. "Through Toil and Tribulation: Funding Theological Education, 2001–2011." *Auburn Studies* 18 (2014) 1–26.

Schumpeter, Joseph A. *Capitalism, Socialism, and Democracy*. London: Harper Perennial, 2008.

Taylor, Charles. *Sources of the Self: The Making of the Modern Identity*. Cambridge, MA: Harvard University Press, 1989.

Waters, Brent. *Christian Moral Theology in the Emerging Technoculture: From Posthuman Back to Human*. Burlington, VT: Ashgate, 2014.

———. "Creative Destruction, the Market-State, and the Holy Spirit." In *Just Capitalism: A Christian Ethic of Economic Globalization*, 60–79. Louisville: Westminster John Knox, 2016.

Wolf, Martin. *Why Globalization Works*. New Haven, CT: Yale University Press, 2004.

4

Globalizing the Campus
Implications for Theological Schools

Luis R. Rivera

IN THIS ESSAY, I propose that the Association of Theological Schools (ATS) and its member schools will benefit greatly if they sustain dialogue and collaboration with other professional communities in higher education to address the emphasis ATS calls "global awareness and engagement"[1] and many in US higher education call *internationalization*.[2] Theological schools' reflection and work on this learning and institutional goal could be strengthened by engaging critically the visions and resources developed by peer organizations of educators in higher education that have been doing reflection, research, experimentation, and training in the area of global learning for some time. This is not an invitation to mimic or assimilate what they have done, but to explore selectively and engage critically the body of knowledge, research, and expertise developed by these educators and leaders in higher education.

A wealth of easily accessible information and resources is readily available. One advantage of these resources is that they reflect current academic

---

1. See Aleshire and Ruiz, "New Global Direction," 1.
2. Olson et al., *Comprehensive Internationalization*.

research and the most recent practices in thinking about curriculum and program design, student learning assessment, faculty development, and institutional capacity. In what follows, I highlight and review three programs developed by the American Council of Education that I have found particularly valuable in my personal and professional quest to clarify the notion and practice of "global awareness and engagement" in theological education.

ATS IN THE PURSUIT OF "GLOBAL AWARENESS AND ENGAGEMENT"

Since the 1980s, member schools of the Association of Theological Schools in the United States and Canada (ATS) have been engaged in reflection, research, and pedagogical and institutional practices that promote what ATS used to call "globalization of theological education" and now names "global awareness and engagement."[3] Research conducted in 1998 under a previous ATS initiative called Incarnating Globalization Project established clearly that practices related to "globalizing" curriculum and schools have been present in a significant cluster of US-based ATS schools.[4] These past theoretical, missional, and practical efforts constitute what Lester Ruiz and David Esterline (in this volume) identify as "the long tradition of 'globalization' in accredited graduate theological education." This history, legacy, and tradition are also part of the background to understand the ATS's most recent plan called "Global Awareness and Engagement Initiative."[5]

In December 2013, the ATS Board of Directors approved and issued a statement renewing its commitment to "globalizing" theological education. This convocation invited member schools and the Association itself to explore and improve ways of understanding and practicing the goal of teaching and collaborating for "global awareness and engagement." The plan included the following five strategic directions: (1) understand and build effective partnerships with theological institutions abroad; (2) reflect on and engage with the social and religious global realities present in the North American contexts; (3) facilitate the creation of "bilateral and multilateral flow of scholarship, resources, and expertise" between theological

---

3. ATS, "Global Awareness." For a reflection on the content and transition of these terms in ATS, see Ruiz and Esterline's chapter in this book.

4. See Berling, "Collective Wisdom," 85–139; "Our Words," 63–80.

5. ATS, "Global Awareness."

partners in the Global South and the Global North; (4) promote a broad ecumenical (pan-Christian) and international conversation on the future of theological education; and (5) continue to improve or initiate new collaborative efforts to develop joint degree programs, recognize international degree programs, and clarify guidelines and practices for online degrees exported by North American schools.[6]

Dan Aleshire and Lester Ruiz highlighted four strategies to implement a portion of the Initiative: "(1) conversations with member schools already engaged in global partnerships, (2) discussion with international theological educators, (3) conversations about global patterns of Catholic theological education, and (4) an international gathering of evangelical theological educators."[7] The first strategy of convening schools engaged in global partnerships was incorporated and implemented through the Lilly-funded research project on Educational Models and Practices in Theological Education.[8] This project conducted a comprehensive study of theological education in ATS schools organized in eighteen peer groups.[9] Two of these groups worked and reported on global partnerships.[10]

The second strategy, to promote dialogue among international theological educators, was implemented through two dialogue events. First, ATS convened an ecumenical group of sixteen theological educators from the North American context to reflect on the practices and learnings in what their schools are doing on "global awareness and engagement."[11] Second, ATS supported the organization of an international group of theological leaders (Global Forum of Theological Educators), who organized a conference where an international and ecumenical group of theological educators from thirty-five countries reflected on theological education around the globe.[12] The last two strategies were implemented through dialogues with Evangelical (Spring 2013) and Catholic (January 2015) leaders in theological education. The "Global Awareness and Engagement Initiative" is an effort to continue to clarify and document principles, guidelines, and best practices to support the activities and relationships ATS and its

6. ATS, "Global Awareness."
7. Aleshire and Ruiz, "New Global Direction," 1.
8. Graham, *Educational Models*.
9. Graham, "Midpoint Reflections," 1. Kern, "Inter-group Conversations," 1.
10. See the final reports of all groups in ATS, "Educational Models."
11. Brown, "Global Engagement," 1.
12. Brown, "Global Forum of Theological Educators," 1.

member schools pursue toward theological education that practices "global awareness and engagement."

Most likely, ATS schools in the United States can be located in a spectrum of practices and success when it comes to infuse curricula and campuses with global and intercultural analysis, perspectives, viewpoints, and practices. To my knowledge, no one has developed a typology or a developmental flow chart as a theoretical tool to differentiate patterns or models of teaching and enacting "global awareness and engagement" in ATS theological schools. One can only speculate (with a measure of confidence) that most schools are located on a continuum from one end of *minimum* "globalizing or internationalizing" activities to the opposite end of *maximum* engagement.

Based on past evidence and present anecdotal information one can attempt to identify and organize the variety of formal practices that move schools to be more aware, connected, and responsive with international environments and global dynamics. The internationalization or globalization of theological education is conducted through different formal and informal practices that involve people in learning contexts, educational programs, and institutional connections. A school can globalize its education and campus by engaging in several practices at home and abroad.[13] These multiple formal practices can be classified in four spheres of practices and two domains of action.[14]

---

13. The following characterization on practices for "globalizing" education is more descriptive of predominantly "non-immigrant" theological schools in the United States. We need to recognize the emergence in ATS of a cluster of about twelve Asian-serving schools that require a study to describe the ways they practice "global awareness and engagement." See ATS, "Asian Schools," 140–44.

14. This is a provisional classification to help organize and differentiate between practices related to academic programs, people, and institutions at home and abroad. This table takes the US, or domestic schools, as the main point of reference. There is a sense in which all of these practices are institutional, that is, validated and supported by the appropriate school's offices and officers. The category of "institutional capacity" is one way of recognizing that sometimes the collaboration extends beyond the primary educational agents (faculty and students) and traditional products (degrees, programs, and courses) and involves more directly executive administrative leaders working to strengthen the school's resources and infrastructure.

Action sphere	At-home domain/on-campus globalizing practices	Abroad domain/off-campus globalizing practices
Curriculum-centered practices	Degree and non-degree programs focused on global learning for domestic and/or international learners living at or traveling to the home school; transfer of credits for education abroad; regular lecture series or conferences on global or international topics; incorporating the teaching resources and/or sites of local, international, or cultural-ethnic organizations and leaders; teaching of or in a second language; etc.	Export of degrees and non-degree programs for international learners in host countries; study abroad programs for domestic students conducted independently or jointly by home or host schools; dual degree programs or joint degree programs; educational programs with nonacademic partners (churches; NGOs; indigenous or social activist organizations); etc.
Student-centered practices	Exchange programs for international students; recruitment of international students for degree programs; residential internships or service opportunities in local cross-cultural sites for domestic and international students; student research opportunities in local cross-cultural sites; language-culture immersion programs in local cross-cultural programs for domestic or international students; student organizations or services focused on international students in the host school; etc.	Study abroad programs for domestic learners conducted by home or host schools with or without credit; travel seminars; residential internships or service opportunities abroad; research opportunities overseas; language/culture immersion programs abroad; programs or services for international alumni; etc.

Action sphere	At-home domain/on-campus globalizing practices	Abroad domain/off-campus globalizing practices
Faculty-centered practices	Trainings on global and cross-cultural issues and pedagogies for domestic faculty; internationalizing syllabi and courses; visiting scholars program; hiring of international professors and domestic professors with international experience; on-line or residential bi/multi-national team-taught courses; international faculty serving as PhD dissertation consultants, advisors or examiners; endowed chairs (term or tenure) for international scholars; support for learning international languages; using technology to incorporate international resources in courses; etc.	Faculty exchange programs with schools abroad; sabbatical time abroad for research, teaching or enrichment of domestic faculty; travel seminars for faculty; domestic faculty serving abroad as PhD dissertation consultants, advisors or examiners; global teams collaborating in research, teaching, and curriculum projects; leading travel seminars for students; attending international conferences; etc.
Institutional capacity-centered practices	Memoranda or covenants generated by domestic schools; local or joint research, teaching or training centers focused on global or cross-cultural learning; officers or offices devoted to work with international students or faculty; agreements for access to local library resources and other services for learners or schools abroad; etc.	Memoranda or covenants generated by schools abroad; creation of satellite campus abroad; offering consulting or administrative services overseas; partnership with research, teaching or training centers established abroad; training of administrators, faculty and staff abroad; agreements for access for domestic students and faculty to library resources and other services overseas; etc.

The more a school engages in these practices across these four spheres and two domains of action, the wider is the scope of "global awareness and engagement" involvement. But a wider scope does not necessarily mean a deeper form of practice. Sometimes, schools engage in several of these practices in peripheral or fragmentary ways, and without much assessment. "Deeper" implies a more intentional and integrated way of conducting these practices by relating them to: (1) the school's mission and goals; (2) the curriculum goals; (3) other programs and activities that promote the "global" at home and abroad in the school; (4) the institutional budget; and (5) assessment systems.

It is likely that there is only a small group of schools whose history, vision, capacity, connectivity, and financial resources allow them to have a high volume of cross-border and intercultural activity that globalizes both curriculum and campus. Of particular importance is the experience of those schools with a greater international footprint in foreign countries due to their capacity to sustain overseas degree programs, satellite campus abroad, or online education delivered internationally. It would also be interesting to know more about the experience of Catholic seminaries, which in some cases receive more international students due to their structural connections with orders and dioceses that import and export international seminarians. We need to explore if seminaries embedded in universities with emphasis in recruiting international students are impacted in different ways than seminaries in universities that are more domestic in orientation and outreach. Finally, 2015 ATS statistics reveal that visa students in US-based schools have remained a stable segment of the overall student population. They have constituted an average of 9.3 percent for the past five years, though there has been a slight increase (5 percent) in headcount of visa students during the past three years—from 6,137 in 2013 to 6,448 in 2015.[15] We need research to help us see the distribution of that population and understand the factors that attract and retain them, as well as the quality of their educational and social experience and the impact they have in those schools. We await a comparative study on the experience and impact of ATS schools with low, medium, or maximum ranges of at-home and abroad globalizing practices.

We need to recognize that although US theological schools are part of the larger and complex higher education system in the United States, we belong to another institutional tier, orbit, or network. We are certainly located in the global sphere of US international higher education, but we participate differently in that web, ecology, or market. Nonetheless, the pedagogical, service, and institutional activities and networks our schools have in the pursuit of "global engagement" create challenges, questions, experiences, and pursuits similar to those in universities and colleges with international experience. The insights and wisdom collected among ATS member school leaders who have participated in focus groups[16] and in the

15. ATS, "2015–16 Annual Data Tables," table 2.12-B.
16. Brown, "Global Engagement."

Educational Models and Practices peer groups[17] that focused on "global awareness and engagement" reveal similar or parallel quests, interests, and paths as our colleagues in colleges and universities pursuing "internationalization of higher education."

For example, leaders in theological education are concerned about, attentive to, and intentional in pursuing global learning and relationships in appropriate, effective, and accountable ways. Based on their practice and reflection, they are laying out an expansive and multilayered agenda of issues that require attention. I classify some of these issues under three general categories. The first category of issues I call *the spirit of global engagement*. This has to do with the intention and commitment to participate in these international and cross-cultural endeavors with clarity and transparency of purpose. Many of them highlight the need to engage in this work by being theologically rooted, mission centered, learning focused, and culturally mindful. I call the second category *the ethics of global engagement*. These are concerns with building relationships and practices that foster communities of learning across cultural and geographical borders that are guided by values and principles such as mutuality, reciprocity, flexibility, humility, respect, transparency, honesty, integrity, excellence, accountability, sensibility for differences, and justice in the midst of asymmetries and disparities. Finally, there is a cluster of issues that we can name *the practice of global engagement*. These items are curricular, strategic, organizational, fiduciary, financial, and technical in nature. They have to do with identifying, supporting, and resourcing: (1) the *agents* of/for "global awareness and engagement" within and without the schools (students, faculty, leaders, administrators, partners, stakeholders, etc.); (2) the institutional *agreements* to start, sustain, assess, renew, or even close those relationships and programs; (3) the curricular and pedagogical *agenda* in all its complexity; and (4) the practices of learning and institutional *assessments*, including the assessment of global partnerships.

All of these items find analogues in the larger academy and in professional associations of higher education. Our colleagues have engaged in experiments and research that could provide theories, practices, and resources to enrich our *own* praxis and wisdom in understanding and practicing forms of global, international, and intercultural education in theological schools. An advantage of using these resources is that they reflect current

---

17. See final reports of the two peer groups on Global Partnerships in ATS, "Global Partnerships," 115–30, 131–39.

academic research and the most recent practices developed through peer and project-based methodologies. In the next section, I review a few programs developed by the American Council of Education (ACE) I consider pertinent, relevant, and useful to theological educators and schools seeking to clarify, develop, consolidate, and improve teaching, learning, and service with and for "global awareness and engagement."

ACE IN THE PURSUIT OF INTERNATIONALIZING HIGHER EDUCATION

The ideal and goal of "internationalizing higher education" have been renewed in the past three decades in light of academic and public discussion on globalization. Important segments of leaders in the complex system of US higher education are promoting the idea that, in order to respond strategically to both the challenges and opportunities present in national and international landscapes, public and private universities and colleges need to reenvision their mission, curricula, and educational systems to address the new conditions and aspirations for education in a globalized world, at home and abroad.

The three leading US professional associations in higher education advancing the ideal of the "internationalization" project are the American Council of Education (ACE),[18] the Association of International Educators (NAFSA),[19] and the Association of International Education Administrators (AIEA).[20] They constitute the top key promoters and brokers that have gathered resources, established national and international networks, and conducted research, advocacy, and training to articulate visions and strategies that promote the internationalization of higher education in the United States. These organizations work from the conviction that US universities and colleges are embedded in and impacted by a new globalized context for higher education, and their opportunities for missional impact and growth depend on building capacity for global engagement.

---

18. ACE, "American Council on Education."

19. Previously known as National Association of Foreign Students Advisors (1948) then as National Association for Foreign Students Affairs (1964), and later as NAFSA: Association of International Educators (1990). See NAFSA, "Association of International Educators."

20. AIEA, "Home."

From their perspective, the world and work of higher education in the United States now operates in a larger, complex, international, and interconnected environment. United States universities and colleges with footprints at home and abroad are impacted by some of the following global forces:

- a new economic geography with international corporations, financial organizations, political elites, financial markets, and a diverse migrant work force operating within and across national borders;
- the extraordinary deployment, exchange, and displacement of capital, products, ideas, and people due to new developments in technology, communication, and transportation systems;
- the phenomenal disproportionate concentration of wealth in minority sectors and among leading industrialized nations (G20) seeking access or investing in Western educational programs and institutions;
- the unprecedented growth of international student populations seeking education in First World countries;
- the international collaboration and the commodification of scientific and educational organizations sponsored by governments and corporations;
- the emergence of new networks of global regulatory organizations, on the one hand, and social movements resisting what they perceive as deepening hierarchy and exclusion in these organizations, on the other;
- the appearance of new forms of social consciousness that advocate for unity or diversity or hybridity;
- a new sense of shared problems, cosmopolitan destiny, and planetary responsibility.[21]

The presence and pressure of these economic, political, and cultural forms of globalization spanning geographical boundaries and state borders have prompted some leaders, organizations, and schools in the US higher education system to reconceive and reposition the core practices of teaching/learning, research, and service in terms of global learning, global engagement, and global markets, at home and abroad.

21. For a comprehensive discussion of these and other topics, see Deardorff et al., *SAGE Handbook*.

From my perspective, the organization that has produced the most comprehensive approach to think about internationalizing higher education is the American Council of Education (ACE). I think this is the case for at least three reasons. First, it is an organization with a wide representation of colleges and universities. Its membership provides a diversity of intellectuals, practitioners, and administrators collaborating in forums and projects where research, experimentation, and assessment are brought together. Second, ACE has built a community of learning using effectively the methodologies of consultations, conferences, and project-based collaboration. Finally, ACE engages in research and dialogue with homologous professional associations in other countries and regions around the world.

Three programs developed by the Center of Internationalization and Global Engagement[22] (an ACE initiative) are pertinent to theological educators interested in discerning a vision and a praxis for a curriculum, a campus, and a school that promote "global awareness and engagement." I selected this sample based on the interests, needs, and concerns that have been communicated in the dialogues and reports by leaders of ATS member schools gathered to reflect on their practices of engaging in global learning and relationships.

ACE RESOURCES FOR INTERNATIONALIZING CURRICULUM, CAMPUS, AND SCHOOL

The Center for Internationalization and Global Engagement (CIGE) is one of three centers through which ACE accomplishes its mission and delivers its services.[23] In collaboration with a network of universities and academic leaders in the country, it has developed useful frameworks, trainings, and resources that are available on its webpage to carry its mission for internationalization and global engagement.[24] By "useful," I mean three things. First, these are resources developed by researchers and educators who understand the contemporary practices of curriculum and course design, student-centered pedagogies, institutional action, and assessment processes. Second, the website exhibits the work of several universities that have conducted research and implemented projects on areas and subjects related to international and global education. This means the reader has access to

22. ACE, "Center for Internationalization."
23. ACE, "Higher Education."
24. ACE, "Internalization."

a variety of content and practical ideas from different institutions to help engage in comparative analysis. Finally, because of the variety of sources, the user can examine more critically this material and these case studies by noticing what is different, missing, overstated, or in alignment or not with one's own convictions and perspectives.

Like many others, I am convinced that there is no one way of understanding and practicing global learning in higher or theological education. Each school needs to define its understanding and practices. Nevertheless, the work of ACE scholars and practitioners in this area provides initial resources to those of us who are still trying to find or to refine a path that we know remains an open and experimental journey. I mention just a few.

Comprehensive Internationalization

The signature concept of CIGE is *comprehensive internationalization*. It is defined as "a strategic, coordinated process that seeks to align and integrate policies, programs, and initiatives to position colleges and universities as more globally oriented and internationally connected institutions."[25] This is also the framework that orients and organizes CIGE's research, reflection, communication, and training programs.

Comprehensive internationalization is concept and a process that makes the following proposal. In order for a higher education institution to be successful in preparing professionals and leaders to work successfully and contribute responsibly as citizens in an increasingly diverse and globalized world, the institution needs to develop a curriculum and an institutional plan that supports global learning as a pedagogical and institutional priority. ACE literature works with the following definitions.

- *Global learning* has to do with the learning goals, curricular content, and pedagogical practices that allow students "to understand world cultures and events; analyze global systems; appreciate cultural differences; and apply this knowledge and appreciation to their lives as citizens and workers."[26]

- *Internationalization* refers to all pedagogical and administrative practices that contribute to give priority and enhance "the international,

---

25. ACE, "CIGE Model."
26. Olson et al., *Comprehensive Internationalization*, v.

global, or intercultural dimensions" in the curriculum and in the school's strategic plan.[27]

- *Comprehensive internationalization* is an intentional and concerted effort across the school's systems to give institutional priority and integration to the process of internationalization, that is, the promotion of global learning as a priority in the curriculum and in the organization.[28]

In summary, *comprehensive internationalization* is an invitation to make global learning a priority in the curriculum and in the institutional mission and strategic plan of the school. The vocation of a school committed to internationalization is the formation of people through global learning with the capacity to understand, work, and contribute and to serve as leaders, workers, and citizens in a diverse and globalized world at home and abroad.

The practice of *comprehensive internationalization* requires of a school to engage in two interdependent processes and in this order. First, a process to clarify, establish, and assess student global learning goals and, second, to conduct an institutional review to clarify, integrate, and assess international goals and initiatives that foster global learning in the student body and in the institution. The goals for *global learning* will infuse, lead, and guide the curriculum and all other institutional practices. *Comprehensive internationalization* happens when all of the school's educational and institutional activities promote global learning goals and when the practices of international engagement are connected and coordinated to foster global learning in the school as a community of learning and as an educational institution. *Internationalization* is comprehensive when it impacts and links the following six areas:

- Articulated institutional commitment: Mission statements, strategic plans, and formal assessment mechanisms;
- Administrative structure and staffing: Reporting structures and staff and office configurations;
- Curriculum, co-curriculum, and learning outcomes: General education and language requirements, co-curricular activities and programs, and specified student learning outcomes;

---

27. Olson et al., *Comprehensive Internationalization*, viii.
28. Olson et al., *Comprehensive Internationalization*, viii.

- Faculty policies and practices: Hiring guidelines, tenure and promotion policies, and faculty development opportunities;
- Student mobility: Study abroad programs, and international student recruitment and support; and
- Collaboration and partnerships: Joint-degree or dual/double-degree programs, branch campuses, and other offshore programs.[29]

CIGE uses the framework and method of *Comprehensive Internationalization* to organize all its leadership training programs, guide its research, deliver consulting services, and develop resources for its member schools.[30] The most famous program for schools is the International Laboratory.[31] ACE consultants works with schools in organizing and developing a customized review program to conduct the two processes of establishing global learning goals and institutional international goals and developing a strategic plan for internationalization. More than one hundred schools have participated in this program.

This perspective and program will not be appealing to all theological schools, particularly if the vocation for internationalization is not a missional priority for the school. Nonetheless, some of the practices and resources developed by CIGE can serve well the educational and institutional processes of schools who are interested in promoting some form of global learning as part of its theological curriculum. ATS schools already engaged in some form of global theological learning and international engagement at home and abroad will find good resources and ideas to design and deliver educational programs that form religious leaders with deeper global, cultural, and international awareness and prepare them for cross-cultural ministries at home or abroad.

Internationalization in Action

One of the changes and growing trends in US higher education over the past twenty-five years has been the growth of international engagement and partnerships to deliver education to US nationals going abroad, and also to export US education to local populations in foreign countries. These

29. CIGE, *Mapping Internationalization*, 4.
30. ACE, "CIGE Programs."
31. ACE, "International Laboratory."

two modalities of delivering education abroad have required the development of international partnerships with multiple organizations, including colleges and universities, foreign study providers, nongovernmental organizations, religious and cultural organizations, government agencies, industry companies, city governments, research institutions and laboratories, and more. CIGE has developed initiatives to facilitate collaborative research, leadership training, and the sharing of resources among its member schools and participants in their programs. One focus of those efforts has been the area of launching, organizing, sustaining, and assessing international partnerships.

There are two particular resources that offer frameworks, ideas, examples, and tools to develop strategic planning and actions to support the practices of relating and working with international partners. *Internationalization in Action* is a website with free resources that advises on strategies and best practices to advance internationalization on campus, including international partnerships.[32] One such resource is a four-part series entitled International Partners Series. The series presents a nine-step process to "establish a foundation for collaboration, navigate key decision points in the partnership lifecycle, and promote a robust relationship that adapts to changing needs and expectations."[33] The *Internationalization Toolkit* is a web-portal that provides "policies, programs, surveys, and information" for each of the six aspects of the Comprehensive Internationalization model.[34]

There is one link to a *Collaboration and Partnerships* page with links to universities' websites that provide examples on topics and practices such as "Partnership Programs and Agreements, and Global Engagement Planning Processes and Policies."[35] Another important page with occasional papers is CIGE Insights.[36] The reader will find and have access to the publication *International Higher Education Partnerships: A Global Review of Standards and Practices*, which contains results of a research on US and international literature on standards for global partnerships.[37]

All the issues raised by the two ATS groups on Global Partnerships are addressed and illustrated in one form or another by the sources CIGE has

32. ACE, "Internationalization in Action."
33. ACE, "Internationalization in Action."
34. ACE, "Internationalization Toolkit."
35. ACE, "Collaboration and Partnerships."
36. ACE, "CIGE Insights."
37. ACE, "International Higher Education Partnerships."

collected from their partners and programs to address the area of international partnerships. It is curious that there is no reference to any of these resources in these reports. It is my hope that this simple survey of ACE's resources leads theological educators and leaders to mine selectively and critically available resources from professional communities of learning in higher education.

"AT HOME IN THE WORLD: EDUCATING FOR GLOBAL CONNECTIONS AND LOCAL COMMITMENTS" INITIATIVE

Working with different universities interested in internationalizing higher education, ACE discovered on the ground a rift between two competing and rival fields of scholarship and teaching as well as student services on campuses: international education and multicultural education. In 2006, ACE convened a forum of professors and administrators representing these two academic fields and asked them to explore an alternative way of addressing this divide. They entitled the conference "Educating for Difference: The Intersection Between Internationalization and Multicultural Education."[38]

This conference was the occasion for a publication and the creation of an initiative with the following name: "At Home in the World: Educating for Global Connections and Local Commitments."[39] A three-year initiative funded by the Henry Luce Foundation, CIGE collaborated with eight institutions to "advance new analytical frameworks, enhance pedagogy, and develop innovative ways of fostering collaboration between internationalization and diversity/multicultural education on campus."[40] They define the purpose of this project this way:

> Cultural competency among twenty-first-century graduates has become imperative as the job market globalizes and the workforce continues to diversify. In order to become responsible, productive citizens, our students must understand their own cultures and those of their neighbors at home and afar. By engaging higher education institutions in examining the collaboration potential between diversity/multicultural education and

---

38. Olson et al., *At Home*, 35.
39. ACE, "At Home."
40. ACE, "At Home."

internationalization, we seek to address these needs through the At Home in the World: Educating for Global Connections and Local Commitments initiative. For institutions to fulfill their service mission in a globalized society, they will need to advance the analytical frameworks, pedagogical enhancements, diversification strategies and innovative solutions to societal issues that the work in this intersection affords.[41]

Their agenda was, and still is, to find common ground by identifying learning goals that can be affirmed by educators and leaders of internationalization and multicultural education and adapted by schools. They recognized that these two traditions of study have different trajectories, methodologies, and structures in campus life.

Acknowledging the differences and tensions, the scholars convened by ACE in 2006 accepted the challenge not to dismiss, subordinate, or conflate these distinct approaches, but to construct a common ground defined by shared learning goals. The work group of experts and leaders produced the following statement on learning outcomes for learning and learners.

Knowledge/Content Oriented

- Understand the interconnectedness and interdependence of global systems.
- Understand the historical, cultural, economic, and political forces that shape society and explain their own situation in this context.
- Develop a nuanced/complex understanding of culture as a concept and the deep/complex/dynamic nature of culture.
- Understand various/different cultures and how culture is created.
- Understand the relationship of power and language, and how language interacts with culture.
- Understand the connections between power, knowledge, privilege, gender, and class (locally and globally).
- Understand conflict and power relationships.
- Understand how language frames thinking and perspective; "the language you speak creates the box in which you think."
- Recognize how stereotypes develop and where they come from.

---

41. ACE, "At Home."

Attitudinal/Mode of Being

- Develop a sense of perspective and social responsibility.
- Overcome provincial/parochial thinking.
- Reduce their own prejudice.
- Appreciate difference; value and acknowledge other cultures as legitimate.
- Improve cultural self-awareness and understanding of one's self in the global context (one's own place and connections).
- Demonstrate greater appreciation of or an interest in learning about different cultures.
- Develop empathy and perspective consciousness.
- Demonstrate open-mindedness and an understanding of complexity.

Skills

- Think, work, and move across boundaries—in diverse environments with a range of people.
- Develop and use skills in conflict resolution.
- Develop and use intercultural communication skills.
- Demonstrate language proficiency.
- Take informed responsibility for actions in a globally connected world.
- Link theory and practice through their own experience both as citizens and in professions.
- Internalize and apply cultural understandings and knowledge.
- Seek out multiple perspectives—inside perspectives as well as outside ones.[42]

ACE did not offer this statement as a consensus and normative proposal but as a tool to support critical dialogue and exploration among those who determine learning goals, policies, and structures for educational programs in their institutions. They recommended this methodology (finding common ground) and resource (statement of learning outcomes) as part of

42. Olson et al., *At Home*, 13.

an institutional strategy to organize and promote critical and constructive dialogue in search of discernment for action. The suggestion to focus on the learning and the learner was one way of seeking common ground as people keep exploring their disciplinary and ideological differences and divides.[43]

The debate and challenge for seeking an intersection between those studies that focus on issues of differences, divides, hierarchies of power and privilege, social justice, and social transformation (e.g., critical multiculturalism, critical social sciences, critical philosophical and cultural studies) and those disciplines that are more interested to describe the sociocultural differences in order to promote business, cultural exchange, and social integration still continues.

The debate and tensions between the traditions, practices, and organization of international and multicultural/diversity education have been present in theological education since the 1970s (though not on a grand scale) with the emergence of the many theologies of liberation and the use of social sciences in practical and political theologies. This tension remains, and I hear a similar call for convergence in one of the concerns the sixteen ATS leaders expressed in their commitment to begin global engagement at home. They agreed that "while it can be easier to engage with theological educators abroad, it is just as important to engage with multicultural constituents in the seminary's own campus and context. Local relationships can be complicated by a history of past injustices that must be overcome in order for participants to gain credibility."[44]

The CIGE's webpage has snapshot stories of the eight participant schools and their projects, and toolkit resources to conduct an intentional and structured dialogical process that could be adopted and adapted fruitfully to meet the need for bridging the gap of these important education traditions and approaches that inform theological education in our schools.[45]

CONCLUSION: EXPANDING THE COMMUNITY OF LEARNING

ATS has renewed its call for member schools and the association itself to be concerned about and committed to teaching in new and effective ways the wisdom, habits, and practices that will prepare religious leaders,

43. Olson et al., *At Home*, 27–32.
44. Brown, "Global Engagement," 1.
45. ACE, "At Home." See also Appendix below, 77-78.

congregations, and people of faith to live, lead, and serve with "global awareness and engagement" in a globalized and plural world. In order to hone its self-understanding and practices for this learning goal, ATS educators and leaders could benefit from collaborative work with and resources developed by peer professional associations in US higher education, particularly the research projects and materials of the American Council of Education.

What "global awareness and engagement" means and how we teach it remains an open and experimental path as we seek to respond to the contradictory and still untamed forces and systems of economic, political, and social globalizations that bring and distribute unevenly seeds of life and death, freedom and oppression, wealth and scarcity—or in religious language, a mixed bag of blessings and curses. The practice of global learning is not a new gnosis or a new gospel. Rather, it is an earthly vessel to season theological *sapientia* (wisdom) and marinate ministerial *diakonia* (service) to respond to the signs of the time and the Spirit's leading for this time and place.

APPENDIX

Comparative Table on Educational Approaches Addressing Racial/Ethnic and Cultural Diversities

Luis R. Rivera

	Anti-Racism or Anti-Oppression Education	Multicultural Education	Diversity Education	Intercultural Education
Contextual and Social Challenges	The prevalent damaging impact of institutional structures of domination and oppression (race, class, gender, sexuality, etc.). Anti-racism education focuses on the operations and impacts of institutional white racism (power and privilege) in its economic, political, and cultural manifestations	Global and national demographic changes due to immigration and growth of national minoritized and diaspora populations; political, legal, and social challenges to nationalist, xenophobic, racist, assimilationist politics, institutions, and policies; affirmation of the human rights of migrant workers, indigenous, and minoritized groups to claim and practice freely their cultural differences	Demographic changes contributing to the emergence of a diverse society, work force, and consumer markets, plus new laws that protect the rights of underrepresented minority groups demand the creation of new work environments and organizations	The predominance and persistence of ethnocentric attitudes and practices, and how they block effective cross-cultural communication and relationships in social contexts where people and communities with different cultural identities, practices, and traditions coexist

	Anti-Racism or Anti-Oppression Education	Multicultural Education	Diversity Education	Intercultural Education
Problems to address	Hierarchical systems, structures, and ideologies of oppression and exclusion that promote power and privilege for dominant groups; and domination, subordination, dispossession, and exclusion for racialized subaltern groups	Nationalist, xenophobic, racist, assimilationist institutions, politics and policies that promote power and privilege for dominant groups and economic, political, and cultural subordination, exclusion and oppression for minoritized groups	Individual, group, and organizational patterns of prejudice; exclusionary policies and practices in organizations; lack of compliance with civil rights laws	Cultural misunderstanding, subordination, and exclusion in multicultural environments and interactions due to ethnocentrism and lack of intercultural competence in people, groups, and organizations
Goals and aspirations (social, organizational, and personal)	Dismantling of racist systems and cultures; development of social systems and organizations that promote equity, inclusion, and social justice; promotion of cultural changes that reduce prejudice, discrimination, violence, dispossession against minoritized groups; promotion of politics and policies that empower the agency of subaltern groups for resistance and social change	Promote visions and practices of nation, citizenship, and culture that affirm the value of cultural differences and diversity in any project of unity; resist and challenge hegemonic, homogenizing, and colonializing systems and practices that privilege the Western-Anglo-White populations and traditions; reform education systems to promote cultural diversity, cross-cultural interactions, and equality and equity	Create a workplace or organization with policies, practices, and a culture that promote respect, dignity, and inclusion for all people; use their cultural differences to increase productivity and profitability; comply with federal and state laws that grant and protect civil rights; avoid class-action suits	Development of intercultural competence in people and organizations to be more inclusive, adaptive, and intentional in harnessing the resources of cultural differences and diversities. *intercultural sensitivity* *intercultural competence* *intercultural awareness and knowledge*

BIBLIOGRAPHY

American Council on Education (ACE). "American Council on Education." http://www.acenet.edu/Pages/default.aspx.
———. "At Home in the World Toolkit." http://www.acenet.edu/news-room/Pages/AHITW-Toolkit-Main.aspx.
———. "Center for Internationalization and Global Engagement (CIGE)." https://www.acenet.edu/news-room/Pages/Center-for-Internationalization-and-Global-Engagement.aspx
———. "CIGE Insights." http://www.acenet.edu/news-room/Pages/CIGE-Insights.aspx.
———. "CIGE Model for Comprehensive Internationalization." http://www.acenet.edu/news-room/Pages/CIGE-Model-for-Comprehensive-Internationalization.aspx.
———. "CIGE Programs." http://www.acenet.edu/news-room/Pages/CIGE-Programs.aspx.
———. "Collaboration and Partnerships." http://www.acenet.edu/news-room/Pages/Collaboration-and-Partnerships.aspx.
———. "Higher Education." http://www.acenet.edu/higher-education/Pages/default.aspx.
———. "International Higher Education Partnerships: A Global Review of Standards and Practices." https://www.acenet.edu/news-room/Pages/International-Higher-Education-Partnerships-A-Global-Review-of-Standards-and-Practices.aspx.
———. "International Laboratory." http://www.acenet.edu/news-room/Pages/ACE-Internationalization-Laboratory.aspx.
———. "Internationalization and Global Engagement." http://www.acenet.edu/higher-education/Pages/Internationalization.
———. "Internationalization in Action." http://www.acenet.edu/news-room/Pages/Internationalization-in-Action.aspx.
———. "Internationalization Toolkit." http://www.acenet.edu/news-room/Pages/Internationalization-Toolkit.aspx.
Aleshire, Daniel, and Lester Edwin J. Ruiz. "A New Global Direction for ATS: Five Reflections on the Global Survey on Theological Education." http://www.ats.edu/uploads/resources/publications-presentations/documents/new-global-direction-for-ats.pdf.
Association of International Education Administrators (AIEA). "Home." http://www.aieaworld.org.
Association of Theological Schools (ATS). "2015–16 Annual Data Tables." http://www.ats.edu/uploads/resources/institutional-data/annual-data-tables/2015–2016-annual-data-tables.pdf.
———. "Asian Schools." In *Educational Models and Practices Peer Group Final Reports*, 140–44. Pittsburgh: ATS, 2017. https://www.ats.edu/uploads/resources/current-initiatives/educational-models/publications-and-presentations/peer-group-final-reports/peer-group-final-report-book.pdf.
———. "Global Awareness and Engagement Initiative." http://www.ats.edu/resources/current-initiatives/global-awareness-and-engagement-initiative.
———. "Global Partnerships." In *Educational Models and Practices Peer Group Final Reports*, 115–30, 131–39. Pittsburgh: ATS, 2017. https://www.ats.edu/uploads/resources/current-initiatives/educational-models/publications-and-presentations/peer-group-final-reports/peer-group-final-report-book.pdf.

Berling, Judith A. "Collective Wisdom: What ATS Schools Have Learned About Establishing, Sustaining, and Evaluating Good Cross-Cultural Relationships." *Theological Education* 35.2 (1999) 85–139.

———. "Our Words Are Beginning to Make It So: ATS Schools on Cross-Cultural Relationships and Globalization." *Theological Education* 36.2 (2000) 63–80.

Brown, Eliza Smith. "Global Engagement: Ten Critical Lessons Learned by Theological Educators." Pittsburgh: ATS, 2015. http://www.ats.edu/uploads/resources/publications-presentations/documents/global-engagement-ten-critical-lessons-learned.pdf.

———. "Global Forum of Theological Educators to Hold Inaugural Meeting." Pittsburgh: ATS, 2016. http://www.ats.edu/uploads/resources/publications-presentations/colloquy-online/gfte-to-hold-inaugural-meeting.pdf.

Center for Internationalization and Global Engagement (CIGE). *Mapping Internationalization on US Campuses*. 2012 edition. Washington, DC: ACE, 2013.

Deardorff, Darla K., et al., eds. *The SAGE Handbook of International Higher Education*. California: SAGE Publications, 2012.

Graham, Stephen. "Educational Models and Practices in Theological Education." https://www.ats.edu/resources/current-initiatives/educational-models-and-practices-theological-education.

———. "Midpoint reflections on Educational Models Project—Peer Groups Share Ten Themes." Pittsburgh: ATS, 2016. https://www.ats.edu/uploads/resources/publications-presentations/colloquy-online/midpoint-reflections-on-ed-models.pdf.

Kern, Lisa. "Inter-Group Conversations Introduced at Educational Models and Practices Peer Group Forum." Pittsburgh: ATS, 2017. https://www.ats.edu/uploads/resources/publications-presentations/colloquy-online/intergroup-conversations-introduced.pdf

National Association of Foreign Student Advisers (NAFSA). "NAFSA: Association of International Educators." http://www.nafsa.org.

Olson, Christa L., et al. *A Handbook for Advancing Comprehensive Internationalization: What Institutions Can Do and What Students Should Learn*. Washington, DC: ACE, 2006.

Olson, Christa L., et al. *At Home in the World: Bridging the Gap Between Internationalization and Multicultural Education*. Washington, DC: ACE, 2007.

5

Church Affiliation and Higher Education in a Secularizing World
Insights and Questions for Theological Education

E. Byron Anderson

DENOMINATIONAL AFFILIATION REMAINS A factor for many religiously affiliated colleges and universities (for example, the hundred-plus higher education institutions affiliated with The United Methodist Church). But how do these institutions negotiate that affiliation in light of the rapidly changing US higher education scene, including increasing competition for students, declining mainline churches, greater cultural and religious campus diversity, and expanding global competition?

Shifting the conversation from US higher education in general to graduate theological education in particular complicates this question. The questions asked by colleges and universities, even in relationship to the question of church relationship, have not been the primary questions asked by theological schools, even when some schools have begun to redefine their relationship to the church. Nevertheless, theological schools have much to learn from the higher education debates as they confront the need to rethink and recalibrate their commitments to the church and the education of its leaders today. In this task, I suggest below, the higher education discussion about church affiliation correlates with recent discussions about globalization in theological education. The intersection of the two, as I attempt in the final section of this chapter, offers seminaries and theological schools a framework in which to navigate this complex challenge.

I begin with an overview of some of the conversation about church affiliation, secularization, and higher education. I then review a series of taxonomies that have been used to categorize types of relationships between churches and universities, with attention to one particular taxonomy, indicating implications for how we think about theological education. Finally, I attempt to correlate this taxonomy with a set of definitions of globalization that reflect differing understandings of the church's mission in the world. I conclude with several questions for our continued conversation.

FAITH AND EDUCATION: THE SECULARIZATION THESIS

One of the issues that shapes the question of church affiliation is the widespread perception that we live in a "secularizing world" that has experienced a corresponding secularization of higher education. Some assumptions in this perception require our attention. Douglas and Rhonda Jacobsen argue that, although church-university relationships had begun to be severed far earlier,

> by the late 1970s, religion as a matter of living faith and practice had essentially been bleached from the goals and purposes of higher education at the nation's major universities. Higher education was about public knowledge, and public knowledge was defined in purely secular terms. . . . Students, if they were so inclined, could hold onto their religious beliefs in private, but those personal religious beliefs and practices were considered to have scant connection with the public knowledge that was being developed and disseminated in the classroom.[1]

The history of Northwestern University's relationship to The Methodist Church serves as an example. The university, though envisioned as a "non-sectarian institution," was established by Methodists, and its first presidents were ordained Methodists. Its first non-Methodist president was

---

1. Jacobsen and Jacobsen, "Postsecular America," 10.

not installed until 1920. It was not until 1972 that the university moved to fully sever its ties to the church, with its formal affiliation ending in 1974.[2]

The Jacobsens' claim echoes what several scholars label as James Burtchaell's "secularization thesis," proposed in his book *The Dying of the Light: The Disengagement of Colleges and Universities from Their Christian Churches*. This thesis suggests that "given enough time, church-related colleges leave their founding denominations and their founding principles for the greener grass of some combination of better funding, increased prestige in the eyes of the academy, choice and quality in faculty hiring and more open student recruitment."[3] From Burtchaell's perspective, "even on most of the campuses which are still listed by churches as their affiliates, there is usually some concern . . . about how authentic or how enduring that tie really is; and often wistful concern is all that remains."[4] For Northwestern, it seemed to be not so much a departure from its founding principles as a confirmation of what the university intended at its founding and had become before the mid-twentieth century.

Writers such as Jacobsen and Jacobsen challenge this secularization thesis. "The way people sometimes talk about faith and higher education," they argue, "[uses] a bipolar frame of reference [that is, the poles of religious/non-religious or church-related/secular] that ignores actual diversity." Rather, they claim, "religion is present in many different forms and to varying degrees on public and private school campuses across the nation,"[5] as is evident in the strength and number of parachurch as well as church-sponsored ministries on (or adjacent to) many state university campuses. What may be more true, therefore, is what Peter Berger calls a shift in the "institutional location of religion,"[6] away from formal relationships with or sponsorships by churches and schools. The Jacobsens go on to argue that "the gap between church-related higher education and mainstream non-religious higher education has, in some ways, shrunk" as church-related as well as nonreligious schools work to balance "critical thinking and academic excellence" with concerns for "purpose, meaning, values, and even faith."[7]

2. Marshall, "Keeping the Faith."
3. Badley, "Whither Church-Related Higher Education Now?," 339.
4. Burtchaell, *Dying of the Light*, ix.
5. Jacobsen and Jacobsen, "Ideals and Diversity," 65–66.
6. Berger, "Desecularization of the World," 10.
7. Jacobsen and Jacobsen, "Ideals and Diversity," 79.

While I agree with the Jacobsens' perspective, I note two concerns. First, they imply that religiously-affiliated schools had been historically uncommitted to "objective inquiry and critical rationality," an argument I think many church-affiliated schools can and would readily challenge. Second, where Burtchaell is concerned with church-relationships and the practices he thinks should be evident from those relationships, the Jacobsens are focused primarily on the "presence of religion" on campus. These are related but not equivalent concerns and need to be treated as such.

If the bipolar frame is inappropriate as the Jacobsens claim, so too is a frame that suggests the merger of the two domains, of the secular and the religious, even if "the public does not perceive a sharp difference between church-related colleges and other kinds of educational institutions."[8] As they suggest, "The two domains . . . continue to have different goals . . . circumscribed by different regulations regarding what is and is not appropriate. The tradition-informed instruction . . . of many church-related colleges and universities would be clearly out of bounds at public institutions of higher learning where neutrality toward religion is the legal standard."[9] Here the Jacobsens offer another implicit and, I think, problematic assumption, that "tradition-informed instruction" is the only model for church-related higher education, when in fact there are several different models, as we will see.

CHURCH FOUNDED, CHURCH-RELATED, OR "ECCLESIALLY BASED"

The simple bipolar structure of the religious/secular distinction conceals the more diffuse reality of church-related colleges and universities. That is, even when we look at schools that were or remain church-affiliated, even schools affiliated with one church tradition such as those affiliated with The United Methodist Church (my own tradition, which I use as an example here), there are several ways in which to name the relationship between a school and a church. In some cases, again such as with United Methodist colleges and universities as well as seminaries, "church relationship" has no one definition, not even at the denominational level. For example, schools approved by the United Methodist University Senate—a kind of accrediting body of United Methodist-affiliated schools—are assessed on

8. Cunniggim, *Uneasy Partners*, 23.
9. Jacobsen and Jacobsen, "Ideals and Diversity," 79–80.

"institutional integrity, well-structured programs, sound management, and clearly defined church relationships."[10] A church-related school, from a United Methodist perspective, is therefore a school that has been so assessed and approved by the University Senate.[11] Any further definition of that relationship is "of institutional design," because of the diverse histories, heritages, and institutional practices of the schools.[12]

This somewhat ambivalent description of church-relatedness appears in the 2016 United Methodist *Book of Discipline*, which sets out a statement of support for higher education and for the church's relationship to it. But, as Thomas Trotter notes, such support has not always been the case. In 1972, shortly after the merger of the Evangelical United Brethren and Methodist churches that created The United Methodist Church and about the time that Garrett and Evangelical were playing out that merger in their own merger, The United Methodist Church considered giving up on higher education. Some in the church at the time argued that "it was time to abandon the mission of higher education and turn it over to the public universities."[13] Part of the rationale for such a consideration, Trotter suggests, was that "the church schools, seeking survival, have tended to be smaller versions of the mega-university," which are "focused on producing graduates who are more oriented toward jobs than social responsibility, toward personal autonomy than service, and toward indifference to religious traditions as defining human accountability."[14]

Trotter's description seems to suggest that church-relationship requires more than institutional or accrediting approval. It requires some sense of shared purpose and common mission. Merrimon Cunniggim's description of the church-related school addresses this point, emphasizing history, identity, and values. He argues that "a church-related college must possess a sense of its past, its rootage, and must show by its life—that is, by both its professions and its practices—that it has a lively appreciation of its

---

10. United Methodist Church, *Book of Discipline*, ¶1415.3.

11. That the United Methodist Church has a "university senate" as a kind of accrediting body of United Methodist-affiliated schools is interesting. What does it mean for the denomination to "accredit" schools alongside of the Association of Theological Schools and the Higher Learning Commission or other "secular" accrediting bodies, especially when there seems to be no specific doctrinal expectations of that accreditation?

12. United Methodist Church, *Book of Discipline*, ¶1416.5.

13. Trotter, "Church's Mission," 76.

14. Trotter, "Church's Mission," 74.

history and present character."¹⁵ And, he continues, it must believe "deeply in the academic values of truth, freedom, justice, and kinship, and . . . have a relationship with its church that is credible and mutually understood."¹⁶ Others, such as Samuel Schuman, press to make identity and values more explicit, arguing that church-related schools are distinguished by "their strong sense of a focused mission" and the ways in which their tight hold on "a central religious core . . . sharpens their identity, internally and to the external world."¹⁷ Where Cunniggim seems to emphasize more general academic values, Schuman calls for schools to affirm and adhere to particular church doctrines and beliefs.

Another group of scholars suggest that "church-related" does not go far enough to counter the secularization of the university. However, rather than pressing for adherence to some form of doctrinal orthodoxy or belief system, they propose something they call the "ecclesially-based" university. Their description shares much with Cunniggim and Schuman but adds a concern for and emphasis on vocation and practice. Such a university, they argue, exists not primarily "to transmit the technical expertise for the future economic success of its students within the broader horizons of the nation and the world," a form of globalization [or internationalization] we might find described in the mission statements of state research universities, but "to initiate and socialize its members into the polity and practices of the church within, for, and often against the polity and practices of the liberal democratic society."¹⁸ Michael Budde suggests that

> the purpose of ecclesially based higher education is to make participants more fully into disciples shaped by the priorities and practices of Jesus Christ; to help them discern their vocation as members of the transnational body of Christ; and to contribute to the mission of the church—to help the church serve more fully and faithfully as a foretaste of the promised kingdom of God, on earth as it is in heaven.¹⁹

Such a claim about Christian vocation seems to be more common to and to align better with the mission and purpose of a theological school

---

15. Cunniggim, *Uneasy Partners*, 99.

16. Cunniggim, *Uneasy Partners*, 117.

17. Schuman, *Seeing the Light*, 227. The conclusion of the book provides a helpful overview of the literature. See Schuman, "Essay on Sources," 281–318.

18. Wright, "How Many Masters?," 14, 26.

19. Budde, "Assessing," 256.

than with a university. At the same time, it proposes an alternate, perhaps even eschatological, understanding of globalization.

This group of scholars is suggesting not only that the church-related schools are increasingly secularized in their approaches to vocational and educational formation but also that there is a necessary missional divide between secular and "ecclesially-based" institutions. Yet Michael Cartwright, an advocate of the ecclesially-based institution model, suggests that they need not be mutually exclusive. Cartwright believes that it is possible for church-related schools to exist "where the organizing paradigm remains secular but where it is also possible to frame the mission of the institution in ways that not only are consonant with the Christian vision but also make available Christian articulations of that vision in a variety of forms accessible to students and faculty alike."[20] Cartwright himself has sought to realize such a possibility through the development of the Lantz Center for Christian Vocations at the University of Indianapolis.

In several publications, Cartwright has described the journey the University of Indianapolis has taken from its origins as a college of the United Brethren Church, largely destroyed by intra-denominational politics early in its history, to a marginally church-related school, to what he calls an "intentionally pluralist school" that has simultaneously sought to strengthen its relationship to The United Methodist Church and to broaden its interfaith and ecumenical concerns.[21] He contrasts this history with what he sees happening more broadly in church-related, or formerly church-related, colleges. He notes: "It has become increasingly common for church-related colleges to image students as 'consumers' and themselves as 'product providers' seeking to provide 'customer satisfaction' in education. In the midst of the competition for students, church-related colleges and universities have been known to downplay [or even erase] their relationship to the church in order to compete in the marketplace" even as churches themselves increasingly "use the metaphors of 'personal spirituality' instead of 'organized religion,' as if vital piety is not embodied socially in ways that are not easily 'marketable.'"[22] Faced with declining enrollments and denominational funding, some theological schools have begun to make similar moves.

20. Cartwright, "Moving Beyond," 187.
21. See Cartwright and Strege, *Called to Unite*.
22. Cartwright, "Moving Beyond," 195.

Cartwright offers a number of proposals in response to these concerns, three of which seem most relevant to this conversation. First, he argues, "instead of assuming segregated missions, church-related colleges and universities must begin to think conjunctively about their missions in relation to the church's mission." He encourages schools to recontextualize their mission statements and mottoes "in ways that recover at least some of the significance of the Christian vision that informed the institutions when they were founded." Second, "instead of acting as if students are 'unencumbered' [by religious belief], ecclesial-based universities must learn to think of faculty and students alike as persons formed by conviction." Here Cartwright's claims are consistent with those made by the Jacobsens, namely, that religion remains on campuses even without formal church affiliations. Just because a college or university has shed it religious identity does not mean (or require) that its students and faculty do the same. More important, he understands that those "encumbering" religious convictions may be increasingly non-Christian. Third, Cartwright argues, "the ecclesially based university must help [students] be reoriented as explorers on a quest for self-understanding [rather than as consumers] or as actors in a drama with multiple 'acts.'" He qualifies this "quest for self-understanding" by suggesting that such a quest is oriented not toward self-fulfillment but "toward the vision of human flourishing to which Christians bear witness,"[23] a quest that links values, identity, vocation, and practice. Cartwright's own work as [now former] dean of ecumenical and interfaith programs at the University of Indianapolis seems to model such an orientation.

The concern for vocation and practice that Budde and Cartwright identify is a concern shared with most theological schools (and is, in fact, an accreditation standard for the Association of Theological Schools). For example, we find such "conjunctive thinking" about a school's mission in relation to the church's mission at the heart of The United Methodist Church's understanding of the purpose of its denominational seminaries. According to the *Book of Discipline*, "Theological schools of the UMC share a common mission of preparing persons for leadership in the ministry of The United Methodist Church; of leading in the ongoing reflection on Wesleyan theology and of assisting the church in fulfilling its mission to make disciples of Jesus Christ for the transformation of the world."[24] More,

---

23. Cartwright, "Moving Beyond," 209.
24. United Methodist Church, *Book of Discipline*, ¶1422.1.

> The United Methodist schools of theology located in the USA shall acquaint students with the current polity, theology and programs of The United Methodist Church and shall offer practical experience in administration, evangelism, stewardship, and other areas which will prepare them for effective Christian ministry in a multicultural society. Each school of theology . . . shall provide the courses in United Methodist history, doctrine, and polity specified in ¶335.(3) and seek to form persons for ministry in the Wesleyan tradition.[25]

Note how in these two statements the mission of the church seems to take the lead in establishing the mission of the seminary. The "shalls" in this last quotation result in specific curricular requirements that some seminaries, or at least non-United Methodist faculty in United Methodist seminaries, experience as an imposition, especially since these factors are at play in University Senate approval and financial support from the denomination.

SECULAR AND GLOBAL, RELIGIOUS AND DIVERSE

Whether or not we connect to the notion of the ecclesially-based rather than church-related school, one of questions that continues to emerge is that of ecclesial and theological diversity, inclusion, and hospitality. Elizabeth Newman frames the question well: "How can an academic institution identify with a particular religious tradition and at the same time be 'open to diversity'?"[26] This question becomes especially important if, as Cartwright suggests, students and faculty do not arrive unencumbered by religious convictions. Newman uses an interesting analogy in approaching this question, suggesting that many schools approach the question of religious diversity as if they were a kind of "hotel" that may provide space for other persons, but fail to extend true hospitality, because these schools have no real sense of place. "Hospitality," she argues, "can only be fully practiced when a concrete sense of place sustains the life of an institution."[27]

Cartwright picks up on this question of hospitality. His starting point is the need to "pay attention to the local 'membership' that comprises particular institutions of higher education." He notes:

---

25. United Methodist Church, *Book of Discipline*, ¶1422.3(c).
26. Newman, "Hotel or Home?," 91.
27. Newman, "Hotel or Home?," 91.

> On the one hand, our rhetorics of 'diversity and inclusion' often are ungrounded, divorced from the particularities of our campuses, including the fact that many of the faculty, staff and students are, by either background or profession, Christian. On the other hand, it is equally possible to discuss membership without recognizing the ways that we end up creating patterns of 'second-class citizenship' that send the deadly message that *only Christians* can be full participants in the mission of the church-affiliated university.[28]

It is all too easy, he argues, to set up "a conversational dynamic in which it might appear that the United Methodists occupy an inner circle, with another circle that finds itself on the outside looking in, and a third circle of those who feel that they do not belong at all to the mission of the institution."[29] An institution may appear to be religiously inclusive "but in practice the agency of hospitality appears to be governed more by *administrative tolerance* than by the kind of *enriched hospitality* in which all parties are invited to participate in the mission of the institution while giving and receiving hospitality."[30] The question for both Newman and Cartwright becomes how an institution invites those "outside" its church relationship to help the institution think about its relationship to the church's mission, a question that becomes even more pronounced in a denominationally-identified seminary.

Lauree Hersch Meyer offers a similar argument, but with more attention to concerns for diversity and globalization: "Christianity and higher education face the challenge of embodying their traditional vision of universal truth in ways that honor people from diverse cultures and contexts." The question for her, then, "is how we shall hear and honor multiple voices, learn from and teach one another, graciously sharing common living space and activities while engaging and interpreting them from our rich variety of perspectives."[31] And, as Cartwright suggests, how do we listen to and honor those multiple voices when they are already part of our "local membership"? While Newman, Cartwright, and Meyer do not provide answers to these questions, they imply that how an institution identifies its sense of place in relationship to its church-relatedness conditions, and for some,

---

28. Cartwright, "Mission of the University," 1.
29. Cartwright, "Mission of the University," 3.
30. Cartwright, "Mission of the University," 20–21 (emphasis added).
31. Meyer, "Christianity," 91.

determines if and how it will listen to and honor diverse voices as well as if it will do more than tolerate diversity.

TAXONOMIES OF CHURCH-RELATED SCHOOLS

These challenges and concerns inform the ways in which colleges and universities negotiate their relationships to the church, if they choose to have any relationship. And, once we move beyond the simple bipolar distinction between secular and religious, we can begin to describe multiple forms of relatedness. As we can see in Table 1, it has been addressed in various ways since the late 1960s. (I have constructed the table to best reflect the similarities between the models. Unpacking each model is beyond the scope of this essay.)

Robert Benne's framework seems to be the reigning structure in current conversations, so I focus our attention there. As I do so, it is important to note that Benne's goal is not simply descriptive. He is seeking to provide a framework by which schools that had moved to what he calls "intentional pluralism" can find their way back to some significant connection with their ecclesial home. He is particularly troubled by the loss of the role pre-1960s Christian colleges had played in a larger ecological system of Christian formation, from schools to Sunday schools, family camping programs to youth ministries (a concern shared by denominational theological schools).[32] The way back to "genuine Christian colleges and universities," he argues, requires that the religious ethos of the tradition "must in some relevant way condition and affect the life of the college. . . . And persons who bear the vision and the ethos [of the tradition] must participate influentially in the life of the school."[33] When one or more of these things disappear, such as when a church-related school previously headed by an ordained member of that church selects either a non-ordained or unaffiliated person as president, or when a school assumes that the founding vision and ethos will carry the identity without more intentional reflection, schools becomes increasingly "unable or unwilling to articulate their identity and mission in substantive terms."[34]

---

32. Benne, *Quality with Soul*, 34.

33. Benne, *Quality with Soul*, 8.

34. Benne, *Quality with Soul*, 17. This is often of greater concern for denominational theological schools.

Before proceeding with a description of Benne's model, I want to note some of the assumptions it makes and the limitations that come from these assumptions. First, Benne's agenda seems a bit nostalgic. The pre-1960s system is not likely to reappear any time soon. Second, he clearly implies that church-affiliation and "intentional pluralism" are incompatible partners, although there is significant evidence to the contrary. Third, like some of the scholars identified earlier, he has bought into the secularization thesis, arguing that most church-established colleges have relinquished any meaningful connection to their church home, following Enlightenment/secularization processes that restrict questions of faith to the private and subjective realm.[35] Finally, his concern is not simply for the reestablishment of church-relatedness, but for a return to "genuine Christian colleges." In doing so, he seems to be seeking not only some form of institutional relationship or commonality of mission, but also a specific form of religious conviction that is part of the school's identity.

With these concerns before us, we can turn to Benne's model. Benne sets out a fourfold typology of church-relatedness in which he identifies church-related colleges and universities as orthodox, critical mass, intentionally pluralist, or accidentally pluralist. I briefly summarize each category, supplementing Benne's examples of colleges with examples of theological schools.

Orthodox:

- subscribes to a statement of belief;
- exhibits overt piety, religious practice, and denominational loyalty;
- proceeds from a "common Christian commitment [and] all personnel are assumed to live out that commitment at the school"; and
- sees "communication of the ethos" as the main point.[36]

Wheaton College, with its "For Christ and his Kingdom" motto, is a good example of this model. In 2015, it terminated the employment of a faculty member after she chose to wear a hijab as a sign of solidarity with Muslims and claimed that Christians and Muslims worshiped the same God.[37]

---

35. Benne, *Quality with Soul*, 5.
36. Benne, *Quality with Soul*, 50.
37. Pashman, "Wheaton College."

Asbury Theological Seminary provides a similar ethos with a clearly defined statement of faith.[38]

Critical mass:

- not all members of the community must be believers in the school's theological or denominational tradition, but "a critical mass of adherents from [that] tradition inhabit all the constituencies of the educational enterprise";
- "the critical mass must be strong enough to define, shape, and maintain the public identity and mission of the college consonant with the sponsoring tradition";[39]
- "Christian commitment conditions everything that goes on there...[and] is an honored partner in ongoing dialogue"; and
- "an inner core of members of the tradition are expected to bear its vision, teach it to others, and connect that vision with all facets of the school's life."[40]

Benne offers the ELCA-affiliated St. Olaf College as an example of this perspective. According to the school's mission statement, students should "examine faith and values, and explore meaningful vocation in an inclusive, globally engaged community nourished by the Lutheran tradition."[41]

Most United Methodist seminaries, including my own institution, also fit this category. Despite a desire among some United Methodist theological schools to move toward a more pluralist position, The United Methodist Church provides significant financial incentive to its seminaries to maintain a "critical mass" of Methodist faculty: "United Methodist theological schools where less that 40 percent of the regular rank faculty are United Methodist or another historic Wesleyan denomination . . . forfeit 1/3 of their Ministerial Education funding."[42] A 2016 document laying out the principles of the United Methodist University Senate makes the "critical mass" language more explicit: "The commission shall assess a school's ability to provide United Methodist students with an opportunity for growth

---

38. Asbury Theological Seminary, "Our Statement of Faith."
39. Benne, *Quality with Soul*, 50.
40. Benne, *Quality with Soul*, 54.
41. St. Olaf College, "Mission."
42. United Methodist Church, *Book of Discipline*, ¶816.2.a.

in the United Methodist tradition. This shall include discussion and mutual inquiry into United Methodist history and theology. To nurture such a tradition, there must be a critical mass of persons who claim the tradition and an environment in which such an ethos can flourish."[43]

Intentionally pluralist:

- describes liberal arts colleges with a Christian heritage but which have removed all religious expression from their campus;
- the dominant atmosphere is secular, yet there is an open minority of students and faculty who support the sponsoring tradition;
- Christianity is one perspective among others, but it has no privileged place in the school's life and it "is not *the* honored partner in every major intellectual engagement; it is one among many"[44];
- the religious paradigm has been "dethroned" by secularization or some other organizing model;
- commitment to representation of the vision and ethos of the tradition are present only "here and there in the school's life"; and
- maintaining sufficient numbers of persons within the community from the tradition has become increasingly difficult.[45]

A good example of this model is the University of Indianapolis, described earlier. It has worked to both reclaim its church-affiliation and to become intentionally pluralist in perspective. It is perhaps not surprising that when we look at other United Methodist colleges and universities, we see a strong inclination toward intentional pluralism. The 1976 statement *A College-Related Church: United Methodist Perspectives* makes this inclination quite clear: "The Wesleyan tradition in education has endeavored to avoid narrow sectarianism. Cosmopolitan and ecumenical in nature, Methodist institutions have been open to all."[46]

However, when it comes to United Methodist theological schools, we see a different picture, as suggested earlier in the discussion of "critical mass" schools. Claremont School of Theology's short-lived venture

---

43. United Methodist Church, *Organization, Policies, and Guidelines*, 38–39.
44. Benne, *Quality with Soul*, 55.
45. Benne, *Quality with Soul*, 51–52.
46. United Methodist Church, *College-Related Church*, 13.

with Claremont Lincoln University to offer an interreligious program of theological education and formation provides one example. Some within the denomination and the University Senate questioned whether United Methodist Ministerial Education funds, which provide funding to United Methodist seminaries, would underwrite the training of imams and rabbis.[47] In the end, to preserve access to those funds "Claremont altered its original plans to train Christian, Muslim and Jewish students in one college, instead creating a new university with separate graduate schools for Muslim and Jewish students."[48]

Yet we know that Claremont is not alone in the challenges it faces. Church-related colleges and theological schools, in Richard Ray's words, "must address pressures to increase revenue and enrollment in unique and dynamic ways that are true to their intrinsic values. Stated differently, they must find mission-based ideas and practices that will enable them to increase revenue, resources, and enrollment while remaining faithful to their historic missions."[49]

A contrast to Claremont's experience is the University of Chicago Divinity School, which describes itself as "a tough-minded, sprawling, rigorous and dynamic conversation about what religion is and why understanding it is so vitally important . . . where all ideas are subject to uncompromising standards of argument and evidence" and, combined with the university, "represent an unparalleled depth of expertise in all five major world religions."[50] Nevertheless, the University of Chicago Divinity School is also free from particular denominational identity and the financial restrictions such a tie might require, therefore making it free to pursue such a conversation.

Accidentally pluralist:

- more-or-less secular schools with little or no allusion to their original Christian heritage (remember Benne is concerned with Christian, church-affiliated schools that have drifted from their source);

---

47. Gilbert, "United Methodist."
48. Landsberg, "United Methodist."
49. Ray, "Purpose, Provender, and Promises," 30–39.
50. University of Chicago, "About."

- an inexpressibly small and reclusive minority of denominationally-affiliated administrators and faculty may still exist, but they are unorganized and unrecognized;
- "does not have enough commitment to its sponsoring tradition to push for its representation in key facets of the school" leadership; and
- does not operate "out of a religious vision" for the school; such vision is "largely left to chance."[51]

Benne seems unable to provide examples of "accidentally pluralist" schools. More, where his description suggests an unintentional drift away from the church, the histories of many formerly church-affiliated schools suggest this is inaccurate. Their separation from their founding traditions seems quite intentional, even if the initial impetus was a kind of inattention to that tradition. In such schools, theology departments are now clearly identified as religious studies programs. In some cases, such as in the historic relationship between Butler University and Christian Theological Seminary in Indianapolis, what was formerly the "school of religion" within the university was reestablished as an independent institution and religious studies within the university program was recast as the department of Philosophy, Religion and Classics. Lake Forest College, Illinois, is another example of an intentional decision. As they note, after 1955 "traditional ties to the Presbyterian denomination seemed less relevant to a nation challenged by Sputnik and by the diversity of a shrinking world." The college thus decided to sever that relationship and broaden the "faculty's cultural base."[52] Butler and Lake Forest, then, seem to be intentional rather than accidental in their move away from church affiliation and their concern for pluralism.

CHURCH-AFFILIATION IN A GLOBAL CONTEXT: WHITHER THEOLOGICAL EDUCATION?

What does all of this mean for the questions about globalization and theological education—a key concern of this book? At the very least, it is possible to see a correlation between perspectives on church affiliation as represented in the work of Robert Benne and approaches to globalization in theological education as represented in the work of Don Browning and

---

51. Benne, *Quality with Soul,* 52.
52. Lake Forest College, "History."

Mark Heim.[53] It is a correlation that raises more questions than it answers, but offers a framework within which we might continue the conversation.

In 1990, Heim provided a "cartography" for the question of globalization in theological education, setting on one axis four definitions of globalization used in theological education (paraphrased from work by Browning) against a second axis of modes of interpretation, including questions about symbol, philosophy, function, economy, and power. Three of his four definitions of globalization suggest a ready correlation to Benne's categories (see Table 2).

In Heim's first definition, "globalization is the church's universal mission to evangelize the world."[54] This correlates with Benne's description of the "orthodox" church-affiliation, with its concern for the expression of overt piety and commitment and for the development and transmission of a Christian ethos throughout the school's life. It is a perspective that seeks and maintains strong boundaries, providing a kind of "intra-theological security." But here other theological traditions, especially the non-Christian world, remain "other" and, as such, they either must be brought within those theological boundaries (often expelled when those boundaries are violated), or they must be resisted, if not defeated.

Second, "globalization is ecumenical cooperation between the various manifestations of the church throughout the world, including growing mutuality and equality among these churches and respect for their differences."[55] This definition fits Benne's description of the "critical mass" school, which remains overtly Christian in its identity and mission even as it expresses an awareness of Christian difference and a commitment to engaging those differences. The boundary of denominational identity is still present, but seems far more permeable, especially in ecumenical collaboration. Although "classical ecumenism" may have begun in the mode of the first definition, seeking the ideal of "the Christian century," conciliar ecumenism of the last half century seems much more in the mode of this second definition. Ecumenical encounters with Pentecostalism and African indigenous churches still presume the "critical mass" of Western Christianity as a theological voice.

---

53. Heim, "Mapping Globalization," 7–34. Heim draws on Browning, "Globalization," 43–59.
54. Heim, "Mapping Globalization," 12.
55. Heim, "Mapping Globalization," 12.

Third, Heim suggests, "globalization is the dialogue and cooperation between Christianity and other religions."[56] This definition seems to correlate, at least in part, with Benne's description of "intentional pluralism." But as I noted earlier, Benne seems to think that strong church-affiliation and intentional pluralism are incompatible. More in evidence, however, is that it is possible to hold the two together—just difficult to develop, thus the importance of intentionality. Although denominations are seeking to preserve "market share" as well as the theological distinctiveness of their traditions, this definition and model seem to hold more promise for development of theological education in a globalizing world. The challenge here, perhaps, is to pay attention to the ways in which Christianity beyond the West has, as Lamin Sanneh argues, "emerged from a profoundly pluralist religious and cultural world," and how that pluralistic context has deepened their understanding of the gospel.[57]

In his fourth definition, Heim claims that "globalization is the mission of the church to be in solidarity with the poor and oppressed in their struggle for justice."[58] Unfortunately, this definition does not seem to correlate with any of Benne's models. It has some affinity for the ecclesially-based schools which, as described earlier, emphasize vocation and formation. It also has some affinity with Cartwright's sense that such schools should be oriented "toward the vision of human flourishing to which Christians bear witness."[59] This definition also seems to fit the direction that various councils of churches, including the World Council of Churches and Churches Uniting in Christ, have taken in recent years.[60] But it is also a definition that presses us to be more conscious of what Fumitaka Matsuoka calls the "global in our own backyards within North America" and to our interaction "with women, with people of color, with linguistic and ethnic minorities, with the native dwellers of the continent,"[61] that is, to our interaction with our neighbors.

---

56. Heim, "Mapping Globalization," 12.
57. Sanneh, "Universal and Particular," 104.
58. Heim, "Mapping Globalization," 12.
59. Cartwright, "Moving Beyond," 209.
60. The WCC 10th Assembly, held in Busan, Korea in 2013, called the churches "to join a pilgrimage of justice and peace" (WCC, "What We Do"). In 2002, CUIC committed itself to a greater public witness of reconciling the baptized and seeking unity with justice. See CUIC, "Unity."
61. Matsuoka, "Pluralism at Home," 35.

CONTINUING QUESTIONS

The various models of church-related undergraduate education and their correlates in theological education as described here both enact and problematize particular understandings of pluralism and globalization. Yet, as I anticipated at the beginning of this essay, I end not with a conclusion but with several questions that I hope can shape future conversation.

1. In what ways are these understandings of pluralism and globalization carried forward into, confirmed, challenged, or transformed by the models of church-relatedness enacted in theological schools?

2. If the "orthodox" and "critical mass" models of denominational schools are inadequate to both a globalized church and to post-Christian social contexts, might some combination of the "intentionally pluralistic" and "ecclesially-based" models provide a more adequate response?

3. If such is required for a more adequate response, what would such a model look like, especially if we are not to remake theological education into another version of "religious studies"?

All of these questions require attention from North American theological schools, perhaps especially from those within mainline/oldline Protestantism. Without exploring such questions, we cannot address contemporary questions about the need for the church raised by a generation of "nones" (no ecclesial affiliation) and of the "spiritual but not religious," even as these very persons present themselves on our doorsteps and in our classrooms.

Table 1
A Comparison of Recent Taxonomies of Church-Affiliated Schools[62]

Pattillo and Mackenzie, *Church-Sponsored*	Pace, *Education and Evangelism*	Cunniggim, "Categories of Church-Relatedness"	Sandin, *Autonomy and Faith*	Benne, *Quality with Soul*
Defenders of the faith: campus an extension of local church (64)	Institutions governed by churches (66)	*Embodying*: "purist reflection of the sponsoring denomination or church"; "strive to demonstrate denominational faith and values in . . . institutional operations" (68)	*Pervasively religious*: adopt "primary Christian convictions into the totality of college life" (68)	*Orthodox*: subscribe to a statement of belief; overt piety, religious practice, and denominational loyalty (70)
	Nominally related to church but in process of disengagement (66)			

62. This table summarizes in comparative form Garrison, "Taxonomies," 63–72. In the comparison, I have attempted to show the parallels between the different systems. Quotes within the table are from Garrison. In Pace's reading of this relationship, institutional success was correlated with strength of denominational affiliation; "the most distinctive church-related institutions are the ones most likely to survive and prosper" (Pace, *Education and Evangelism*).

Pattillo and Mackenzie, Church-Sponsored	Pace, Education and Evangelism	Cunniggim, "Categories of Church-Relatedness"	Sandin, Autonomy and Faith	Benne, Quality with Soul
		Proclaiming: "give witness or proclamation to its denomination as an affiliated partner" (67); "openly admit their connection to the church and its religious beliefs" (68)	*Religiously supportive:* largely shaped but not determined by religious tradition (69)	*Critical Mass:* "majority of its students, faculty, board and administrators are members of the denomination"; "have a defined identity and mission which highly reflects the denomination." (70)
Free Christian colleges: "loosely guided by a religious framework"; religious faith and liberal arts complementary (65)		*Consonant:* "ally with the denomination, or a certain faction within the denomination, but speak infrequently of its church relationship" (67)	*Nominally church-related:* view church-relatedness "as an important symbol of historic association," but "under no obligation to follow any institutional directive or theological conviction held by the denomination" (69)	*Intentionally Pluralistic:* "liberal arts colleges with a Christian heritage," dominant atmosphere is secular, yet "an open minority of students and faculty who support the sponsoring tradition"; "has removed all religious expression from their campus." (70)

Pattillo and Mackenzie, Church-Sponsored	Pace, Education and Evangelism	Cunniggim, "Categories of Church-Relatedness"	Sandin, Autonomy and Faith	Benne, Quality with Soul
Church-related (focuses on UM and RC): "a pluralistic worldview by design" and limited or "barely evident" denominational involvement (65	Established by church and retain some connection to founding tradition (66)			
Non-affirming: affiliated but downplay relationship to denomination, upholds "religious living" but not specific religious/moral teachings (65)	Church (Protestant) roots, but no longer so in any legal sense (66)		Independent with Historical Religious Ties: at one time "closely identified with the denomination but have long since dropped any such ties" (69)	Accidentally Pluralistic: secular schools with little or no allusion to their Christian heritage"; a small minority of denominationally affiliated administrators and faculty "still exist, but are unorganized and unrecognized" (71)

Table 2
Parallels between Church-Affiliation and Globalization

Benne, *Quality with Soul*	Heim, *Mapping Globalization* (12)
Orthodox: • subscribes to a statement of belief; • overt piety, religious practice, and denominational loyalty; • "communication of the ethos is the main point." (50)	1. Globalization is the church's universal mission to evangelize the world.
Critical Mass: • "does not insist that all members of the community be believers in their tradition, though they do insist that a critical mass of adherents from their tradition inhabit all the constituencies of the educational enterprise." (50) • "an inner core of members of the tradition are expected to bear its vision, teach it to others, and connect that vision with all facets of the school's life." (54)	2. Globalization is ecumenical cooperation between the various manifestations of the church throughout the world, including growing mutuality and equality among these churches and respect for their differences.
Intentionally Pluralist: • dominant atmosphere is secular; • Christianity one perspective among others; the religious paradigm "dethroned" by secularization or some other organizing model. (51) • "some straightforward or tacit commitment to representation of the vision and ethos of the tradition . . . in the school's life" but the tradition has no privileged place in that life. (52)	3. Globalization is the dialogue and cooperation between Christianity and other religions.
Accidentally Pluralist: • secular schools with little or no allusion to their Christian heritage; • "does not have enough commitment to its sponsoring tradition to push for its representation in key facets of the school" leadership, (55) • does not operate "out of a religious vision" for school; it is "largely left to chance" (55)	4. Globalization is the mission of the church to be in solidarity with the poor and oppressed in their struggle for justice.

BIBLIOGRAPHY

Asbury Theological Seminary. "Our Statement of Faith." http://asburyseminary.edu/about/theological-orientation/statement-of-faith.

Badley, Kenneth. "Whither Church-Related Higher Education Now?: A Review Essay of Six Recent Titles." *Journal of Research on Christian Education* 19 (2010) 338–44.

Benne, Robert. *Quality with Soul: How Six Premier Colleges and Universities Keep Faith with Their Religious Traditions*. Grand Rapids: Eerdmans, 2001.

Berger, Peter. "The Desecularization of the World: A Global Overview." In *The Desecularization of the World: Resurgent Religion and World Politics*, edited by Peter Berger, 1–18. Grand Rapids: Eerdmans, 1999.

Browning, Don S. "Globalization and the Task of Theological Education." *Theological Education* 23.1 (1986) 43–59.

Budde, Michael. "Assessing What Doesn't Exist: Reflections on the Impact of an Ecclesially Based University." In *Conflicting Allegiances: The Church-Based University in a Liberal Democratic Society*, edited by Michael L. Budde and John Wright, 255–71. Grand Rapids: Brazos, 2004.

Burtchaell, James. *The Dying of the Light: The Disengagement of Colleges and Universities from their Christian Churches*. Grand Rapids: Eerdmans, 1998.

Cartwright, Michael G. "The Mission of the University, *Reincorporated*?: Membership Matters at the Intentionally Pluralist Church-Related University." Paper presented at Exiles from Eden conference, Valparaiso University, June 7, 2014.

———. "Moving beyond Muddled Missions and Misleading Metaphors: Formation and Vocation of Students within an Ecclesially Based University." In *Conflicting Allegiances: The Church-Based University in a Liberal Democratic Society*, edited by Michael L. Budde and John Wright, 185–216. Grand Rapids: Brazos, 2004.

Cartwright, Michael G., and Merle D. Strege, eds. *Called to Unite Knowledge & Vital Piety: Indiana's Wesleyan-related Universities*. Indianapolis: University of Indianapolis Press, 2012.

Churches Uniting in Christ (CUIC). "Unity in the Midst of Strife." http://www.churchesunitinginchrist.org.

Cunniggim, Merrimon. "Categories of Church-Relatedness." In *Church-Related Higher Education: Perceptions and Perspectives*, edited by Ronald Parsonage, 78–95. Valley Forge, PA: Judson, 1978.

———. *Uneasy Partners: The College and the Church*. Nashville: Abingdon, 1994.

Garrison, Michael Shane. "Taxonomies for Church-Related Schools: How Christian Colleges and Their Denominations Relate." *Campbellsville Review* 5 (2009–10) 63–72.

Gilbert, Kathy L. "United Methodist Ties to Claremont Lincoln University End." *UM News*, April 21, 2014. http://www.umc.org/news-and-media/united-methodist-ties-to-claremont-lincoln-university-end.

Heim, S. Mark. "Mapping Globalization for Theological Education." *Theological Education* 26.s (1990) 7–34.

Jacobsen, Douglas, and Rhonda Hustedt Jacobsen. "The Ideals and Diversity of Church-Related Higher Education." In *The American University in a Postsecular Age: Religion and the Academy*, edited by Douglas Jacobsen and Rhonda Hustedt Jacobsen, 63–80. New York: Oxford University Press, 2008.

———. "Postsecular America: A New Context for Higher Education." In *The American University in a Postsecular Age: Religion and the Academy*, edited by Douglas Jacobsen and Rhonda Hustedt Jacobsen, 3-15. New York: Oxford University Press, 2008.

Lake Forest College. "History of the College." http://www.lakeforest.edu/about/history/#1970.

Landsberg, Mitchell. "United Methodist Church Lifts Sanctions Against Claremont Theology School." *Los Angeles Times*, June 27, 2010. http://articles.latimes.com/2010/jun/27/local/la-me-claremont-20100629.

Marshall, Jon. "Keeping the Faith: Students of Diverse Beliefs Find Fertile Ground to Grow Their Spiritual Lives at Northwestern." *Northwestern* (Summer 2002). http://www.northwestern.edu/magazine/northwestern/summer2002/features/coverstory.

Matsuoka, Fumitaka. "Pluralism at Home: Globalization within North America." *Theological Education* 26.s (1990) 35-51.

Meyer, Lauree Hersch. "Christianity, Higher Education, and Socially Marginalized Voices." In *Should God Get Tenure: Essays on Religion and Higher Education*, edited by David W. Gill, 86-102. Grand Rapids: Eerdmans, 1997.

Newman, Elizabeth. "Hotel or Home? Hospitality and Higher Education" In *Conflicting Allegiances: The Church-Based University in a Liberal Democratic Society*, edited by Michael L. Budde and John Wright, 91-100. Grand Rapids: Brazos, 2004.

Pace, Robert. *Education and Evangelism: A Profile of Protestant Colleges*. Hightstown, NJ: McGraw-Hill, 1972.

Pashman, Manya Brachear. "Wheaton College Could Face Long-Term Fallout Over Professor Controversy." *Chicago Tribune*, February 22, 2016. http://www.chicagotribune.com/news/ct-wheaton-college-professor-fallout-met-20160222-story.html.

Pattillo, Manning M., and Donald M. Mackenzie. *Church-Sponsored Higher Education in the United States: Report from the Danforth Commission*. Washington, DC: American Council on Education, 1966.

Ray, Richard. "Purpose, Provender, and Promises." *The Cresset* 77.4 (2014) 30-39. http://thecresset.org/2014/Easter/Ray_E14.html.

Sandin, Robert T. *Autonomy and Faith: Religious Preference in Employment Decisions in Religiously Affiliated Higher Education*. Atlanta: Center for Constitutional Studies, Mercer University, 1990.

Sanneh, Lamin. "The Universal and the Particular in Muslim-Christian Dialogue." In *Ecumenical and Interreligious Perspectives: Globalization in Theological Education*, edited by Russell E. Richey, 91-107. Nashville: GBHEM, 1992.

Schuman, Samuel. "Essay on Sources." In *Seeing the Light: Religious Colleges in Twenty-First-Century America*, 281-318. Baltimore: Johns Hopkins, 2010.

———. *Seeing the Light: Religious Colleges in Twenty-First-Century America*. Baltimore: Johns Hopkins, 2010.

St. Olaf College. "Mission." http://wp.stolaf.edu/about/mission.

Trotter, F. Thomas. "The Church's Mission in Higher Education in the Twenty-First Century." *Quarterly Review* 23.1 (2003) 71-77.

United Methodist Church. *Book of Discipline*. Nashville: United Methodist, 2016.

———. *A College-Related Church: United Methodist Perspectives*. Nashville: National Commission on United Methodist Higher Education, 1976.

———. *Organization, Policies, and Guidelines*. Nashville: United Methodist, 2012.

University of Chicago, Divinity School. "About." https://divinity.uchicago.edu/about.

World Council of Churches (WCC). "What We Do." https://www.oikoumene.org/en/what-we-do.

Wright, John. "How Many Masters? From the Church-Related to an Ecclesially Based University." In *Conflicting Allegiances: The Church-Based University in a Liberal Democratic Society*, edited by Michael L. Budde and John Wright, 13–28. Grand Rapids: Brazos, 2004.

6

The Glocalization of Theological Education
A Roman Catholic Perspective

MARGARET ELETTA GUIDER, OSF

INTRODUCTION

MINDFUL OF THE ECCLESIAL, local and global dynamics affecting Roman Catholic seminaries and schools of theology and ministry within the context of the United States, specifically in relationship to Catholic identity, diversity and internationalization, I begin this essay with a brief personal narrative that serves as the backdrop for this essay. I proceed to explain the concept of glocalization and discuss its importance for theological education at this moment in time. Next, I draw upon selected insights from the history of Catholic higher education (of which graduate theological education is a part) in order to provide some points of reference for making connections between past experiences and current realities. I then offer a constructive proposal for reimagining theological education in the light of globalization and provide a few practical examples of specific glocal challenges and opportunities that have direct bearing on human formation for contemporary mission and ministry. Finally, I conclude with a brief reflection on Pope Francis and his glocal way of proceeding.

MY NARRATIVE

For the past twenty-seven years, I regularly have taught an introductory course in ecclesiology at an institution that evolved from being a freestanding school of theology and ministry to being a professional graduate school of a major Catholic university. In the early 1990s, the students enrolled in the course included well-educated young men, most of whom were of European descent and born in the United States. They were members of religious orders, and the majority were preparing for ordained ministry. Present in their company were one or two religious sisters and a few laywomen and men, including the occasional cross-registrant from other graduate theological schools in the area. Rare was the student who was married or raising children. While differences existed in terms of gender, vocational paths, professional backgrounds and age, there was minimal ethnic and racial diversity and limited internationality.

By the Spring of 2016, the demographics of my classroom were amazingly different. The students enrolled in the course represented fourteen countries and five continents. Nearly half of the students were women. In a course where first-year seminarians once constituted the vast majority of students, only 36 percent of the students were candidates for ordination and 12 percent were ordained already. More than half of these men were international students. As for the lay students, who once constituted a small percentage of the students enrolled in the course, aspiring lay ecclesial ministers made up 52 percent of the class. Half of them were married with children. A fifth of them were men, the rest were women. Women religious, who technically fall under the category of lay students, remained few in number and came from countries in Africa and Asia. With regard to under-represented minorities from the United States, three students were Hispanic. There were no African Americans or Native Americans. Though additional differentiations could be noted, between 1991 and 2016 many changes occurred in my classroom. Such changes were evident not only in terms of the composition of students, the content of my syllabus and advances in new instructional technologies but also, and perhaps most importantly, in terms of what I would describe as the glocal nature of students' individual hopes, perceived needs, and envisioned futures in mission and ministry. That is to say, the desire on the part of students to achieve an ecclesial-local-global balance between the ecclesial identities they claim, the local context they bring with them and to which they are accountable, and the global context they seek to better understand.

As a comparative assessment of these two scenarios reveals, viewed in contrast to 1991, the reality of 2016 carried with it some new challenges and opportunities that were distinct, though not unrelated, from those of twenty-five, fifteen, or even five years ago. There was a more equal ratio of men and women and a more even breakdown between US students and international students. There was a more diverse balance of life commitments, ranging from vowed celibates and singles to spouses and parents, often with young children. The nature and quality of relationships within and outside of the classroom context were discernably different and in some ways more complex.

In light of my experience and given the focus of this edited volume, I would like to address three interrelated questions: What is glocalization and why does it matter for Roman Catholic theological education today? How do historical perspectives on the evolution of Catholic identity, diversity and internationalization in Catholic higher education serve as warrants for greater attentiveness to the processes that are contributing to glocalization? Moreover, in what ways might the glocalization of Roman Catholic theological education contribute to an integral formation for mission and ministry?

WHAT IS GLOCALIZATION AND WHY DOES IT MATTER FOR THEOLOGICAL EDUCATION TODAY?

"Glocalization is the way in which ideas and structures that circulate globally are adapted and changed by local realities"[1]

RICHARD TIPLADY

"Glocal theology implies that every local theology has the responsibility to be both context relevant and at the same time to remain in touch with the global church and the rest of the world."[2]

MARTIN ACCAD

1. Tiplady, *World of Difference*, 21.
2. Accad, "Middle Eastern Theology," 161.

The definition of glocalization set forth by Richard Tiplady and the description of glocal theology articulated by Martin Accad serve as starting points for understanding the concept of glocalization and its theological relevance. While theorists in a variety of disciplines have used the concept, including some theologians and missiologists,[3] its appropriation and explicit usage in discourse on theological education has been somewhat limited.[4] In my own efforts to understand the implications of diversity and internationalization for theological education, I have been informed and influenced by the theological works of Robert Schreiter as well as the sociological-philosophical works of Roland Robertson and Victor Roudometof.[5]

In 1997, when Robert Schreiter published his classic text *The New Catholicity: Theology between the Global and the Local*, he presciently explored the evolving reality of the Church and its diverse contexts.[6] He described "global flows" and "cultural [local] logics"[7] and identified "important global/universal concerns that transcend geographical and cultural boundaries."[8] Laying out the distinguishing characteristics of globalization, Schreiter offered specific ways of seeing and making meaning of the globalized context in which the Church found itself. Attentive to the claims made in his earlier work, *Constructing Local Theologies*,[9] Schreiter brought a theological voice to the encounter between the global and the local—and an emerging awareness of the phenomenon of glocalization.[10]

Over the course of the next two decades, Schreiter, in the company of many colleagues, continued to provide theological educators with the interdisciplinary insights needed to understand global Catholicism and its

---

3. See Küster, "Contextualization to Glocalization," 203–26; Lo, "Paul and Ethnicity," 184–98; Beyer, "Globalization and Glocalization," 98–117; Roberts, *Glocalization*.

4. See Kang, "Radical Border-Traversing."

5. For more on *glocalization*, see Robertson, *Globalization*; "Glocalization," 25–44; Roudometof, *Glocalization*, 1–19. "The word glocal is a neologism; that is, it is a new word constructed by fusing of global and local." From the notion of glocal emerge "the more specific terms glocalization, glocality, and glocalism." Roudometof traces the origin of the word to two sources: the English rendering of the Japanese word *dochakuka* (becoming deeply rooted) and the *depth* dimension of a three-dimensional orthogonal "Rubik's Cube of Ecology" (Roudometof, *Glocalization*, 1–3).

6. See Schreiter, *New Catholicity*.

7. Schreiter, *New Catholicity*, 15–27.

8. Rajashekar, "Theological Education."

9. Schreiter, *Constructing Local Theologies*.

10. See Schreiter, *New Catholicity*, 12, 21. See also Robertson, "Glocalization."

contextual/local expressions. Some of these insights included contemporary models of mission and contextual theologies, global and local perspectives on a wide range of ethical concerns such as poverty, racism, human sexuality, violence and ecology, and outlooks on the ways in which the migration and immigration of peoples are shaping our interreligious, ecumenical, and pastoral commitments. Through their contributions, these theologians and theological educators, without necessarily using the word *glocal*, provided the foundations for thinking glocally, acting glocally, and for coming to terms with the increasingly glocal nature of our Roman Catholic identity and social location.

As the research of Nancy T. Ammerman,[11] Katarina Schuth,[12] Mary Gautier[13] and others demonstrates, there are new influences and qualitatively different challenges and opportunities being set before theological educators at the present time. In the interest of providing concrete examples, I highlight three. Firstly, when it comes to Roman influences on theological education and their effects on ministerial formation within the context of a world church, Pope Francis has given voice to a set of concerns and imperatives that have considerable implications for the formation of future priests, religious, and ecclesial lay ministers. Since becoming pope, he has lost no time in identifying the temptations and "curial diseases" to which all pastoral agents are susceptible.[14] Secondly, when it comes to local influences on theological education and their implications for diversity and equity, the effects of the political and ideological divisions in the United States are consequential in a number of anticipated and unanticipated ways. While social realities such as racism, ethnocentrism, xenophobia, and sexism are not unfamiliar, these realities have taken on added significance and urgency for faith communities as well as for ministerial leaders. Thirdly, when it comes to global influences on theological education and the internationalization of many of our institutions, the effects of world events on the personal lives of students, faculty members, administrators and staff serve as constant reminders of what it means to be in solidarity with the world and the world church.

These three examples of influences affecting Roman Catholic theological education at this moment in time are by no means exhaustive.

11. See Ammerman, "America's Changing Religious," 27–34.
12. See Schuth, *Seminary Formation*.
13. See Gautier and Holland, *Catholic Ministry*.
14. See Francis, "*Evangelii gaudium*," 76–109; "Roman Curia."

However, they are representative of the converging forces that contribute to glocalization. They also draw attention to the exigencies that seminaries and schools of theology and ministry must be prepared address. For some, this is uncharted territory, and as of yet, ecclesial documents dealing with theological education and ministerial formation[15] provide little in the way of theoretical guidelines or practical suggestions. When it comes to addressing formative issues that deal directly with the human, spiritual, intellectual and pastoral demands related to diversity, internationalization, and Roman Catholic identity in a religiously pluralistic world, ecclesial resources are limited. Even the most recent document, *Ratio fundamentalis institutionis sacerdotalis (The Gift of the Priestly Vocation)*[16] stops short of offering any new directions other than highlighting the importance of social media.[17] While acknowledging aspects of internationalization and the importance of attending to local realities in the formative process for mission and ministry, specific guidelines are lacking.

Mindful of the observations made in the first part of this essay, I now offer two potentially helpful resources for engaging theological educators in further reflection and discussion on Catholic identity, diversity, internationalization and glocalization. One of these resources is historical and the other is constructive.

ECCLESIAL IDENTITY, DIVERSITY, AND INTERNATIONALIZATION IN ROMAN CATHOLIC HIGHER EDUCATION

"The cultural atmosphere in which a human being lives has a great influence upon his or her way of thinking and, thus, of acting."

John Paul II[18]

"Born from the heart of the Church, a Catholic University is located in that course of tradition which may be traced back to the very origin of the University as an institution.

---

15. John Paul II, "*Pastores dabo vobis*"; "*Christifideles laici*"; USCCB, *Priestly Formation*; *Co-Workers in Vineyard*.
16. Congregation for the Clergy, "*Ratio fundamentalis*."
17. Congregation for the Clergy, "*Ratio fundamentalis*," §97–98, 182, 185.
18. John Paul II, "*Sapientia christiana*," 1.

> *It has always been recognized as an incomparable center of creativity and dissemination of knowledge for the good of humanity."*
>
> JOHN PAUL II[19]

> *The Church is called to realize that the very catholicity that makes her a leaven of unity in diversity and communion in freedom both demands and favours "the polarity between the particular and the universal, between the one and the many, between the simple and the complex. To annihilate this tension would be to go against the life of the Spirit." What is needed, then, is to practice a way of knowing and interpreting reality in the light of the "mind of Christ" (cf. I Cor 2:16), wherein the model for approaching and resolving problems "is not the sphere . . . where every point is equidistant from the center, and there are no differences between them," but rather "the polyhedron, which reflects the convergence of all its parts, each of which preserves its distinctiveness."*
>
> POPE FRANCIS[20]

Looking Backward in Order to Go Forward

History often holds insights and inspirations that can guide us in our efforts to move forward into an unfolding future. Mindful of this fact, the second part of this essay offers some perspectives on the ways in which Catholic higher education (of which graduate theological education is a part) has endeavored to respond to the exigencies associated with Catholic ecclesial identity, diversity and internationalization over time.

For centuries, Roman Catholic institutions of higher education have been recognized as "centers of creativity and dissemination of knowledge for the good of humanity." Serving as centers of learning where scholars and students from diverse cultures met and interacted, the medieval universities of Europe[21] experienced for their time in history something analogous to what we have experienced in our own, namely, inquiring minds crossing

---

19. John Paul II, "*Ex corde ecclesiae*," 1.
20. Francis, "*Veritatis gaudium*," 3d.
21. See de Ridder-Symoens, *University in Europe*.

boundaries and entering into new cultural contexts in pursuit of higher education.[22]

As the Age of Exploration dawned, Spanish colonial powers and ecclesiastical authorities moved quickly to establish centers of higher learning in the so-called New World.[23] Bound by imperial systems of patronage, these universities, while subject to the charters that kept them tethered to imperial powers and papal authority, enabled teachers and learners to discover creative ways of preserving and advancing their respective cultural patrimonies, ethnic heritages, and contextual particularities. By nurturing desires for freedom, autonomy, and independence, they, too, experienced for their time in history something analogous to what we have experienced in our own, namely, the potential and power of Catholic higher education to uphold, defend, and sustain the integrity of local identities, interests, and initiatives.

As for the North American context, the complex cultural history of Catholic higher education in New France began with the establishment of the Collège de Québec in 1635. A residential seminary was later established alongside, driven by colonial interests in the training of local clergy and in time became the first university in French Canada. After the British Conquest of 1760, Catholic higher education in Canada languished for close to a century. By the mid-nineteenth century, despite ongoing religious, ethnic, racial and political tensions, founders and administrators of Roman Catholic institutions created models for affiliations and partnerships. Through negotiation, innovation and reconciliation, they endeavored to overcome the acrimony of cultural hostilities as well as ethnic and racial divisions between the Protestant British and the Catholic French.[24] They experienced

---

22. See Odin and Manicas, *Globalization*; Vaira, "Globalization," 483–510; Killick, *Developing Global Student*; Westover, *Globalization*.

23. See Roberts et al., "Exporting Models," 256–84.

24. See Magnuson, *New France*. The Jesuits established the Collège de Québec first as a school for Native and French children. Bishop François de Montmorency-Laval founded the Séminaire de Québec in 1663. After the British Conquest, the Séminaire took over the teaching component from the Jesuit Collège. In 1848, the Jesuits founded the Collège Sainte-Marie de Montréal and the Oblates of Mary Immaculate established the College of Ottawa (St. Paul's University). By 1852, Queen Victoria issued the Université Laval (previously the Séminaire de Québec) a royal charter and decades later Pope Benedict XV granted pontifical recognition. By 1881, the Basilian College of St. Michael was affiliated with the University of Toronto. Advancing into the twentieth century, more Catholic university colleges and seminaries emerged, including Brescia University (Ursuline) College for Women, founded in 1919 by the Ursuline Sisters who had offered

for their time in history, something analogous to our own, namely the enduring effects of dangerous memories and the haunting legacies of deeply rooted prejudices and regional differences.

Within the context of New England, British colonial rule also impeded and limited opportunities for Catholic education. However, following the American Revolution, the Declaration of Independence, and the drafting of the US Constitution and Bill of Rights, the historical, political, and educational landscape of the United States changed significantly. As freedom of religion facilitated the establishment of Catholic schools, new pathways for Catholic higher education were created.[25] Moving through the nineteenth century into the twentieth, the development and chartering of Catholic colleges became an attainable goal not only for men but also for women. In accord with the mission and vision of the founders and/or the founding religious institutes, Catholic higher education sought to provide for many forms of higher education meeting the needs and aspirations of people from diverse backgrounds.

As the twentieth century approached, Vatican concerns about Americanism and Modernism in matters of orthodoxy intensified.[26] Catholic seminaries and colleges in the United States began to organize among themselves.[27] Such alliances proved to be strategic in securing and sustaining a delicate balance when it came to being perceived as sufficiently Catholic in the eyes of Roman "insiders" and sufficiently American in the eyes of "insider" Nativists.[28]

---

noteworthy educational leadership for centuries. See Association of Catholic Colleges and Universities in Canada, "Mission."

25. See Gleason, "Bibliographic Essay," 95–113. Beginning with the founding of Georgetown in 1789 and the establishment of St. Mary's Seminary in Baltimore in 1792, eighty-four Catholic men's colleges were founded by 1860. See Dosen, "Catholic Higher Education," 32; Power, *Catholic Higher Education*. Though the process of securing higher educational opportunities for women was more gradual, by 1896, Notre Dame of Maryland became the first four-year Catholic women's college to be chartered in the United States. See Schier and Russetts, *Catholic Women's Colleges*; and Cameron, *College of Notre Dame*.

26. See Fogarty, "Reflections," 1–12.

27. In 1898, the Educational Conference of Seminary Faculties came into existence. See Ellis, *Seminary Education*. In 1899, representatives of fifty-three colleges gathered in Washington, DC, to establish the organization for colleges. Eventually these separate organizations became one organization known as the Association of Catholic Colleges and Universities (ACCU). For additional information, see ACCU, "Home."

28. Today, the ACCU represents 261 Catholic colleges and universities, 16 of which are seminaries or schools of theology and ministry. See 2016 statistics from ACCU,

For the first half of the twentieth century, the numerical growth and ongoing expansion of institutions of Catholic higher education proved to be an impressive accomplishment for American Catholicism.[29] However, tensions and struggles increased proportionately as schools endeavored to define and sustain their respective missions and visions. Within the Catholic church, as well as in American society, the consequences of rapidly changing cultural, political, and socioeconomic conditions—local and global—were affecting every sphere of life in the United States. Immigration, labor movements, world wars, women's struggles for equality, economic turmoil, along with racism and prejudice of every sort were but a few of the social concerns confronting Catholic institutions of higher learning. Moving into the mid-twentieth century, an urgent question in search of a timely answer emerged: *To what degree would seminaries, colleges, and universities recognize and assume their social and moral responsibilities for Catholic formation in the midst of so much diversity and internationality?*[30]

Catholic Higher Education, Culture Change, and Social Responsibility

From within and outside of Catholic higher education, advocates of the social Gospel, agents of social action and promoters of the social teachings of the Church began to make their voices heard.[31] So began the initial strivings and hesitancies on the part of Catholic colleges, universities and seminaries to deal with (or not) the pressing issues and concerns of ethnicity and race, social location and class, access to education and gender, the melting pot of assimilation into the dominant culture, and the mosaic of cultural identity and differentiation. These issues and concerns, along with others, served as the early foundations for institutional commitments that later would find fuller expression in the advancement of diversity/equity and internationalization.[32]

"Catholic Higher Education FAQs."
    29. Gleason, *Contending with Modernity*.
    30. See O'Brien, "Social Teaching," 195–224.
    31. An example of this that focuses on the beginnings of the Young Christian Student Movement at the University of Notre Dame is discussed in Putz, "Specialized Catholic Action," 433–39.
    32. See Sullivan and Pagnucco, *Vision of Justice*; ACCU, *Catholic Higher Education*.

As the 1950s unfolded into the 1960s, some Catholic colleges and universities were thriving, others were surviving, and still others were closing their doors.[33] Viewed from an ecclesial perspective, the effects of changes in the Church on Catholic higher education in the United States prior to the Second Vatican Council (1962–1965) cannot be underestimated, nor can the various consequences of Vatican II and its aftermath.[34] The directions set by the Council's documents[35] were challenging, demanding and unsettling, not only religiously but also socially, culturally, economically, and politically.[36] Catholic seminaries underwent considerable turmoil as well as transformation.[37] Viewed from a secular perspective, many events, such as the Cold War, the Cuban Revolution, the war in Vietnam, the Peace Movement, the sexual revolution, the Women's Movement, the Civil Rights Movement, violence and poverty, student protests, nuclear proliferation and the coming of age of a generation of Baby Boomers, had a dramatic influence not only on American culture and consciousness, but also on the degree to which Catholic higher education could and would respond to these signs of the times.

At the forefront of offering leadership in dealing with societal challenges, threats, opportunities, and hopes—ecclesial, local and global—were a number of Catholic university and college presidents as well as seminary rectors. Three individuals who gave witness to a Roman Catholic spirit of civic and ecumenical leadership at the time were Reverend Theodore M. Hesburgh, CSC (1917–2015),[38] Sister Ann Ida Gannon, BVM (1915),[39] and Bishop Harold R. Perry, SVD (1916–1991).[40] Hesburgh, Gannon, and Perry

33. O'Brien, "Catholicism," 16–31.

34. See Donovan, *Vatican Council II*, 9.

35. See selected documents of the Vatican Council II in Flannery, *Documents of Vatican II*, especially the Pastoral Constitution on the Church in the Modern World, *Gaudium et spes*; the Declaration on Christian Education, *Gravissimum educationis*; the Declaration on Religious Freedom, *Dignitatis humanae*; the Decree on Ministry and the Life of Priests, *Presbyterorum ordinis apostolicam actuositatem*; the Decree on Priestly Training, *Optatam totius*; the Decree on the Lay Apostolate, *Apostolicam actuositatem*; and the Decree on the Renewal of Religious Life, *Perfectae caritatis*.

36. See Greeley et al., *Social Effects*; *Catholic Americans*; *Changing Catholic College*. See also Dosen, *Catholic Higher Education*.

37. See USCC, *US Catholic Seminaries*; Klimoski et al., *Educating Leaders*.

38. University of Notre Dame, "Man of the World."

39. Aguirre, *Sister Ann Ida Gannon*.

40. Prior to his episcopal appointment as Auxiliary Bishop of New Orleans, Louisiana, in the Fall of 1965, Bishop Perry served as Rector of St. Augustine Divine Word

exemplified for Catholic institutions of higher education the importance of Catholic leadership in preparing men and women, not only for the professions (the arts and sciences) but also for citizenship—locally, nationally, and globally. This was no small task in turbulent and transformative times. Reflecting the positive face of Catholicism, they provided direction and inspiration, not only for the University of Notre Dame, Mundelein College, and St. Augustine Seminary but also for other Catholic universities, colleges, and seminaries in the United States and elsewhere. In their company stood countless other priests, sisters, brothers, and lay leaders—equally prophetic, visionary, and daring—who served as examples of what it meant to be leaders in higher education as well as faithful Catholics and engaged citizens of the United States and the world.

Over the course of the next six decades, congresses, documents, discussions, debates, divisions, and developments, marked efforts to envision, implement, and assess the advancement of many goals and objectives,[41] including the existing programs and new initiatives that focused on internationality, diversity, and equity. The face of Catholic higher education within the context of the United States was being transformed, in some cases at break-neck speed, in other cases at a turtle's pace. Not unlike their peer institutions, whether public or private, it was evident that the learning curve was steep when it came to navigating the often-choppy waters of higher education in America.

When Pope John Paul II issued the Apostolic Exhortation *Ex corde ecclesiae* in 1990, it served as an ecclesial instruction for Catholic institutions of higher education around the world.[42] Seeking to inspire, support, and exhort these institutions, *Ex corde ecclesiae* also raised a number of issues and concerns. The reception of the document in the United States was mixed. It was welcomed by some and contested by others.[43] Whether or not the document was coincidental or causal to renewed interest in Catholic

---

Seminary in Bay St. Louis, Louisiana, from 1958 until 1964. A prominent figure in the civil rights movement, he was one of the first African American Roman Catholic Bishops. See Francis, "Homily."

41. See Curran, *Catholic Higher Education*.

42. It is important to note that not all institutions are governed by *Ex corde ecclesiae*. Pontifical colleges and universities as well as pontifical theological faculties are governed by the Apostolic Constitution *Sapientia christiana*. Still, *Ex corde ecclesiae* remains an influential document for all of Catholic higher education.

43. See Hendershott, "Catholic Culture Wars," 227–43.

identity, founding charisms and the rediscovery of the "deep story"[44] of every institution, the fact remained that Catholic colleges and universities became increasingly more intent on articulating their respective missions and living out their respective visions, some in complete compliance with the document, others with more qualified deference. While the Vatican unambiguously asserted that Catholic colleges and universities were "born from the heart of the Church," it was evident to bishops, administrators, faculty, students, benefactors, and alumni/ae that these Catholic colleges and universities had grown, developed, and matured in the heart of the world—the real world of diversity, internationality, and the struggle for equity and access. Managing culture change, preserving the Catholic intellectual tradition, and overcoming the obstacles that often contributed to polarization were unavoidable challenges in the American context.[45] Doing so in the light of the Gospel, church teachings, civil laws, governmental regulations, and accreditation standards was a daunting task and a multifaceted undertaking[46] as the historical interplay between Catholic identity and social location took on new significance amidst the forces of globalization.

Contemporary Questions Regarding Diversity/Equity and Internationalization: Mutually Reinforcing Goals or Dueling Agendas?

For theological educators in search of answers to the question: *How should institutions of Catholic higher education deal with the demands of an increasingly more complex and fragmented world?*, Michael Buckley's book, *The Catholic University as Promise and Project*, and John C. Haughey's *Where Is Knowing Going? The Horizons of the Knowing Subject* offer some important perspectives. More recently, the proceedings from the annual meetings of the Association of Catholic Colleges and Universities [ACCU][47] as well as recent issues of the *Journal of Catholic Higher Education*, the *Journal of Diversity in Higher Education* and *International Higher Education* provide insights into current trends, challenges, and opportunities. Specifically, such research and scholarship reveal the ways in which commitments to

44. See Lee, "Charism," 124–35.
45. See O'Brien, "American Catholic History," 93–100.
46. See Morey and Piderit, *Catholic Education*, 21–48.
47. See ACCU, "ACCU Annual Meeting."

Catholic identity, diversity/equity, and internationalization, remain an ongoing challenge, particularly when it comes to strengthening and advancing the mission and identity of each institution. This is most evident when the expectations and competing claims of multiple stake-holders and constituencies (such as religious sponsors, trustees, administrators, faculty members, staff, students in general, students from under-represented minorities, international students, alumni/ae and benefactors, etc.) are in play and, at times, in conflict.

When reflecting on Catholic identity, diversity/equity and internationalization, recent data from 2015 offers insight into the magnitude of the phenomena that is the subject of inquiry. Viewed collectively and comparatively, statistics from the ACCU[48] shed additional light on the demographic realities of Catholic higher education in the United States. In this regard, the research of Kathrina Anderson Bell, *Similar Goals and Dueling Agendas: Perceptions of Campus Internationalization and Equity Policies*,[49] makes an important contribution to understanding and interpreting the possibilities and limitations faced by Catholic institutions. Indeed, the complexities and challenges are numerous as they endeavor to manage and negotiate the scrutinies of guardians of the Roman Catholic tradition as well as the competing claims of business-minded proponents for internationalization and radicalized advocates for diversity.

Building on the earlier work of Chris Argyris,[50] Bell draws important distinctions between espoused theories (the words used by institutions to convey what they do or what they would like others to think they do) and theories-in-practice (the action[s] that govern actual behavior).[51] When applied to Roman Catholic theological education, the value of Bell's insights is found in her identification and comparative analysis of the tensions existing within and between institutional efforts to advance diversity/equity on the one hand and efforts to promote internationalization on the other.[52] While

---

48. For further information, see ACCU, "Catholic Higher Education FAQs."
49. See Bell, *Dueling Agendas*.
50. See Argyris, *Theory in Practices*.
51. See Bell, *Dueling Agendas*, 24–25.
52. Drawing upon the work of Jonas Stier, Bell explores his *Typology of Understanding of Comprehensive Internationalization*. See table adapted from Stier, "Taking a Critical Stance," 83–97. Bell juxtaposes Stier's work with her own "Typology of Understandings of Equity in Higher Education." See Bell, *Dueling Agendas*, 54–58. Though a point-by-point analysis of Stier's and Bell's respective typologies is beyond the scope of this particular essay, I draw attention to their research because their analytical framing of the issues is

many institutions of higher education acknowledge the complementarity and development of internationalization and diversity since the 1980s, evidence suggests that institutional commitments to equity and diversity as reflected in the enrollment of students coming from under-represented minorities in the United States has not kept pace with strides made in internationalization and the enrollment of international students.[53] In this regard, Bell's overall analysis in *Dueling Agendas* is particularly important for seminaries and schools of theology and ministry facing similar disparities.

In summary, this brief historical overview of Catholic higher education provides three specific advantages. First, it offers a perspective on the realities that have brought us to where we find ourselves today. Second, it alerts theological educators to the importance of paying greater attention to higher education initiatives, programs, and research in order to deal more effectively with the complex dynamics of Catholic identity, diversity/equity and internationalization in seminaries and schools of theology. Third, it provides a starting point for examining with greater intentionality how the influences of Catholic identity, diversity and internationalization are contributing factors to the glocalization of Roman Catholic theological education.

REIMAGINING THEOLOGICAL EDUCATION IN THE LIGHT OF GLOCALIZATION

Throughout the United States, seminaries and schools of theology and ministry continue to seek out sustainable ways of guaranteeing that commitments to Catholic identity, diversity and internationalization are advanced in equitable ways. Conscious of these commitments, my investment in promoting more intentional institutional reflection on glocalization is driven by the conviction that Catholic identity, diversity and internationalization are requiring us to reimagine theological education in more complex and integrated ways. The question before us is this: What can we do to enhance the human, spiritual, intellectual and pastoral formation of all of our students and prepare them as adequately and appropriately as we can for their unfolding futures?

---

not only instructive for Catholic colleges and universities but also potentially helpful for Catholic seminaries and schools of theology and ministry.

53. See Dungca, "Lost on Campus," A-1, A-6-7; Killick, "Internationalization," 11–14.

Understanding the Interactive Processes of Romanization, Localization, and Globalization

According to 2017 statistics from the Center for Applied Research in the Apostolate, there are 41 seminaries and schools of theology and ministry in the United States preparing candidates for ordination and lay ecclesial ministry in the church and the world.[54] Among these, 25 are diocesan, regional, or national seminaries, where seminarians and lay students often receive similar instruction in separate programs. The other 16 constitute freestanding institutions, graduate professional schools, or departmental programs that are operative within a university setting. While the personal narrative that I provided at the outset of this essay is more representative of the graduate professional school (specifically with regard to lay students, especially women, and broad-based internationality), most institutions have shared, to greater and lesser degrees, the challenges and opportunities posed by the three processes indicated below, one of which is unique to Roman Catholic theological education. These processes include Romanization, localization, and globalization.[55]

1. *Romanization* is the process through which the Pope and the Roman Curia set forth expectations and norms for theological and ministerial formation that are universal in scope and implemented by National Conferences of Bishops, the designated offices and other representative bodies, such as the Conference of Major Superiors of Men. Ideally, this process contributes to ecclesial consciousness, identity and engagement. It can be coupled with a commitment to Catholic identity.

2. *Localization* is the process of creating, customizing and implementing theological education programs for students from a specific geographic location and similar socio-cultural backgrounds. Ideally, this process contributes to local consciousness, identity and engagement.[56] It can be coupled with a commitment to diversity.

3. *Globalization* the process of designing, developing and implementing theological education programs for students from multiple cultural backgrounds and diverse global contexts. Ideally, this process

---

54. See Gautier and Holland, *Catholic Ministry*, 9.

55. I am grateful to Professor Francine Cardman for her helpful suggestions in the drafting of these definitions.

56. See Schreiter, *Constructing Local Theologies*, 1.

contributes to global consciousness, identity and engagement. It can be coupled with a commitment to internationalization.

Historically, the interactive dynamic between Romanization and localization predates the Second Vatican Council and continues to prevail in a number of seminaries and schools of theology and ministry around the world. Similarly, the interactive dynamic between Romanization and globalization has historical antecedents as well as recent manifestations in the late 1960s and beyond. While Romanization, localization and globalization have been operative in the world of theological education for quite some time, looking to the demands of the future these processes may no longer be sufficient in and of themselves. Given the contemporary exigencies associated with Catholic identity, diversity and internationalization, I believe that reimagining theological education in the light of glocalization could help in anticipating, identifying and addressing unmet needs.

Currently, the forces of glocalization that are affecting the world are being felt in both subtle and obvious ways at seminaries and schools of theology and ministry. This is particularly true in settings where concerns regarding Catholic identity, diversity and internationality are no longer exceptions to the rule of institutional homogeneity but, rather, the hallmarks of an evolving heterogeneity. While the dynamics are readily perceptible "to those who have eyes to see and ears to hear," it may be more difficult to rightly name and accurately interpret glocalization, especially when a certain reliance on more familiar categories such as Romanization, localization or globalization is determinative of what people see and hear and how they make meaning.

By making the assertion that I do regarding the significance of glocalization for Roman Catholic theological education, I do not mean simply attending more intentionally to the social and ecclesial conditions that are present in the geographical area in which a seminary or school of theology and ministry happens to be situated. What I am suggesting is that our institutions need to find ways of more adequately and appropriately attending to the localities from which every one of our students has come, as well as those localities to which each student is likely to minister in the near future. Currently, numerous complexities and competing claims, apparent and elusive, inform and influence the realities—ecclesial, local and global—in which our students have ministered, are ministering, and will minister. To the extent that these complexities and competing claims are not acknowledged with intentionality, both inside and outside the classroom, we must not ignore or abdicate our responsibility as theological educators for engaging the theological, ministerial, and vocational imaginations of our students in ways that are interactively ecclesial, local and global. In the interest of assuming such responsibility, I offer the following proposal.

A CONSTRUCTIVE PROPOSAL FOR THE GLOCALIZATION OF ROMAN CATHOLIC THEOLOGICAL EDUCATION

This proposal for the glocalization of Roman Catholic theological education is a hybrid conceptual framework that is student-centered and made up of three inter-related processes that can be described in the following manner:

1. As a process of adapting and modifying ecclesiastically-oriented theological education programs to meet the formative needs of students who, while consciously desiring and, in some cases, needing to have a theological education that is recognized by Rome, do not want their desire or need to be fulfilled at the expense of a diminished capacity for critical thinking, prudential judgment and pastoral engagement that is guided by the principle of mercy,

2. As a process of adapting and modifying locally-oriented theological education programs to meet the formative needs of students who, while consciously committed to honoring the local from which they come or in which they are currently immersed or embedded, do not want this commitment to come at the expense of foregoing a world-church identity and a deeper knowledge of the contributions, struggles, hopes, and anxieties of global Catholicism, and

3. As a process of adapting and modifying globally-oriented theological education programs to meet the formative needs of students who, while fully understanding the value of having a world church/global Christianity consciousness, do not want that consciousness to come at the expense of losing their local identities, along with the loss of their awareness of the local needs, norms, and cultural practices of their respective communities of accountability.

Ideally speaking, these inter-related processes cannot be undertaken separately because the transformative work of faculty, staff and administrators needs to take place at the intersection of all three. In imagining the glocalization of theological education, the formative needs of our students—as individuals and as members of a community of learners—must be a non-negotiable priority. Achieving a glocal balance, while critical to every pillar of formation, is particularly critical to human formation, precisely because of the ways in which identity, self-understanding, self-esteem, and integrity are the preconditions for mutuality, empathy, respect, and trust. In the absence of a glocal balance, evidence of resentment, withdrawal, resistance, hostility, resignation, indifference, entitlement, and obliviousness is likely to build up. When the causes go unrecognized or minimized, there may be no way of effectively addressing the glocal challenges that involve dealing with relational dislocation, breaking habits of micro-aggression, challenging pedagogies of abdication, and becoming consciousness of the privileges that one enjoys because of globalization or localization. However, if glocal opportunities for advancing a culture of encounter,[57] cultivating the harmony of goodness,[58] promoting pedagogies of engagement,[59] and embracing the demands of missionary discipleship[60] are taken up by those committed to Catholic identity, diversity and internationalization, seminaries and schools of theology and ministry will be positioned to achieve a constructive glocal balance. Progress in this regard will be demonstrated in the measure that appreciation, participation, mutuality, reconciliation, interest, enthusiasm, stewardship, and solidarity are in evidence, not only among the few, but the many (see Table 1).

Table 1

Evidence of Glocal Imbalance	Engaging Glocal Challenges	Embracing Glocal Opportunities	Evidence of Glocal Balance
resentment withdrawal	1) dealing with relational dislocation	1) advancing a culture of encounter	appreciation participation
resistance hostility	3) breaking habits of micro-aggression	2) cultivating the harmony of goodness	mutuality reconciliation

57. Fares, *Heart of Pope Francis.*
58. See Ingham, *Harmony of Goodness.*
59. Bareness and Kim, "Pedagogy of Engagement," 89–106.
60. See Gittins, *Way of Discipleship.*

| resignation indifference | 3) challenging pedagogies of abdication | 3) promoting pedagogies of engagement | interest enthusiasm |
| entitlement obliviousness | 4) becoming conscious of globalization/localization privilege | 4) embracing the demands of missionary discipleship | stewardship solidarity |

As theological education moves forward into the third decade of the twenty-first century, more critical thinking on the subject of glocalization will be needed. If our expressed institutional commitments to Catholic identity, diversity and internationalization are to be deemed credible, they must be coupled with our faith-based commitments to justice, peace, and the integrity of creation. The exigencies by which our credibility as theological educators is measured must be taken very seriously. Past approaches and the often siloed processes of Romanization, localization and globalization will not meet the expectations of a new generation of students. We cannot abdicate responsibility for doing the work of integrated learning and helping to create the conditions in which the glocalization of theological education can flourish. We can no longer do what we consider to be "our work" and leave students from Uganda, Vietnam or Brazil to figure out on their own how to apply a general concept or a global insight to their respective contexts. We cannot leave students from Newark, El Paso or Sioux City to figure out on their own the global implications or imperatives of a contextual issue or perspectival viewpoint. We cannot leave diocesan seminarians, Franciscan novices or returning lay missioners to figure out on their own how to measure the theological distance between Rome and the margins and peripheries of the world. The work of glocalization is a common endeavor that needs be done *in common*. This institutional, curricular and collegial work cannot be delegated to a few designated individuals or relegated to consultants. Given our Catholic identity, our diversity, and our internationality, *de facto* pedagogies of abdication must be seen for what they are—impediments to advancing the glocalization of theological education in response to the signs and needs of these times.

Although this brief consideration highlights only a few of the challenges and opportunities associated with the glocalization of theological education, it provides a point of entry for further investigation, discussion, and debate.

CONCLUSION

Theological Education in the Era of Pope Francis: Toward a Glocal Way of Proceeding

"Work for the culture of encounter, in a simple way, as Jesus did."

POPE FRANCIS[61]

After the resignation of Pope Benedict XIV in December 2012, the papal election of the Argentinian Jesuit Cardinal Jorge Bergoglio in March 2013 ushered in a new era in the history of the Roman Catholic Church and a new moment for theological education. The glocal nature of contemporary Catholicism became more visible and vibrant. The papacy of Pope Francis—and, indeed, the person of Pope Francis himself—became emblematic of a glocal way of proceeding, of redefining power[62] and of manifesting a kind of ecclesial hybridity.[63]

Throughout the world, pockets of resistance to glocalization are in evidence. Such resistance is especially evident in those places where people struggle to maintain the primacy of the local over the global or vice versa, and where communities of faith are polarized by their acrimonious disputes about what constitutes real and true Catholicism. Amidst these realities, Pope Francis embodies a way of being in the church and in the world that is attuned to the positive dynamics of glocalization; yet, at the same time, acutely aware of the competing and divisive forces characterized by Benjamin Barber as "Jihad vs. McWorld."[64]

Leading by example, Pope Francis invites those who seek to minister in God's name and that of the Church to be attentive to the local and the global, conscious of the implications for mission and ministry. Focusing on insights from his Christmas Messages to the Curia, his Chrism Liturgy homilies, his Easter Vigil homilies, his Pentecost Homilies, his encyclical *Laudato si'*, his Apostolic Exhortations *Evangelii gaudium*, *Amoris laetitia*, and *Gaudete et exsultate*, and his Apostolic Constitution *Gaudium et*

---

61. Francis, "Culture of Encounter."

62. Francis, "*Evangelii gaudium*"; "Overcome Indifference and Win Peace."

63. See Fulkerson, "They Will Know," 265–79.

64. See Troy, "Invisible Legions." Troy refers to Barber, *Jihad vs. McWorld*; Zakaria, *Post-American World*.

veritatis, one gets a sense of just how Pope Francis understands the glocal nature of human formation. Clearly, he is attuned to the expectations, demands, temptations, competencies, and commitments of those entrusted with responsibility for the formation of ministers and the exercise of ministries within the church and the world.

Over the course of the past five years of teaching and learning in the era of Pope Francis, I have grown increasingly more conscious of the ways in which glocal challenges and glocal opportunities exist on a continuum. As I have described in this constructive proposal for the glocalization of Roman Catholic theological education, the key task involves recognizing that, within the classroom or the institution, the intersectionality of the ecclesial, the local and the global cannot be ignored or underestimated. To be more specific, localization no longer means focusing solely on the immediate and obvious local, as in the location of a given seminary or school of theology and ministry such as the Archdiocese of Chicago. Rather, it means being attentive to the concerns and aspirations of every local that each student represents—from the outskirts of Kampala to the mountainous region of Chiang Mai. Similarly, globalization involves more than attentiveness to regions of the world that are at a distance. It also involves an attentiveness to the global that is present in the local though often rendered invisible. It means making connections between the writings of Jon Sobrino and the pastoral care of Salvadoran migrants in a local shelter.

As we enter into the third decade of the twenty-first century, institutions must find ways of responsibly meeting the demands of preparing the next generation of ecclesial ministers, both ordained and lay, in ways that are appropriate and adequate as well as efficacious and effective. If we want these men and women to deal with the complex and interactive dynamics of thinking and feeling with the church in their ministerial, diocesan, and national contexts as well as in the broader context of the world church, then it is incumbent upon theological educators to recognize, analyze, and critically reflect upon the formative challenges and opportunities discussed above as well as their glocal significance for mission and ministry. This is not a responsibility to be undertaken *apart* from our students, but rather, *with* them. Creating the conditions for authentic encounter is at the heart of reimagining theological education in the light of glocalization.

"Today our proclamation of the Gospel and the Church's doctrine are called to promote a culture of encounter, in generous and open cooperation with all the positive forces that contribute to the growth of universal human consciousness. A culture, we might say, of encounter between all the authentic and vital cultures, thanks to a reciprocal exchange of the gifts of each in that luminous space opened up by God's love for all his creatures."

POPE FRANCIS[65]

BIBLIOGRAPHY

Accad, Martin. "Middle Eastern Theology in Evangelical Perspective." In *Global Theology in Evangelical Perspective: Exploring the Contextual Nature of Theology and Mission*, edited by Jeffrey P. Greeman, et al., 148–62. Downers Grove, IL: InterVarsity, 2012.

Aguirre, Robert. *Sister Ann Ida Gannon, BVM: A Life Time of Leadership*. Chicago: Center for Women and Leadership of Loyola University, 2014.

Ammerman, Nancy T. "America's Changing Religious and Cultural Landscape and Its Implications for Theological Education." *Theological Education* 49.1 (2014) 27–34.

Argyris, Chris. *Theory in Practices: Increasing Professional Effectiveness*. San Francisco: Jossey-Bass, 1974.

Association of Catholic Colleges and Universities (ACCU). "Association of Catholic Colleges and Universities: Home." https://www.accunet.org.

———. "Annual Meeting." *Association of Catholic Colleges and Universities*. http://www.accunet.org/Programs-Events/AnnualMeeting.

———. *Catholic Higher Education and Catholic Social Teaching*. Washington, DC: Association Of Catholic Colleges And Universities, 2012. http://www.accunet.org/Portals/70/Docs/Publications/CHE_CST_VisionStatement_2012.pdf?ver=2017-04-28-143619-610.

———. "Catholic Higher Education FAQs." *Association of Catholic Colleges and Universities*. http://www.accunet.org/About-Catholic-Higher-Ed/Catholic-Higher-Ed-FAQs#HowMany.

Association of Catholic Colleges and Universities in Canada (ACCUC). "Mission—About Us—Who We Are." https://www.stmu.ca/accuc/.

Barber, Benjamin R. *Jihad vs. McWorld*. New York: Times, 1995.

Bareness, Roy E., and Richard D. Kim. "A Pedagogy of Engagement for the Changing Character of the Twenty-First-Century Classroom." *Theological Education* 49.2 (2015) 89–106.

Bell, Kathrina Anderson. "Similar Goals and Dueling Agendas: Perceptions of Campus Internationalization and Equity Policies." PhD diss., San Francisco State University, 2013. http://scholar.dominican.edu/cgi/viewcontent.cgi?article=1000&context=geo-staff.

---

65. Francis, *Veritatis gaudium*, 3B.

Beyer, Peter. "Globalization and Glocalization." In *The Sage Handbook of the Sociology of Religion*, edited by James A. Beckford and N. J. Demerath III, 98–117. London: Sage, 2007.

Buckley, Michael. *The Catholic University as Promise and Project: Reflections in a Jesuit Idiom*. Washington, DC: Georgetown University Press, 1998.

Cameron, Mary D. *The College of Notre Dame of Maryland 1895–1945*. New York: D. X. McMullen, 1947.

Congregation for the Clergy. "The Gift of the Priestly Vocation: *Ratio Fundamentalist Institutionis Sacerdotalis*." December 8, 2016. http://www.clerus.va/content/dam/clerus/Ratio%20Fundamentalis/The%20Gift%20of%20the%20Priestly%20Vocation.pdf.

Curran, Charles E. *Catholic Higher Education, Theology, and Academic Freedom*. Notre Dame: University of Notre Dame Press.

De Ridder-Symoens, Hilde, ed. *Universities in the Middle Ages*. Vol. 1 of *A History of the University in Europe*. New York: Cambridge University Press, 1992.

Donovan, George F., ed. *Vatican Council II: Its Challenge to Education*. Washington, DC: Catholic University of America, 1966.

Dosen, Anthony J. "Catholic Higher Education in the United States: An Historical Context." In *Catholic Higher Education in the 1960s: Issues of Identity and Governance*, by Anthony J. Dosen, 27–46. Charlotte, NC: Information Age, 2009.

Dungca, Nicole. "Lost on Campus, as Colleges Look Abroad." *Boston Globe*, December 13, 2017.

Ellis, John Tracy. *Essays in Seminary Education*. Notre Dame, IN: Fides, 1967.

Fares, Diego. *The Heart of Pope Francis: How a New Culture of Encounter Is Changing the Church and the World*. New York: Crossroad, 2015.

Flannery, Austin P. *Documents of Vatican II*. Grand Rapids, MI: Eerdmans, 1975.

Fogarty, Gerald P. "Reflections on the Centennial of *Testem benevolentiae*." *US Catholic Historian* 17.1 (1999) 1–12.

Francis. "*Evangelii gaudium*: Apostolic Exhortation to the Bishops, Clergy, Consecrated Persons and the Lay Faithful on the Proclamation of the Gospel in Today's World." November 24, 2013. http://w2.vatican.va/content/francesco/en/apost_exhortations/documents/papa-francesco_esortazione-ap_20131124_evangelii-gaudium.html.

———. "For a Culture of Encounter: Morning Meditation in the Chapel of the *Domus sanctae marthae*." September 13, 2016. https://w2.vatican.va/content/francesco/en/cotidie/2016/documents/papa-francesco-cotidie_20160913_for-a-culture-of-encounter.html.

———. "Overcome Indifference and Win Peace: Message for the Celebration of the XLIX World Day of Peace." January 1, 2016. http://w2.vatican.va/content/francesco/en/messages/peace/documents/papa-francesco_20151208_messaggio-xlix-giornata-mondiale-pace-2016.html.

———. "The Roman Curia and the Body of Christ: Presentation of the Christmas Greetings to the Roman Curia." December 22, 2014. https://w2.vatican.va/content/francesco/en/speeches/2014/december/documents/papa-francesco_20141222_curia-romana.html.

———. "*Veritatis gaudium*. Apostolic Constitution on Ecclesiastical Universities and Faculties." December 8, 2017. https://w2.vatican.va/content/francesco/en/apost_constitutions/documents/papa-francesco_costituzione-ap_20171208_veritatis-gaudium.html.

Francis, Joseph A. "Homily—Twenty-Fifth Episcopal Anniversary of Most Reverend Harold Robert Perry." New Orleans, Louisiana, January 12, 1991. http://www.inaword.com/assets/francis-1991-homily.pdf.

Fulkerson, Mary McClintock. "They Will Know We Are Christians by Our Regulated Improvisation: Ecclesial Hybridity and the Unity of the Church." In *The Blackwell Companion to Postmodern Theology*, edited by Graham Ward, 265–79. Malden, MA: Blackwell, 2001.

Gautier, Mary L., and Jonathan Holland. *Catholic Ministry Formation Enrollment: Statistical Overview for 2016–2017*. Washington, DC: Center for Applied Research in the Apostolate, Georgetown University, 2017.

Gittins, Anthony J. *The Way of Discipleship: Women, Men, and Today's Call to Mission*. Collegeville, MN: Liturgical, 2016.

Gleason, Philip. "A Bibliographic Essay on the History of Catholic Higher Education." In *Handbook of Research on Catholic Higher Education*, edited by Thomas C. Hunt, et al., 95–113 Greenwich, CT: Information Age, 2003.

———. *Contending with Modernity: Catholic Higher Education in the Twentieth Century*. New York: Oxford University Press, 1995.

Greeley, Andrew. *The Changing Catholic College*. Chicago: Aldine, 1967.

———. *The Education of Catholic Americans*. Chicago: Aldine, 1966.

Greeley, Andrew, et al. *The Social Effects of Catholic Education*. Chicago: National Opinion Research Center, University of Chicago, 1964.

Haughey, John. *Where Is Knowing Going?: The Horizons of the Knowing Subject*. Washington, DC: Georgetown University Press, 2009.

Hendershott, Anne. "Continuing the Catholic Culture Wars." In *Status Envy: The Politics of Catholic Higher Education*, by Anne Hendershott, 227–43. New Brunswick, NJ: Transaction, 2009.

Ingham, Marybeth. *The Harmony of Goodness: Mutuality and Moral Living*. 2nd ed. St. Bonaventure, NY: Franciscan Institute, 2012.

John Paul II. "*Christifideles laici*. Post-Synodal Apostolic Exhortation on the Vocation and the Mission of the Lay Faithful in the Church and in the World." December 30, 1988. http://w2.vatican.va/content/john-paul-ii/en/apost_exhortations/documents/hf_jp-ii_exh_30121988_christifideles-laici.html.

———. "*Ex corde ecclesiae*. Apostolic Constitution on Catholic Universities Ex." August 15, 1990. http://w2.vatican.va/content/john-paul-ii/en/apost_constitutions/documents/hf_jp-ii_apc_15081990_ex-corde-ecclesiae.html.

———. "*Pastores dabo vobis*. Post-Synodal Apostolic to the Bishops, Clergy and Faithful on the Formation of Priests in the Circumstances of the Present Day." March 25, 1992. http://w2.vatican.va/content/john-paul-ii/en/apost_exhortations/documents/hf_jp-ii_exh_25031992_pastores-dabo-vobis.html.

———. "*Sapientia christiana*. Apostolic Constitution on Ecclesiastical Universities and Faculties." April 29, 1979. http://w2.vatican.va/content/john-paul-ii/en/apost_constitutions/documents/hf_jp-ii_apc_15041979_sapientia-christiana.html.

Kang, Namsoon. "Radical Border-Traversing: Theological Education in a Glocalized World of Disjuncture." *Spotlight on Theological Education* (March 2014). https://www.aarweb.org/publications/spotlight-on-theological-education-march-2014-radical-border-traversing-theological-education-in-a-glocalized-world-of-disjuncture.

Killick, David. *Developing the Global Student: Higher Education in an Era of Globalization*. New York: Routledge, 2015.

———. "Internationalization, Equality and Diversity." In *The Internationalization and Diversity in Higher Education: Implications for Teaching, Learning, and Assessment*, by David Killick, 11–22. New York: Palgrave MacMillan, 2017.

Klimoski, Victor J., et al., eds. *Educating Leaders for Ministry: Issues and Responses*. Collegeville, MN: Liturgical, 2005.

Küster, Volker. "From Contextualization to Glocalization: Intercultural Theology and Postcolonial Critique." *Exchange* 45.3 (2016) 203–26.

Lee, Bernard J. "A Socio-Historical Theology of Charism." *Review for Religious* 48.1 (1989) 124–35.

Lo, Lung-Kwong. "Paul and Ethnicity: The Paradigm of Glocalization." In *Jesus and Paul: Global Perspectives in Honor of James D. G. Dunn for His 70th Birthday*, edited by B.J. Oropeza, et al., 184–98. Library of New Testament Studies 414. New York: T. & T. Clark, 2009.

Magnuson, Roger. *Education in New France*. Montreal: McGill-Queen's University, 1992.

Morey, Melanie M., and John J. Piderit. *Catholic Education: A Culture in Crisis*. New York: Oxford University Press, 2006.

O'Brien, David J. "American Catholic History and American Catholic Higher Education: Memories and Aspirations." *US Catholic Historian* 28.3 (2010) 93–100.

———. "Catholicism, American Style." In *From the Heart of the American Church: Catholic Higher Education and American Culture*, by David J. O'Brien, 16–31. Maryknoll, NY: Orbis, 1994.

———. "Social Teaching, Social Action, Social Gospel." *US Catholic Historian* 5.2 (1986) 195–224.

Odin, Jaishree K., and Peter T. Manicas, eds. *Globalization and Higher Education*. Honolulu: University of Hawaii, 2004.

Power, Edward J. *Catholic Higher Education in America: A History*. New York: Appleton-Century-Crofts, 1972.

Putz, Louis J. "Reflections on Specialized Catholic Action." *US Catholic Historian* 9.4 (1990) 433–39.

Rajashekar, J. Paul. "Theological Education in an Era of Globalization: Some Critical Issues." *Journal of Lutheran Ethics* 15.1 (2015). https://www.elca.org/JLE/Articles/1069.

Roberts, Bob. *Glocalization: How Followers of Christ Engage the New Flat Earth*. Grand Rapids: Zondervan, 2007.

Roberts, John, et al. "Exporting Models." In *Universities in Early Modern Europe (1500–1800)*, edited by Hilde de Ridder-Symoens, 256–84. Vol. 2 of *A History of the University in Europe*. New York: Cambridge University Press, 1996.

Robertson, Roland. *Globalization: Social Theory and Global Culture*. London: Sage, 1992.

———. "Glocalization: Time-Space and Homogeneity-Heterogeneity." In *Global Modernities*, edited by Scott Las and Roland Robertson, 25–44. London: Sage, 1995.

Roudometof, Victor. *Glocalization: A Critical Introduction*. New York, NY: Routledge, 2016.

Schier, Tracy, and Cynthia Russetts, eds. *Catholic Women's Colleges in America*. Baltimore: Johns Hopkins University Press, 2002.

Schreiter, Robert J. *Constructing Local Theologies*. Maryknoll, NY: Orbis, 1985.

———. *The New Catholicity: Theology between the Global and the Local*. Maryknoll, NY: Orbis, 1997.

Schuth, Katarina. *Seminary Formation: Recent History, Current Circumstances, New Directions*. Collegeville, MN: Liturgical, 2016.

Stier, Jonas. "Taking a Critical Stance toward Internationalization Ideologies in Higher Education: Idealism, Instrumentalism and Educationalism." *Globalisation, Societies, and Education* 2.1 (2004) 83–97.

Sullivan, Susan Crawford, and Ron Pagnucco, eds. *A Vision of Justice Engaging Catholic Social Teaching on the College Campus.* Collegeville, MN: Liturgical, 2014.

Tiplady, Richard. *World of Difference: Global Mission at the Pic'n'Mix Counter.* Carlisle, UK: Paternoster, 2003.

Troy, Jodok. "Invisible Legions: The Pope and International Relations." *E-International Relations*, April 10, 2013. http://www.e-ir.info/2013/04/10/invisible-legions-the-pope-and-international-relations.

United States Catholic Conference (USCC). *US Catholic Seminaries and Their Future.* Washington, DC: United States Catholic Conference, 1988.

United States Conference of Catholic Bishops (USCCB). *Co-Workers in the Vineyard: A Resource for Guiding the Development of Lay Ecclesial Ministry.* Washington, DC: USCCB, 2005.

———. *Program of Priestly Formation.* 5th ed. Washington, DC: USCCB, 2006.

University of Notre Dame. "A Man of the World." http://hesburgh.nd.edu/fr-teds-life/a-man-of-the-world.

Vaira, Massimiliano. "Globalization and Higher Education Organizational Change: A Framework for Analysis." *Higher Education* 48 (2004) 483–510.

Westover, Jonathan H. *Globalization and Higher Education.* Champaign, IL: Common Ground, 2017.

Zakaria, Fareed. *The Post-American World.* New York: Norton & Norton, 2011.

7

"Made in the USA"
A Chinese Perspective on US Theological Education in Light of the Chinese Context

K. K. Yeo

This essay draws not from library research primarily, but from my engagement with US theological education in a global context over the past fifteen years.[1] The purpose is to explore whether global theological education is *possible*, as we look to a future based on current or "pilot" programs that I and many others have been initiating. Drawing on my own anecdotal study of various developments in Chinese higher and theological education—as well as Chinese engagement with US theological institutions (institutional partnerships, faculty exchanges, students receiving American theological degrees, etc.)—this essay seeks to identify concerns, questions, and possibilities for US theological institutions to consider, specifically the way in which their visions, efforts, and core values are preparing Christian leaders for local communities and churches, the academy, and the world.

The essay uses the metaphor of "Made in the USA" to frame its rethinking of US theological education and the retooling needed for a robust model of theological education in a world of change and difference.

---

1. See the collection of essays in ATS, *Theological Education* 35.2.

Whether printed on their certificates or not, "Made in the USA" here refers to graduates as the "final products" we[2] send out to serve within the United States and also overseas. Obviously, there are many differences between commercial products and graduates of higher education, a topic I will not address here. However, I use the metaphor to raise the following questions:[3]

1. What does it look like biblically and theologically to say the MDiv and PhD degrees we produce are "Made in the USA"? Is our assumption that theological education completed in the US is identical to other programs completed elsewhere in the world?

2. Are we proud of our "products," i.e., graduates going to serve in (and some returning to) Chinese communities? How do we prepare them pedagogically so that their work enables them to become ambassadors of their home institutions? The term "Made in the USA" is not only a heuristic device for marketing and purchasing power, but it also raises an important issue of whether doing theological education uncritically in a global context may result in exporting our problems to other nations—problems such as English hegemony (only English) as the *globalizing* tongue, causing destruction of languages and cultures elsewhere; or expecting the world to address problems such as democracy, eliminating evil via warfare, or a narcissistic culture leaning toward segregation and homogeneity, on terms set by the United States.

3. Do we simply "export" theological education in a stiff "free-market economy" of theological education, just as other transnational or international companies are doing? Have we prepared our students well for them (students) as ministers of the gospel and for us as teaching faculty, to be concerned with a "branding" (making a distinguished mark or contribution) that pays attention to the socio-political situation and reconfiguration of the global church in ministry?

4. Can we (institutions in the US) be held accountable for a "brain drain," e.g., for not encouraging Chinese students to be national leaders in

---

2. The "we" and "our" usage in this chapter reflects my nomadic consciousness of living in at least two worlds (US and China), and should thus be read as connoting a Chinese person teaching in a US institution, constantly negotiating and compromising on the methods, values, languages, and perspectives of my research and teaching in the US and China.

3. An excellent and expansive resource to compare and contrast with my work here is Altbach, *International Imperative*.

China and simply letting the laissez-faire force of the job market determine their professional roles? Will a shared value and "mega corridor"[4] of knowledge one day overcome a brain drain? Will "cloud technology" equalize space-time and make a brain drain obsolete?

5. In light of our shrinking world, can theological education be based simply on a "Made in the USA" model? Does the theology of the global church not call for collaborative effort, just as the increasing number of US products are assembled or even made overseas? A related question is: How significant is it for the United States to maintain its own institutional boundary?

LANDSCAPING US THEOLOGICAL EDUCATION IN RELATION TO CHINA

Autobiographical Reflections on Cross-Border Theological Education

The biographical material on which this essay is based serves to confirm that this work is not simply an intellectual exercise of *outopia* (no-place; unrealizable dream), but an *eutopia* (ideal place) that is possible.[5] During eight years of formal theological training in the United States (1984–1992) and my first teaching appointment in Hong Kong (1993–1996), I had various opportunities to make contact with students, scholars, and Christian leaders in China. My work at Garrett-Evangelical Theological Seminary and Northwestern University, in Evanston, Illinois (since 1996), Peking University (as a visiting professor since 2006)[6] and more than ten years of academic directorship (since 2006) of running Christian, classical, and comparative literature studies programs in more than four universities in

---

4. As metro areas around the world continue to expand, their boundaries blur, forming new areas known as mega-cities or mega-regions—areas that have large populations and share natural resources, economic systems, and ecosystems. Mega-corridors are the transport corridors that connect two or more of these areas. See Efrat, "World's Top Global Mega."

5. See Yeo, *Chairman Mao*, 218.

6. Later, other universities also invited me to be a visiting professor: Zhejiang University, HuaQiao University, Fudan University, Peking Normal University, and Tsinghua University.

China—has made me aware of the great challenges and possibilities ahead for US theological institutions.

Since 2012, I have been writing a series of theological textbooks with Majority-World[7] scholars, who were all trained in the West. In reminiscing about their education in the West, some of them have lamented about how "unprepared" they were when they returned home to teach and pastor. I remember how much more "translating" and critical thinking I needed to do myself in almost all courses I took as a seminarian in the United States. Through the research group on "reading Scripture in a global context," which draws Majority-World scholars together, I became even more aware of a cultural-contextual approach to higher education.

I am still revising a model of teaching and learning for theological education in China I hope will be more effective. However, over the past ten years, I have become committed to the following visions and programs to ground this model:

1. *Producing a cadre of indigenous Chinese theological teachers who can reproduce the leadership of China's official and "family" churches.* Whether the "production line" is in China or in the United States does not matter, except that I am convinced that no one locale can accomplish the job on its own. For a number of reasons, the Christian Study program I did in China is primarily implemented in China to lower costs, be contextually relevant, and avoid a brain drain. However, US institutions have been supportive of visiting Chinese scholars; and a number of Chinese scholars have even completed graduate degrees in the United States.

2. *Mentoring faculty in religious studies, cross-cultural studies, and comparative literature studies at universities in China (all state institutions), thus strengthening Christian programs by supporting faculty development and expanding their contribution to the university curriculum.* It has proved necessary to use a cross-cultural, cross-national approach to sharing resources in order to achieve the most efficient and effective results. This program is implemented both in China and in the United States. Workshops, seminars, or conferences are organized in China for faculty and scholars, but all of them are given opportunities to visit the United States for their own or for collaborative research.

---

7. The term "Majority World" is used here in preference to largely outdated, inaccurate, and biased terms such as "developing world," "third world," "two-thirds world," "three-fourths world," or the "global South."

3. *Creating a corpus of Chinese-adapted, Chinese-relevant Christian literature for China's church and academia, through the publication of Christian textbooks and Bible commentaries.* Three series from three separate publishers have been up and running for more than ten years, with approximately thirty-five titles published so far.[8] I believe Chinese Christians have much to offer the global church, but the first step is for them to have their own theology and Bible commentaries—part of the *zhongguohua* (中国化, sinification) the Chinese academy and government also endorse. What is the role of US theological institutions in this endeavor? I will deliberate this question in the next section as I explore the themes of friendship, midwife, and surrogate.

The long-term vision for Christian literature is to build in China a core residential, research library of biblical and theological collections to support graduate Christian Studies programs there. Currently, there is no library in China properly set up yet able to provide that support.

4. *Equipping Christian leaders in public sectors (government departments, businesses, and public schools) to make an impact on society through a biblically-grounded Christian witness and Chinese praxis.* For example, it is an honor to work with the Chinese Christian businessmen and entrepreneur training programs (currently in seven cities). Here, my role is as consultant on public theology[9] and faculty development, while China provides all the resources and personnel. I have learned much from my colleagues about how to connect the church with society and how to be faithful Christians as biblical teaching is translated into the public square.

All the visionary programs mentioned above have sociological and theological underpinnings that are dynamically contextual, and thus deserve our critical reflection so that theological education is not conceived as a static program, but as learning receptive to God's Spirit in engagement with our changing contexts. Therefore, this essay will first observe the complex relationship between the two worlds of the United States and China. Second, it will observe the challenges in theological education in

---

8. Peking University Christian Culture series (Beijing: Religious Culture); Biblical Library series (Shanghai: Huadong Normal University Press).

9. My use of the term "public theology" includes "political theology, public discourse, public ethics, public intellectual, and social ethics." See Breitenberg, "To Tell the Truth," 57.

a changing world and speak of what theological education in a US school ideally would look like.

CONTEXTS MATTER: COMPLEXITIES BETWEEN THE US AND CHINA

There are many possible relationships between an overseas seminary and the varieties of China's Protestant witness, and those relationships must be handled with the greatest care. Almost two decades ago (2002), in his book *Third Delight: The Internationalization of Higher Education in China*, Rui Yang proposed the best of "globalization" and "internationalization"[10] in general of higher education. I am less optimistic than Rui, mainly because of my work in *theological* education, and therefore its related sociopolitical complexity in both countries. Let me elaborate briefly.

China is by nature both "a dragon" and "a panda." Thus, theological education since the "Heavenly-Lord Religion" (*Tianzhujiao*, i.e., China Catholicism [e.g., the Jesuit Ricci]) or the "New Religion" (*Xinjiao*, i.e., China Protestantism [e.g., Robert Morrison]) has always been colored by political control (signified by a dragon) and the laity-led "cultural revolution" of the meek spirit (signified by a panda). China is full of paradoxes, as reflected in the various geographic landscapes and cultural mélanges. Ever since antiquity, when China prided itself on being the "Land of God" (*Shenzhou*), the royal cult of the overlords already claimed its divine right to dominate the people. Out of such cultural "fallenness" (Confucius's "propriety [is] fallen and aesthetic [is] broken") came various schools: the teachings and education of the Yin-yang worldview, Daoist philosophy, Confucian morality, and so forth.

Ancient China, since the Han dynasty (206 BCE–220 CE), exhibited its imperial virtue by being receptive to foreign ideas and trading via the Silk Road into this "Middle Kingdom" (*Zhongguo*). As a sovereign state today, China views "globalization" and "internationalization" differently, often perceiving foreign states as threats. Buddhism was "imported" in the Han dynasty and became a Chinese religion, Chán (Zen), by the fifth century. In contrast, even today, Christianity is mistaken as a "foreign religion." The

---

10. Yang, *Third Delight*. On the four usages of the term *globalization* by Don S. Browning (world evangelism, ecumenical cooperation, interfaith encounter, and universal work for justice) and Brubacher's insight on globalization in mission and theological education, see Brubacher, "Globalization of Theological Education," 5–23.

Syrian Nestorians brought Christianity to North China (known then as Cathay) under imperial sponsorship, but over the next fourteen centuries, intermittent foreign missionaries came to China in the names of Christ, civilization, science, trade, freedom/democracy, literacy/education, medicine, etc., complicating the identity of Christianity in the sociopolitical culture of China.[11]

By the turn of the twentieth century, China's soul was weak and its conscience fragile. So, the rise of Red China responded with a strong tone of nationalism to the coming of the Christian gospel that sought to "occupy China."[12] The decade of the Cultural Revolution (1966–1976) is considered the dark ages of Chinese Christianity and "cultural destruction."[13] The haunting past still lingers as a nightmare. Yet, despite chaos and bloodshed, an estimated 80 to 120 million Christians (Protestant and Catholic) live in China today[14] (with a margin of error of 40 million). Perhaps no one knows where the Wind blows (John 3:8); yet the headwind is strong, as we read in the media today.

There are no definitive statistics on the number of Christians or religious workers traveling from the United States to China each year to complete some sort of theological education there. However, out of 25 million US tourists to China, we can assume that the numbers are significant. We also know that there are no fewer than 300,000 Chinese students presently studying at universities, colleges, or seminaries in the United States (comprising 30 percent of the country's international students).[15] There are many Confucius Institutes in the US that promote cultural and academic

---

11. Even in modern day China, China specialist Randall Peerenboom is optimistic about China's "four main pillars of modernity," i.e., the economic, human rights, the legal system ("socialist rule of law"), and democracy. See Peerenboom, *China Modernizes*.

12. Although the Chinese title can be translated literally as "Blessings Upon China," the printed English title of a Chinese book published in 1922 by the China Continuation Committee is "The Christian Occupation of China," with the subtitle: "A general survey of the numerical strength and geographical distribution of the Christian forces in China." See Stauffer, *Christian Occupation*.

13. See Yeo, *Chairman Mao*, 152–62.

14. Aikman, *Jesus*, 7–8.

15. According to The Traveling Team observation, "80 percent of those international students will return to their countries having never been invited to an American home; 40 percent of the world's 220 Heads of State once studied in the US; and only 10 percent of international students are reached by ministries while in the US" (TTT, "Mission Stats").

exchange, and possibly the intention is to advance "soft power" of China via educational means.[16]

Notwithstanding this robust US-China higher education commerce, the two contexts are very different. For example, religious education is carefully monitored in China. I wonder if those who engage in teaching in churches in China know and abide by the *Mandate from the Government*, via SARA (State Administration for Religious Affairs), to:[17]

- thoroughly implement the Party's directives;
- thoroughly implement the central decision-making arrangements on religious work, via the rule of law to promote religious work in the spirit of innovation—such as realizing the Chinese dream of the vast majority of believers to gather strength, to strive for building a prosperous society in a comprehensive reform, and to create a united and stable society;
- continue to implement the "religious qualification of teachers' colleges and title review appointment" and "religious degree granting institutions"—such as for SARA to guide the Chinese Buddhist Institute, the Chinese Academy of Taoism, the China Islamic Institute School of Philosophy, Chinese Catholic Seminary, Nanjing Union Theological Seminary, and Christian Philosophy Catholic Seminary in their mission, curriculum, accreditation, etc.; and
- monitor unauthorized construction (e.g., outdoor religious statues and places of religious activity) and illegal engagement in religious activities that cause chaos.

That there are many restrictions within China is clear. At the same time, it does not help to adopt US-China specialists' own paranoia or superiority (depending on whom you read) when speaking of the state of the nation. Thus, one encounters prognostications, alternatively, of the rapid

---

16. Confucius Institute is administered by China's Ministry of Education and overseen/funded by the Office of Chinese Language Council (国家汉办), and the goal is to have 1,000 institutes worldwide by the year 2020. The model of China's non-profit organization working within affiliate colleges or universities overseas has received criticism on issues related to academic freedom of the host institutions, suspicion of the Institute's industrial espionage activity, and advancing the "soft power" of China via educational means. See Volodzko, "China's Confucius Institutes."

17. See the section titled "Loyal to the State vs. Love for God" in Huang, "'Who Am I.'" In February 2018, the Chinese government issued "Revised Regulations on Religious Affairs." See Zhang, "China."

rise of China and thus the shrinking global influence of the United States,[18] the inevitable increasing competition and limited cooperation between the United States and China,[19] or the "fragile superpower" China that is heading towards domestic chaos and, subsequently, war with the United States.[20] Neither unbridled optimism nor sober pessimism is realistic.

I find Robert Sutter's posture on a *bilateral partnership* model for US-China relations[21] more palatable—a model with important insights for theological education in and between these two nations. Especially important is the idea that theological education institutions in the United States and China can be *mutual friends*. Indeed, at some points, they may even function as *surrogates* or *midwives* to one another. For example, US theological schools can serve as surrogates for Chinese universities that wish to start a curriculum in Western philosophy; and Chinese universities can be midwives for US theological schools to begin a program in Chinese philosophy. Yet, eventually it is their friendship with one another that will enrich Western philosophy from a Chinese perspective, Chinese philosophy from a Western perspective, and *global* philosophy that embraces more than its own culture and context.[22]

Because of the unique sociopolitical situation, sometimes expressed in Chinese as *Zhongguotese* (中国特色), Protestant Christianity in China is exceedingly diverse, not only *between* official churches (the Three-Self Patriotic Movement and China Christian Council, with many "meeting points" [*juhuidian*]) and unofficial family churches [*jiating jiaohui*], sometimes called house churches), but also *among* these groups themselves in their relations with one another and especially with the government.[23] I prefer not to characterize theological education according to source—churches, seminaries, or higher-education institutions, including research institutes. But the fact is that, because of particular historical and sociopolitical contexts in China, there are two main avenues for theological education—and substantial support from outside China, especially the United States.

18. Cohen, *America's Response*.
19. Shambaugh, *Tangled Titans*.
20. Shirk, *China*.
21. See Sutter, *US-Chinese*; Mann, *About Face*.
22. Friends in both China and the United States have spoken proudly of both nations as the "Group of Two" (G2). My understanding of the catholic, ecumenical church does not allow me to agree with their aspiration, though the scope of this essay is focusing on these two countries. The world is constituted of more than G2, or even G20.
23. See Yeo, "Church and State," 31–33.

The first avenue comprises *church-related theological education* offered by the following groups.²⁴

1. *Local churches as training programs (peixun,* 培训*)*, especially in family churches, where foreign Christian groups have a strong presence in the teaching faculty, strong denominational theology (especially Reformed), and accreditation for awarding certificates of completion.

2. *Bible schools and theological seminaries (provincial, regional, and national seminaries)*, including nineteen schools in the Three-Self Patriotic Movement (TSPM)/Christian Council Churches (CCC), and a growing number in family churches. These schools are characterized generally by very few PhD teaching faculty and comparatively little research and writing by faculty members; strength in spirituality, mission, and preaching, but not in biblical studies; and limited attempts to engage Christian theology with Chinese culture. In the late 1990s, Bishop K. H. Ting proposed the "Reconstruction of Theological Thinking," as he considered the context of socialism seriously. Ting's new emphases on social exegesis, an open theology based on the idea of God's freedom, and self-realization through love are radical ideas, raising challenges to the traditional Christian doctrine of "justification by faith."

3. *The "Third Church" of young intellectual and professional members*, who conduct seminars and training programs to fill the need for rigorous faith seeking understanding and constructive faith for the good of China.

The second avenue for Christian education and research is not the institutional church or seminaries, but *institutions of higher education—* colleges and universities, including some predecessors of Christian universities.²⁵ A new movement of academic interest and research on Christianity as the core of Western civilization has developed in China, led by scholars based primarily in humanities and social-sciences institutions, e.g., Peking University, People's University in Beijing, Chinese Academy of Social Sciences in Beijing, Fudan University in Shanghai, and Sun Yat-sen University in Guangzhou.²⁶ Much of the funding for these programs comes from

---

24. See the outdated discussion in Miao, *Education for Service.*

25. On the history of higher education in China from 1880–1975, see Fenn, *Christian Higher Education; Ever New Horizons.*

26. Many universities in China have set up Centers for Christian Studies (e.g.,

the Chinese government, perhaps with the goal of demonstrating to the world China's academic and religious freedom. The government no doubt assumes that academic research of religions as philosophies or cultural phenomena will benefit the modernization of China. It is not surprising that, with resources and support available, many scholars, the majority of whom may not be professing Christians, are able to produce a greater quantity and quality of work than that of Christian theologians in seminaries and churches.

A few of these scholars call themselves "cultural Christians," meaning that they become Christians not through the church (not necessarily through baptism or joining the church), but through reading foreign literature or studying Christian philosophy. Therefore, these scholars study Christianity less as a theological discipline to enhance their faith development or service to the church than as a cultural phenomenon and an academic discipline. Therefore, US theological institutions do not need to export the unhealthy binary educational system of "school of religion" and "seminary/Bible college" to China, for it would only further fracture knowledge and life.

Putting sociopolitical differences and phobia aside, it is sound to propose that these two entities—the US seminary system and China's

---

Peking University, Chinese People's University, Beijing Normal University, Fudan University, Sun Yat-sen University, Shanxi Normal University, Sichuan University) and, in their Philosophy or Religion Departments, offer courses in Christian studies, and some offer extensive courses in classical languages. Wuhan University, for example, has offered courses such as Guided Reading of the Bible (survey), Biblical Exegesis, Subjects on Western Philosophy, History of Christian Church, History of Christian Thought, Systematic Theology, Dialogue between Religions and Social Harmony, and Comparative Studies of Religions. Scholarly journals also are published, such as *Academic Journal of Christian Culture* (Chinese People's University) and *Christian Academia* (Fudan University). Additionally, there are many conferences organized by these universities as well. The China Academy of Social Sciences in Beijing has its own Center for Christian Research (affiliated with the Research Institute for World Religions) and publishes a journal, *Studies on the Religion of Christianity*, as well as organizing symposia. Henan University has The Institute for Jewish Research, and the Research Institute for Biblical Literature publishes the *Journal of Biblical Literature*.

Great work has been done. Stretching points include: (1) contextual *and* global theologies to overcome nationalistic bias; (2) the need to be self-critical of the alienation between *Historie* and *Geschichte* in current teaching and research methods, although in the name of "academic" study (*xueshu* 学术); (3) a methodological reconsideration of text-history-philosophy (文史哲), rather than the reverse in the current state. Thus, what is the role US scholarship or scholars or institutions play—surrogate, midwife, or friend? Friendship looks more promising to me.

institutions of higher learning—must mutually enrich each other. Their relationship cannot be one-way—solely from the US to China. The balance of this essay will help us discern the calling and gifts of a US seminary in this globalized (often hegemonic secular) and changing world. I will use the concept of "communion," akin to *perichoresis* in Trinitarian theology, to speak of the dynamic life of theological education of a US school that does not forget the changing reality it finds itself in.

CHANGING WORLD, OPPORTUNITIES AMID CHALLENGES[27]

Borderless Theological Education—The World Keeps Changing, and It Is Still Flat

The ancient Chinese held a worldview of change as constant and composed *The Classic of Change* so that they could find wisdom to thrive amid the vicissitudes of life. In his 2005 book *The World is Flat: A Brief History of the Twenty-First Century*, Thomas Friedman argued that globalization in the twenty-first century presents all competitors, countries, and companies in the world of trade and commerce with equal opportunities. The idea of a "level playing field" and a constantly shifting environment can be applied to theological education, suggesting that, since global citizenship and mobility will gradually erase nation-state identity and related restrictions, those unprepared to accept flux and change will soon be obsolete. With a passport, we all can travel from Chicago to Beijing on a superliner comfortably and not worry about governments knowing our GPS coordinates. Yet it is also true that many are fearful of traveling to places wherein they perceive terror, or on which a "travel ban" has been imposed by the White House in January 2017.

Change, even crisis, brings opportunity and creativity, if one accepts or appreciates flux as a catalyst.[28] Despite information technology and vir-

---

27. The theological basis of my reflections are found in my forthcoming essay, Yeo, "Biblical Interpretation."

28. As an overseas Chinese born and raised in Borneo, Malaysia ("in exile"), educated in the United States (Westernized), and currently serving the global church by preparing academic and ecclesial leaders in the United States and China (constantly adjusting to two clocks), I used to have great anxiety over my nomadic consciousness (I never felt "at home" in any geographical locale) until I learned from the book of Hebrews about the notion of "restfulness" in the pilgrimage of life.

tual reality, it is still necessary to *have people on the ground* because we are not robots; we are human beings *and* because cultures are diverse and continually subject to change. Theological education that does not take into account the dynamism of time and space will not prepare graduates to live *in reality*. The reality of change suggests that research and development (R&D) is the brain of any company. Likewise, in theological education, once faculty become interchangeable or charged *to be less than engineers or scientists in their fields*—that is, scholars to do research to create knowledge for the good of the world—the demise of leadership training is certain. Revising curricula by moving furniture, shifting courses, changing emphases or schedules will not do it.

Do we really know who we are? And are we (the United States and China) really that different? Many people are colonized to believe that cultural difference is divinely ordained, that cultural predispositions are all relative and, therefore, do not fall under the power of sin. The fact that cultures of the North Atlantic countries (often erroneously and ideologically termed as "the West") values individualism and freedom while traditional Chinese culture values community and harmony may not be "givens." They are negotiable. But the differences between these cultures do not mean that one is better than the other. The best we can do, therefore, is to pick and choose what works for us today. Both cultures need theological reflection so that they can accept and embody God's grace and love, peace, and justice.

The tendency of Chinese students in US educational institutions to totally reject the traditional Chinese value of community and immediately embrace so-called "Western" values of individual freedom illustrates the "value-free" or "open-market" logic of Western European and North American pedagogy. Colleagues sometimes use loaded terms such as "postcolonialism," "liberation theology," or "justice" primarily to distinguish themselves as Western "progressive," suggesting that those who do not subscribe to their stance are "fundamentalists." So, the extremes of far-right and far-left theological education in the United States look very much alike, especially in their fundamental assumptions, even though on the surface they appear opposed to each other. To wit, both are exclusive, both are ideologically driven, and both are expecting students to subscribe to their ideology in theological education. There are still differences between the United States and China, but I often observe the "empire logic" common to the two political systems—the biases and filtering/controlling nature of media, the Mammoth-driven economy, the thirst for violence in popular culture, etc. And I am afraid that the "empire" militarism, idolatry of market, and degradation of human dignity will bring about a distortion of the human spirit, alienation of human psychology, a breakdown of community, and the disappearance of hope and trust.

So, what are the challenges and the possibilities?

Local Contexts and Catholicity—Communion that Is "Many and One"

Partnership and reciprocity—which are themes of friendship—have a role in administration as well as in curricula. The approach to theological education at a US seminary should be reconsidered, specifically so that churches in the European and US colonial powers can listen and learn from churches in the East and the Global South. This calls for humility and trust as US seminaries exercise the gift of networking and conferencing beyond China and the United States.

It has been a long journey that has led me to see the importance of the *interplay* between local and global cultures in the growth of Christianity and the *vitality* of theological education.[29] When teaching faculty and curricula are not grounded in a cross-cultural understanding of the world, a cross-cultural theology and reading of the Bible, and cross-cultural ministry experience, they will fail to meet the needs of twenty-first-century theological education. For example, Langham Partnership (formerly John Stott Ministries) has been sponsoring and mentoring more than 300 PhD students from the Majority World for the past forty years. More than half of their PhD students are currently trained outside North American and Western European countries, i.e., trained also in their own regional and cultural contexts (such as the Philippines, Hong Kong, Nairobi, South Africa, Central and Latin America),[30] in addition to spending 40 percent of their time in Great Britain, Europe, and the United States. This is a hopeful sign.

Are US theological schools now ready to achieve *organic and symmetrical* partnerships, to become conversant in the language and worldview of China? Most US universities have been offering Chinese language to business people, teachers, and lecturers who wish to work in China, and

---

29. See Yeo, "Theology," 45–61.

30. See the insightful essay of Cunningham, "Doctoral-level Theological Education," 101–34.

these courses are available to the general public as well. Yet, few Christian lecturers have an interest in learning Mandarin, and almost all of them expect translators to be hired for them when they arrive in China. Theological education in the United States would improve if students were required to learn a second language before they matriculated. A mono-linguistic education is a handicapped one, and it breeds a sense of bias and superiority. In addition to second-language learning, the US curriculum could involve a cross-cultural immersion experience or comparative literature studies—especially in world scriptures, interreligious studies experience, etc.

At this point, it is worth recalling a longstanding missionary challenge: How does theological education move toward being "fully Christian and fully Chinese"—to borrow the Christological algorithm of "two natures, one person"—when, unfortunately, missionary history often has issued the cry "one more Christian, one fewer Chinese"? Chinese Christians have been asking how they can be "fully Chinese and fully Christian," as they seek the hypostatic union of Christ's humanity and divinity in their own existence. Except for being dressed in the Chinese language, most Chinese Bible commentaries do not relate to Chinese culture, but simply "re-incarnate" the humanity and divinity of the commentators' Eurocentric mentors. The majority of Chinese theologies still buy into the assumption that it is possible for theologies to be a-cultural, partly because European mentors or US academics continue to expect biblical and theological interpretations that are tacitly Western as "the" scholarship or "good" scholarship. I lament this "disorder" of Chinese churches and scholars in my book *What Has Jerusalem to Do with Beijing?* In the book, I demonstrate that unless Chinese theology is both biblical *and* cultural, both the interpretation and the culture will eventually become diseased and die. Any Christian scholar will need to maintain his or her dual-nature-in-one-person self, for culture without theology is soul-less, but theology without culture is body-less. Both together make an embodied soul. In my work on Christology, I argue that the "dual-nature-one-person" ontology of Christ

> enables "every tribe and language and people and nation" (Rev 5:9, 7:9, 13:7, 14:6; cf. Acts 2:1–13) to be "fully Christian and fully Chinese" in their *theologizing*, which constitutes part of Christian worship. Jesus Christ is the Reality that makes all realities, cultures, and meaning-systems true, beautiful, and good. Because Jesus Christ does not speak heavenly tongues in his revelation of God, Christianity does not have a sacred language. The gospel of the church is neither culture nor language-specific. Jesus is the

Eternal Word enfleshed (John 1:14), as the gospel of Christ and Christian doctrines are always proclaimed and understood "incarnationally" within their own cultures "in-linguistically."[31]

Christianities from Africa, Latin America, and Asia portray a blossoming picture of a "global Christianity"[32] with multiple centers, and US seminaries could benefit from mutual exchange among these centers. In this case, the humanity of a US seminary is its own context, while the divinity is its transcendental being that comes from "others" outside its context. That is, any theological education that wants to care for its own context and survival alone will "lose its life" (Matt 16:25), while those who live in the "indebtedness to love others/neighbors" (Rom 13:8) will fulfill and be rewarded richly by the law of life (Lev 19:18).

There are 1.178 billion Christians in the Majority World (including the Pacific and Oceania), but only 819 million in the Atlantic region.[33] Christianity is not a "white man's religion"[34] anymore. Yet the curricula of many US seminaries still bear the burden and normativity of whiteness. In the US institution at which I have been teaching for the past twenty years, we claim diversity as one of the core values. Yet, I notice still that the dominant ideology is "black and white," and the Latina/o and Asians are often only "ghosts" on campus and in classroom discussions. Very few white students bother to attend Asian Week lectures, not appreciating that these lectures are actually organized for them.

There is an Africa Bible Commentary,[35] and commentary series written by non-European biblical scholars and named as such.[36] But there is no series called "North American Bible Commentary." Is this a naïve omission or a hidden and more dangerous assumption that Western or European theologies or North American interpretations are universal and normative?[37] Majority World students keep reminding me that all theologies are contextual, especially Western European and North American theologies. Theological education will need to acknowledge the ethnocentric posture of the traditional Western colonial powers, and will do well to embrace a healthy

31. Yeo, "Biblical Christologies," 162–79.
32. Tennent, *Theology*.
33. Ostling, "Researcher Tabulates World's Believers."
34. Usry and Keener, *Black Man's Religion*, 7.
35. Adeyemo, *Africa Bible Commentary*.
36. Kanagaraj, *Gospel of John*; Ngewa, *1 & 2 Timothy and Titus*.
37. Bonino, "Latin America," 31.

"contextual-global" hermeneutical stance, i.e., one that embodies the church *catholic* (global) as more and more contextual/cultural theologies are lived out in the matrix of conferencing with one another. The principle of "four selfs" (self-support, self-propagation, self-administration of the Chinese Three-Self, plus Justo Gonzalez's self-theologizing)[38] can serve as a guiding principle of theological education today.

Non-binary Thinking—Communion of "Soulish Body" Unity

Theological concerns in the Majority world are hardly binary—splitting the soul from the body in anthropology, separating spiritual from social needs or, worse, privileging the atomist inner life (private) over the interpersonal, communal reality (public). A binary understanding of the world and theology is inadequate and, therefore, harmful not only to international students but also to US students. I propose a non-binary model of theological education:

1. *Communal living and reading of theology*: Notwithstanding numerous attempts on my part, it is almost impossible to persuade students to do a group project as a course assignment. They are reluctant not because of a concern about "intellectual-property-right" infringement, but because of the competitive spirit for grades and financial aid. Most US seminaries are baptized by Descartes's "*cogito ergo sum,*" but the corrective can be the Chinese understanding of *renren* (co-humanity), or John S. Mbiti's understanding of "I am, because we are; and since we are, therefore I am."[39] The primary problem I have observed among students and colleagues in US seminaries does not involve academic performance, but rather interpersonal relationship. Such is the case also in churches and communities.

2. *Social reality of individual self*: Freedom is less an independence of the individual spirit and more a grafting of one's spirit to a community by means of "serving/enslaving" it (Gal 5), thus restoring the *imago Dei* communally. In light of the christological and anthropological understanding of *imago Dei*, the salvation of "the last, the least, and the lost" cannot simply be a social program or a church's missional program. Instead, it is the very salvific act of God in hearing the "cry of my

---

38. González, *Mañana*, 49.
39. See Yeo, *Theology and the Future*, 270–76, 281–91; Mbiti, *African Religions*, 107–8.

people" (Exod 3:7; Jer 8:19), including that of Abel (Gen 1:1–10) and Jesus, both of whom share the *universal* narrative of "Son of Adam/ Man." Shared commitments and benefits are the virtues of theological education of the future.

3. *The public nature of faith*: What can theology be other than "public"?[40] A privatized faith? Yet another political reading of Paul as a "New Perspective" and a "Fresh Perspective"? Have we not paid attention to Latin American readings in the past fifty years?

4. *Myriad life-experiences as the language of theology, as opposed to logic and critical thinking solely*: My first theological training took place informally in a Chinese church in Malaysia, and I remember stories, songs, drama, and paintings as media used to teach. When I was asked to oversee a Christian Studies program at a premier university in China, I encouraged students to use their myriad life-experiences as an expanding horizon for speaking about God in relation to the world. My formal seminary education in the United States, however, was quite different. Logic, proof, argument, and abstraction were the preferred modes of persuasive discourse. Over the years, I have learned to be "cross-cultural" and to embrace both modes. Yet I believe that theological education in US institutions would do well to recognize not only academic writing, but also "commonplace sources . . . and popular media"[41] as authoritative texts. Diane Stinton points out, "The propositional style of analysis associated with scholastic theology in the West is not the only way of expressing theology."[42] Those outside the First World do not have the luxury of armchairs or the air-conditioned tower of libraries. The messiness of life is the "fact on the ground," out of which come seemingly mundane theological expressions such as the "Crucified-Guru" Christology in India,[43] Kosuke Koyama's "water-buffalo theology" in Thailand,[44] or Hwa Yung's "mango-and-banana theology" in Malaysia.[45] What theological education delivers is not only "content" anymore (e.g., Bible, theol-

---

40. On public theology in Asia, see Yeo, "Theology," 45–61.
41. Jenkins, *Faces of Christianity*, 8.
42. Stinton, "Africa, East and West," 107.
43. Thangaraj, *Crucified Guru*.
44. Koyama, *Water Buffalo*.
45. Yung, *Mangoes or Bananas?*.

ogy, knowledge, or skill) but also other "forms," including experience and method (e.g., online learning, community formation, aesthetic in ministry and self-care).

In the coming years, when the world is coming to us and the globe is shrinking, US theological education that does not speak the language of the "other" will lose its saltiness and wisdom. For example, we can journey with the Chinese (and African and Hispanic and Latino/a) people and appreciate a pictographic language and worldview that enable them to be attracted to the biblical metaphors involving lepers, sheep, serpents, donkeys, dictatorships, or false prophets. The biblical world is alive in their worlds, the worlds in which God continues to work. Stories, parables, Old Testament narratives, and the dramatic language of Revelation are music to their ears. Of course, using local languages and worldviews does not mean being coopted by cultural ills. In fact, the opposite is true: Redemption happens as cultural languages are used in our pedagogy:

> The facts of life on the ground are at odds with the authoritative text, thus socio-political reality, anthropological poverty and linguistic epistemology become filters used by the Majority World to read the Scriptures. These lenses emerged out of the Majority World, contexts that the developed, privileged and resourceful "First World" has long forgotten. The Majority World hears the Bible as speaking to its problems of dictatorship and colonialism, exile and displacement, poverty and famine, plague and pestilence, human trafficking and child labor, child prostitutes and child soldiers, patronage and corruption, pirating and extortion, civil or interreligious wars and ethnic violence, environmental devastation and epidemic outbreak.[46]

My own teaching and research over the past twenty years have been challenged by the variegated, complex, and holistic world in the non-European reality. Consequently, I have been compelled to focus on "Bible and cultures," with commitments to the tasks of building nations, transforming local communities, fulfilling the ideals of culture, saving individuals and societies from chaos, meaninglessness, injustice, and violence, as well as moving them toward wholeness and beauty, *shalom*, and glory.

---

46. Yeo, "Bible Interpretations."

CONCLUSION: NEW MODEL OF THEOLOGICAL EDUCATION—NEW HEAVEN AND NEW EARTH OF "COMPASSIONATE JUSTICE"

The world is flat and shrinking, thus getting more and more interactive, interdependent, and borderless. Zeev Efrat's "World's top Global Mega Trends to 2020 and Implications to Business, Society and Cultures" projects that our world is increasingly urbanized with mega-regions, mega-cities, and mega-corridors, prioritized values on infrastructure development, economy, energy, and environment.[47] Theological institutions may need to consider a "mega-corridor" of seminary education, where storefront schools can be empowered by connecting with the corridor. The combined movement of "green" (eco-friendly) and "smart" (tech-savvy) in theological institutions and curricula will redefine the future of personal and communal lives, mobility, and learning goals—thus impacting our traditional understandings of ecclesiology, pneumatology, and eschatology/ethics, respectively. Most probably, the traditional category will be inadequate to describe our world then, as language, especially theological language, is indeed constantly shaped and reshaped by the emerging, constantly changing reality that theology inspires.

Generation Y will make up of 34 percent of the world population and, because members of this group are educated, resourceful, and IT literate, they will be the movers and shakers of the world. Seminary students of Generation Y will be like their peers—adaptive to change. I venture that their purpose of "getting" theological education is not about skills but about "compassionate justice," i.e., immersing themselves in an experience of solidarity/empathy via virtual reality so that they can inspire others to join them in healing the world (*tikkun olam*).

Because space-time in the next five or ten years will be experienced as truncated and "bent" or "warped," as the border between time and space becomes increasingly indistinct, delivery of seminary education and teaching of spirituality, for example, will require us to experience another "epistemological rupture" (Gaston Bachelard, later used by Louis Althusser). Because centers and capital cities will be decentered, a brain drain will cease or even be reversed. Cloud and satellite technology will make New York and Shanghai unimportant as centers, for emerging outsourcing hotspots can be set up easily in Eastern and Central Asia, Africa, or Latin America.

47. Efrat, "Mega Trends," 3.

I find open-source software powerful and creative, the best tool for sharing information and convenient for customization. The sharing/communion of US seminary resources (i.e., research and teaching of faculty, ministry by students, the aspirations of any US seminary's constituencies, the library, individual consultations, professional development) so that universities/colleges, seminaries/Bible colleges, churches/fellowship groups, and Christian NGOs (businessmen, lawyers, artists) will allow both the US and China to find mutual friendship constructive in advancing the aspirations of both countries. This role calls for empathic sharing, rather than condescending authority, in a relationship of stewardship—the sharing of gifts of any US seminary with all partnered schools or centers of Christian activity in China. The role of networking with leaders in the Chinese government, communities, and churches in the nation-building project can range from co-sponsoring research (e.g., medical, economic, or Christianity issues) to co-funding social services (e.g., youth ministry, senior homes, special education) towards *shalom* and justice. This role for US seminaries calls for faithfulness to the gospel of Christ in the ever-renewed life of discipleship in a changing world.

The business world has been practicing outsourcing as a way to afford companies an efficient and cost-effective means of maximizing profit. Theological education, too, can practice outsourcing, with the difference that the goal is compassionate justice rather than self-interested profit. Perhaps US theological schools can dream of a new model of delivering theological education that (1) takes the changing spatial-temporal reality seriously, not limited to a physical campus, yet living out an incarnational theology at its best; (2) has the courage to be a "global seminary," living out the discipleship of compassionate justice in sharing resources with the Majority world; (3) explores new ways of designing curricula in light of the internationalization of theological education, e.g., "off-shoring," not so much to take advantage of lowered costs but to access the flexibility and specialization found elsewhere; "supply-chaining" to overseas partner schools in areas of one's gifts and concentrations; "in-sourcing" to peer schools such as a consortium (e.g., the Association of Chicago Theological Schools); and (4) anticipating a seminary that is fully automated, not in terms of a robot-faculty, but in terms of students effortlessly embodied with God's grace and kingdom values for the holiness of life as priestly and prophetic ministries.

The new-heaven-and-new-earth is the *telos* of God's creation but, interestingly, is not spelled out in detail in the Bible. Perhaps the intent is to invite us to engage in "R&D," to delineate a blueprint of theological education in the next few decades for the good of all creation and humanity *et gloria in excelsis Deo*!

BIBLIOGRAPHY

Adeyemo, Tokunboh, ed. *Africa Bible Commentary*. Grand Rapids: Zondervan, 2006.
Aikman, David. *Jesus in Beijing*. Washington, DC: Regnery, 2003.
Altbach, Philip G. *The International Imperative in Higher Education*. Global Perspectives on Higher Education 27. Rotterdam: Sense, 2013.
Association of Theological Schools (ATS). "Incarnating Globalization in ATS Schools: Issues, Experiences, Understandings, Challenges." *Theological Education* 35.2 (1999) 1–189.
Bonino, José Miguez. "Latin America." In *An Introduction to Third World Theologies*, edited by John Parratt, 16–43. Cambridge: Cambridge University Press, 2004.
Breitenberg, E. Harold. "To Tell the Truth: Will the Real Public Theology Please Stand Up?" *Journal of the Society of Christian Ethics* 23.2 (2003) 55–96.
Brubacher, Ray. "The Globalization of Theological Education and of Christian Mission." *Mission Focus: Annual Review* 8 (2000) 5–23.
Chester, S. Miao, ed. *Education for Service in the Christian Church in China: The Report of a Survey Commission 1935*. Shanghai: National Committee for Christian Religious Education in China, 1935.
Cohen, Warren I. *America's Response to China: A History of Sino-American Relations*. 5th ed. New York: Columbia University Press, 2010.
Cunningham, Scott. "Doctoral-level Theological Education in Africa for Evangelicals: A Preliminary Assessment." *Africa Journal of Evangelical Theology* 26.2 (2007) 101–34.
Efrat, Zeev. "World's Top Global Mega Trends to 2020 and Implications to Business, Society and Culture." Powerpoint Slides. http://www.bar-oriyan.com/Portals/0/mega%20trands%20exec%20summary%20v3%20(1).pdf.
Fenn, William Purviance. *Christian Higher Education in Changing China 1880–1950*. Grand Rapids: Eerdmans, 1976.
———. *Ever New Horizons: The Story of the United Board for Christian Higher Education in Asia 1922–1975*. Grand Rapids: Eerdmans, 1980.
González, Justo L. *Mañana: Christian Theology from a Hispanic Perspective*. Nashville: Abingdon, 1990.
Huang, Jianbo. "'Who Am I': Identity Tensions among Chinese Intellectual Christians." Paper presented at the Annual Meeting of the Association for the Sociology of Religion, San Francisco, August 14, 2004. http://hirr.hartsem.edu/sociology/huang.html.
Jenkins, Philip. *New Faces of Christianity: Believing the Bible in the Global South*. New York: Oxford University Press, 2006.
Kanagaraj, Jey J. *The Gospel of John: A Commentary*. Asia Bible Commentary Series. Secunderabad, India: OM, 2005.
Koyama, Kosuke. *Water Buffalo Theology*. Maryknoll, NY: Orbis, 1974.
Mann, James. *About Face: A History of America's Curious Relationship with China, from Nixon to Clinton*. 3rd ed. New York: Vintage, 2010.

Mbiti, John S. *African Religions and Philosophy*. London: Heinemann, 1969.

Ngewa, Samuel M. *1 & 2 Timothy and Titus*. Grand Rapids: Zondervan and Hippo, 2009.

Ostling, Richard N. "Researcher Tabulates World's Believers." *Salt Lake Tribune*, May 19, 2001. http://www.adherents.com/misc/WCE.html.

Peerenboom, Randall. *China Modernizes: Threat to the West or Model for the Rest?* New York: Oxford University Press, 2007.

Shambaugh, David, ed. *Tangled Titans: The United States and China*. Lanham: Rowman & Littlefield, 2012.

Shirk, Susan L. *China: Fragile Superpower*. 2007. Reprint, New York: Oxford University Press, 2008.

Stauffer, Milton T. *The Christian Occupation of China: A General Survey of the Numerical Strength and Geographical Distribution of the Christian Forces in China*. Shanghai: China Continuation Committee, 1922.

Stinton, Diane. "Africa, East and West." In *An Introduction to Third World Theologies*, edited by John Parratt, 105–36. Cambridge: Cambridge University Press, 2004.

Sutter, Robert G. *US-Chinese Relations: Perilous Past, Pragmatic Present*. 2nd ed. Lanham: Rowman & Littlefield, 2013.

Tennent, Timothy C. *Theology in the Context of World Christianity*. Grand Rapids: Zondervan, 2007.

Thangaraj, M. Thomas. *The Crucified Guru: An Experiment in Cross Cultural Christology*. Nashville: Abingdon, 1994.

The Traveling Team (TTT). "Mission Stats: The Current State of the World." www.thetravelingteam.org/stats.

Usry, Glenn, and Craig S. Keener. *Black Man's Religion: Can Christianity Be Afrocentric?* Downers Grove, IL: InterVarsity, 1996.

Volodzko, David. "China's Confucius Institutes and the Soft War." *The Diplomat*, July 8, 2015. http://thediplomat.com/2015/07/chinas-confucius-institutes-and-the-soft-war.

Yang, Rui. *Third Delight. The Internationalization of Higher Education in China*. New York: Routledge, 2002.

Yeo, K. K. "Biblical Christologies of the Global Church: Beyond Chalcedon? Towards a Fully-Christian and Fully-Cultural Theology." In *Jesus Without Borders*, edited by Gene Green, et al., 162–79. Grand Rapids: Eerdmans, 2015.

———. "Biblical Interpretation in the Majority World." In *The Twentieth Century: Themes in a Global Context*, edited by Mark Hutchinson, 131–69. Vol. 5 of *Oxford History of Dissenting Protestant Traditions*. Oxford: Oxford University Press, 2018.

———. *Chairman Mao Meets the Apostle Paul*. Grand Rapids: Brazos, 2002.

———. "Church and State in China: Home Grown Faith." *The Christian Century*, January 10, 2006, 31–33.

———. *Musing with Confucius and Paul: Toward a Chinese Christian Theology*. Eugene, OR: Cascade, 2008.

———. "Theology and the Future of Global Christianity: Glocal and Public Theologies." In *Theology and the Future: Evangelical Assertions and Explorations*, edited by Trevor Cairney and David Starling, 45–61. Edinburgh: T. & T. Clark, 2014.

Yung, Hwa. *Mangoes or Bananas? The Quest for an Authentic Asian Christian Theology*. Carlisle: Regnum International, 1997.

Zhang, Laney. "China: Revised Regulations on Religious Affairs." *Library of Congress*, November 9, 2017. http://www.loc.gov/law/foreign-news/article/china-revised-regulations-on-religious-affairs.

8

From "Globalization" to "Global Awareness and Engagement"
Perspectives, Challenges, Futures

Lester Edwin J. Ruiz and David Esterline

FROM "GLOBALIZATION" TO "GLOBAL AWARENESS AND ENGAGEMENT"

"Globalization," or what the current Commission on Accrediting of the Association of Theological Schools (ATS) calls "global awareness and engagement,"[1] has been an explicit and central concern of ATS at least since the 1990s—although one can argue that these concerns reach as far back as 1967 with Harvey Cox's reflections on "church-world dialogue for theological education" in the journal *Theological Education*.[2] There are rich

---

1. ATS, *Commission on Accrediting*.

2. Cox, "Significance of Church-World," 270–79. A bit of historical trivia suggests that the need for both awareness about and engagement with "the rest of the world" goes back even further than the 1990s: "We recommend," the minutes of the Ninth Biennial meeting of the Conference of Theological Seminaries and Colleges in the United States and Canada note, "that this Conference assure the [International Missionary] Council of

traditions, perspectives, resources, and practices on "globalization" within ATS, the significance of some still waiting to be rediscovered, further developed, or critically revisited.³ Formal ATS programming in the past ten years at least has not only built on these resources but has also moved ATS discourse toward even more critical and creative directions. These activities have contributed to the deepening and broadening of diversity, mutuality, and equity—core values that have animated not only the long tradition of "globalization" in accredited graduate theological education in general, and within the Association itself in particular, but also in the larger life and work of the Association's member schools.

The move from "globalization" to "global awareness and engagement"—at least as a normative description of that part of the work of theological education that acknowledges that North American theological education is not (or ought not to be) the center of the theological education universe—was not made lightly. Those familiar with the dynamics of ATS as a membership organization know that by the time a normative statement is adopted (or revised) as part of its Standards of Accreditation, ATS member schools would have already undertaken a long and somewhat complex iterative process, including a formal two-thirds "super majority" vote on the Standards themselves.

These complex conversations included deliberations on the substantive, conceptual, methodological, pedagogical, metatheoretical, and political/institutional dimensions of the notion of "globalization" in the Standards, which included revisiting the 1970s-1990s ATS discussions on "globalization" just noted. In the end, ATS adopted the following standard on the "Theological Curriculum: Learning, Teaching and Research" (Standard 3) which contained a section on "the characteristics of theological scholarship" that included patterns of collaboration, freedom of inquiry, relationships with diverse publics, and global awareness and engagement.

---

our genuine interest in theological education in all lands; that we express our conviction that the educational problems of any particular land must be met primarily from within that land; that we express our readiness to share in any possible and desired way in the meeting of these problems; and that we call attention to significant cooperative undertakings already carried out, such as the Deputation of the American Church History Society . . . the study of Christian education in India . . . and the approaching study of theological education in China" (AATS, *Bulletin*, 15).

3. Even the most cursory review of the issues of *Theological Education* will reveal the depth and breadth of this tradition. See, for example, *Theological Education* 9.4; 21.1; 22.2; 26.1.S; 27.1; 27.2; 29.2; 30.1; 35.2. Of direct relevance for this discussion, perhaps, are: ATS, *Theological Education* 26.1.S; 27.2; 35.2.

By "global awareness and engagement," the member schools signaled their desire that

> 3.3.4.1 Theological teaching, learning, and research require patterns of institutional and educational practice that contribute to an awareness and appreciation of global interconnectedness and interdependence, particularly as they relate to the mission of the church. These patterns are intended to enhance the ways institutions participate in the ecumenical, dialogical, evangelistic, and justice efforts of the church.
>
> 3.3.4.2 Global awareness and engagement is cultivated by curricular attention to cross-cultural issues as well as by the study of other major religions; by opportunities for cross-cultural experiences; by the composition of the faculty, governing board, and student body; by professional development of faculty members; and by the design of community activities and worship.[4]

The clear shift of terminology from "globalization" to "global awareness and engagement" in ATS discourse marks an important move within the organization. While there are multiple reasons for this shift, one reading of the ATS conversations, perhaps the dominant one, is related to the pervasive skepticism about the appropriateness or adequacy of the term *globalization* and its consequences for theological education, given its cooptation by (neoliberal) economic, even political (read "western hegemonic") globalization, to characterize ATS's normative vision in this area of theological education. Another reading of this move is tied to the recognition that there are multiple meanings and emphases of *globalization* among ATS member schools—not always commensurable and sometimes deeply contested. Hence the need for less ideological or less polarizing signifiers that would allow for a more inclusive organizational embrace of diversity in this area of work. To be sure, one of the consequences of such a move, perhaps unintended or unforeseen, is that the substantive, methodological, and metatheoretical dimensions of *globalization* became less denotative, compromising thereby the analytical and explanatory capacity of the term—an argument Hendrik Pieterse makes in his chapter in this volume, and which ATS can ignore only at its own peril.

Still a third reading of this move is rooted in assumptions about the nature of human reality and language itself. Here, human experience, because of its *densities*, is not amenable to or exhausted by what Paul Ricoeur

---

4. ATS, *Commission on Accrediting*, 8–9.

called the "moment of explanation" within the larger interpretive framework of explanation, understanding, and appropriation, which the nature of human reality demands because of these assumed densities. In addition, phenomenologically, human experience and its interpretation always include not only a horizon (i.e., a range of vision that includes everything that can be seen from a particular situation, location or vantage point) but also a particular way of grasping totality as an (intentional) amorphous, undifferentiated whole and as a spatial and temporal extension of a particular [Euro-American] way of life. The move away from (western-style) *globalization* in its Anglophone deployments, in fact, is related both to the concept's limitation as a horizon granted universal status and to the fact that it has led us down a pathway that destroys other ways of life that stand in the way of its geopolitical, geostrategic, and geocultural extensions (e.g., colonialism, imperialism, patriarchy, cultural chauvinism, and, more recently, extractivism). Moreover, globalization such as we have inherited it, is almost always accompanied, particularly in the global North, by a fundamental subterranean epistemological temptation to represent the world as an act of a self-sufficient, autonomous, "subject of history."

In other words, without rejecting the need for clarity and rigor about the substantive, conceptional, methodological, pedagogical, metatheoretical, and political/institutional dimensions of "globalization," we are suggesting that part of the reason (perhaps more implicit than explicit) for ATS's move from "globalization" to "global awareness and engagement" has to do with its acknowledgement of the need for a more fulsome definition of the concept. Such a definition would need to meet several desiderata: it is geophysically broader in reach; offers greater rigor and explanatory capacity for the work we do; and supplies a *linguistic* and normative horizon that can "hold together" the diversity of global experiences, institutional priorities, and personal preferences of ATS member schools while honoring the legacy of accredited graduate theological education in terms of its being decidedly normative, thoroughly performative, and intentionally formative.

In this regard, we find the work of French philosopher Jean-Luc Nancy helpful in bringing together what we understand "global awareness and engagement" to mean at this moment of ATS' history. In his book *The Creation of the World or Globalization*, Nancy argues that "world" (*Mondialisation*) in the French language does not always carry with it the connotations of world as "globalization" noted above. Nancy foregrounds *Mondialisation* as that process of differentiation and formation that "maintains a crucial reference to the world's horizon as a space of human relations . . . of meaning held in common . . . of signification or possible signification."[5] In fact, *Mondialisation* places the emphasis not on the *representation* of the world but on the creative act of *forming* a world. And while it is not clear to us that Nancy fully extricates himself from the representational, apophantic dilemma of globalization conventionally understood, the notion of *Mondialisation* with its implicit relational, dialogical, and personal sensibilities opens to the deeper significance of the shift from "globalization" to "global awareness and engagement."

The ATS Standard, in fact, bridges the substantive and definitional aspects of "globalization" (e.g., interconnectedness and interdependence, as well as its multiple forms like ecumenical, dialogical, evangelistic, and justice efforts), with its conceptual and analytical demands (e.g., curriculum, faculty, study of other religions). More important, it specifies the scope of the term (e.g., patterns of institutional and educational practice; the composition of the faculty, governing board, and student body; and the design of community activities and worship). This list is by no means exhaustive. Indeed, the Standard on "global awareness and engagement" turns out to be not only a practice but also a *dispositif*, a landscape or seascape, if you will. Or, to use Nancy's language, the Standard offers a "space of human relations . . . of meaning held in common . . . of signification or possible signification." That is, "global awareness and engagement" is not in the first instance about the representation of the world but rather, about a creation of worlds. Or, in the language of this chapter, which deserves repeating, the Standard is decidedly normative, thoroughly performative, and intentionally formative.

But, how did ATS get to this place? Is there any evidence in the ATS discursive formations of theological education that warrants such an apophantic, declaratory assertion?

"GLOBALIZATION" OR "GLOBAL AWARENESS AND ENGAGEMENT" IN ATS MEMBER SCHOOLS

Three widely accepted macro-historical developments are worth mentioning at the outset, because they pose significant framing implications for the question of "globalization" or "global awareness and engagement" in ATS discourse: (1) the demographic shifts signaled by the cipher "2040"; (2) the

---

5. Nancy, *Creation of World*, 33–55.

shifting "center" of Christianity from the global North to the global South, and (3) the rapid growth of immigrant churches in North America in the past twenty years.

Many ATS member schools have built "global awareness and engagement" directly into the history, mission, and ethos of their institutions. This decision is framed largely, though not exclusively, by a concern about how best to understand the relationship (broadly conceived) between their particular locations as institutions in the United States and Canada and the rest of the world. The purpose of the relationship varies, depending on factors like the following: the worldwide character of the ecclesial family to which the school belongs; its missionary or evangelistic orientation; its geographical location and nature and composition of its faculty and/or student body; and the communities to which it declares both affinities and accountabilities.

Many schools have collaborative degree programs with partner institutions in the "majority world" at the certificate, baccalaureate, post-baccalaureate, and post-masters levels—some in extension education-, distance learning-, or "global consortiums-" formats. Others have faculty exchanges that involve short-term teaching and/or research. Still others have both credit-bearing and noncredit-bearing intercultural and contextual programs (e.g., travel seminars, immersion and contextualization programs, and "missionary" initiatives). Yet others have partnerships with their historic communities of origin, whether global-global, global-south, or south-south.

Some schools have established centers directly related to global awareness and engagement, such as Trinity Evangelical Divinity School's Center for World Christianity and Global Theology; Ambrose Seminary's Jaffray Centre for Global Initiatives; and New York Theological Seminary's Center for World Christianity. Other schools offer Spanish or Mandarin-language courses, while still others have Korean-language degree programs. Some ATS schools have extension sites in Germany, the Ukraine, Indonesia, Guatemala, and Thailand.

While not always uniformly articulated, member schools, in addition to their missional and theological convictions regarding global awareness and engagement, have a wide range of rationales for their programs and initiatives. These rationales include: (1) a recognition that quality and relevance of theological education in North America must not only have an external global reach but must also integrate non-North American theological resources as constitutive of its North American identity; (2) a realization that sustainable quality education should be a globally-shared enterprise, whose survival is inextricably linked to this "global" reciprocity in the production and reproduction of theological knowledge and wisdom; (3) an affirmation that the educational purpose of a "good theological school" or "good theological education" is to prepare students to be global citizens who have the competencies, capacities, and sensibilities appropriate to a fast-changing, interdependent, and globalizing world; and (4) a conviction that any theological education that deserves to be called "good" must be able to embrace, if not navigate, the difficult but necessary intersectionalities between "the global" and "the local."[6]

In the past ten years, due in part to growing interest in ATS outside North America and the globalization of theological education in a shrinking world, ATS staff and other ATS-related individuals have been involved in transborder, transdisciplinary, transorganizational conversations, resource sharing, and cooperative programming with several international partners. These include the Asia Theological Association (ATA), the Association for Theological Education in Southeast Asia (ATESEA), the Foundation for Theological Education in Southeast Asia (FTESEA), the International Council on Evangelical Theological Education (ICETE), the World Conference of Associations of Theological Institutions (WOCATI), and the World Council of Churches' Program on Ecumenical Theological Education (ETE).

These international faith-based organizations and others like them are important partners who rightly perceive that ATS may have much to offer them. In return, no doubt individual ATS member schools, as well as the Association as a whole, have much to learn from theological education outside North American boundaries. Recognizing this growing rediscovery of mutual need, the ATS Board of Directors began to revisit, at least since 2009, the idea and practice of globalization. They engaged in more structured conversations, first in terms of the notion of "ATS as big tent" and then more recently, in terms of the notion of "ATS and world Christianity."

---

6. See, for example, Guider's essay in this volume. See also Roudometof, *Glocalization*.

"GLOBALIZATION" AND "BIG TENT" ECUMENICITY: INSTITUTIONAL, ORGANIZATIONAL, AND PROGRAMMATIC ISSUES

Where "ATS as big tent" is concerned, The Board of Directors convened a working group to explore the subject and review the practice of "big tent ecumenicity." The working group met several times by conference call, with the work culminating in the November 2012 meeting of the Board of Directors. There, the Board decided to pursue the notion of "big tent ecumenicity" largely within a programmatic rather than an administrative/organizational framework, where "big tent" meant the larger Jewish-Christian tradition. While Board members agreed that the Association has reached a level of maturity that allows for robust conversations on theological diversity among its membership,[7] they acknowledged that the administrative/organizational conditions were not congenial at that time for pursuing the question of diversity across religious and multifaith lines. To be sure, some member schools understand their institutional identity in terms of an interreligious perspective (e.g., Claremont School of Theology, Harvard Divinity School, University of Chicago Divinity School, Hartford Seminary, Graduate Theological Union). However, most member schools continue to understand their missions within a North American Jewish-Christian perspective, notwithstanding their recognition of the importance of addressing interreligious and multifaith issues in a variety of ways.[8] World *Christianity*, rather than world *religions*, was affirmed as the primary organizing metaphor for "big tent ecumenicity."[9]

---

7. One way to read Aleshire's "Community and Diversity" plenary address at the 2012 Minneapolis Biennial is as a cipher of the Association's readiness to explicitly address the fundamental importance of theological/ecclesial diversity, in addition to the more conventionally-accepted racial/ethnic, gender, and missional diversities long recognized by the Association, for the meaning of "big tent" ecumenicity. Aleshire, "Community and Diversity."

8. The present interest of the leadership of ATS in "global awareness and engagement" may appear as a "revival" of the work on "globalization" of the 1990s. However, the context is quite different. "Globalization" is now placed within both "big tent" ecumenism and the emphasis on "pastoral practices," reflected, for example, in the "Christian Hospitality and Pastoral Practices in a Multifaith Society" project. Both initiatives have their origins quite apart from "globalization." In our view, these developments have decisively reshaped—for good—this important dimension of accredited graduate theological education, and will most likely guide the future strategic trajectory of ATS engagement outside North America. See ATS, *Theological Education* 47.1.

9. While not explicitly addressing this notion of "big tent" ecumenicity, Namsoon

Thus, in its meetings during this period, the Board agreed to explore more fully the implications of world Christianity for the future of ATS. A logical next step was focused reflection on the meaning and significance of transdisciplinary, transborder, and transorganizational perspectives and practices. In fact, while racial/ethnic and gender diversity under the sign of multiculturalism had its own specific origins in ATS discourse apart from the discourse on "globalization," their co-constitutive character vis-à-vis global awareness and engagement has come to be recognized more fully. Consequently, the need to deal explicitly with the latter has come to the fore once again, this time within a multicultural, multireligious framework. Necessary steps included an affirmation of the need to pursue more systematically at least two substantive and programmatic questions: what should ATS be doing with its member schools in terms of the question of ATS involvement outside North America? What should ATS be doing with its "partners" outside North America (e.g., ATESEA, ICETE, etc.)? The first question fixes its gaze internally, the second externally. Both are important to how ATS as an organization understands global awareness and engagement. These questions are decisive not only to the programmatic direction that ATS should take but also (perhaps, more importantly) to the future of ATS either as a binational organization or as an organization that seeks to engage the world globally in the service of accredited graduate theological education.

In December 2013, the ATS Board of Directors adopted a framework statement to both authorize and guide future ATS work related to Global Awareness and Engagement in six discrete, though fundamentally interconnected, major areas: (1) understanding effective partnerships; (2) global engagement within North America; (3) cultivating scholarly and programmatic "trade routes"; (4) contributing to a pan-Christian conversation on theological education; (5) educational and degree programs of study; and (6) continuing research and care. The statement also underscored the guiding principle that current and future ATS involvement in programs with a global reach must include constituencies and publics that involve mainline,

---

Kang's essay in this volume raises interesting questions about the adequacy or desirability of "big tent" ecumenicity as a substantive, pedagogical, and political framework not only for ATS as a "global" reaching organization, but also for our understanding of globalization itself. While we are not fully convinced that the notion of "planetarization" successfully moves the discourse into more productive and performative dimensions, Kang's challenge cannot be dismissed.

evangelical, and Roman Catholic/Orthodox individuals and groups—a practice for which ATS is known in its work with member schools.[10]

As if both to prefigure and embody this landmark framework statement, in the fall of 2012 a small group of individuals representing some of the ATS mainline member schools and international partners (ATESEA and WCC) met in Pittsburgh to discuss the present and future shape of theological education and the need for developing systematic and intentional partnerships beyond North America in the service of good theological education. Similarly, in the late spring of 2013, a small group of presidents and deans representing some of the ATS evangelical member schools and organizations (e.g., the Overseas Council) met by conference call to address these same issues. In a consultation in Chicago in January 2015 hosted by Catholic Theological Union, Roman Catholic rectors and presidents met to discuss similar issues. Later, in June 2015, ATS convened representatives of member schools engaged in various global partnership programs in Pittsburgh to explore further the meaning and significance of their global partnerships for theological education. Then, in May 2016, ATS coordinated the first meeting of the Global Forum of Theological Educators (GFTE) in Dorfweil, Germany, gathering possibly for the first time ever in one united forum 86 theological educators from 37 countries from the six major Christian confessional families—Orthodox, Roman Catholic, historic Protestant, Evangelical, Pentecostal, and Independent churches. The aim was to learn from one another and, primarily in the context of fellowship, to share about the current situation of theological education and ministerial formation on a global scale.[11] And finally, ATS staff participated in the consultation of ICETE accreditation agencies in Rome in fall 2017. The purpose of this historic gathering was to develop a structure and process "whereby common accreditation standards and benchmarks [can] be developed within the ICETE network among accreditation agencies in consultation with the church."[12]

Meanwhile, two working groups on "global partnerships" in the ATS Educational Models and Practices Project explored, among other things, two issues: what "global partnerships" under the conditions of diversity,

---

10. ATS, *Guidelines on Global Awareness*.

11. These meetings were made possible through existing ATS undesignated funds, a 2013 planning grant from the Henry Luce Foundation, and other donors including *Evangelisches Missionswerk in Deutschland* (EMW) and the Foundation for Theological Education in Southeast Asia (FTESEA).

12. Kassis, "Rome Roadmap."

mutuality, and equity might look like, and how these partnerships can be enacted where unevenness (political, economic, and administrative) is a dominant reality.[13] One group explored matters related to issues of reciprocity, spiritual formation (study abroad/immersion), and international accreditation. This group identified best practices for initiating, practicing, sustaining, and concluding global partnerships. It identified a number of educational principles, including but not limited to excellence, both institutional and educational; diversity and mutuality; experiential and group learning; interreligious faith dialogue; and integrity and accountability. The other group identified crucial issues that in their shared experience arise when considering, initiating, and sustaining global partnerships. This included faculty ownership of the globalization processes in their respective institutions; the need to establish coherence in articulating degrees offered in different global contexts; and the need to investigate the philosophical and theological mindset behind global partnerships. The group also identified challenges and opportunities in global partnerships, including issues of institutional and educational effectiveness, financial viability, and attentiveness to educational principles.

These ATS staff-supported initiatives may be interpreted as a response to ATS's ongoing commitments noted above. However, these initiatives also serve a further goal, namely to enlist individuals and groups within and without North America to help ATS engage two additional tasks in a framework of collaboration and shared wisdom. The first task is to assist ATS to formally and substantively define its role "in the world" as an organization. The second task is to contemplate its role as an actual participant in the wider conversation of theological education as a bearer of multiple forms of knowledge and wisdom. In other words, these initiatives are the enactment of "global engagement" at the level of everyday practice.

In this regard, WOCATI is an example of an important global institutional initiative in which ATS was involved. With ATS support, accrediting agencies around the world convened for "fellowship, academic research, and mutual support." The WOCATI experience raised large strategic questions for ATS that presupposed even broader substantive, not to mention political, questions. These include:

---

13. See, ATS, *Educational Models*, 115–39.

- If ATS were to be involved outside North America, what should that involvement look like: immersion? solidarity? missionary? contextual? dialogue? bilateral? multilateral?[14] Who should be involved?

- What are the dilemmas posed by such an involvement and how should they be addressed? For example, it seems clear that involvements at any of these levels are welcomed by some, and rejected by others (dependence, interdependence, independence). Put somewhat differently, what are the consequences of such involvement?[15]

- If "being involved" or "being available" is an appropriate stance, how does ATS structure institutionally such availability that avoids past mistakes while rejecting the easy response of non-involvement/non-interference? What would this availability cost, in terms of personnel, finances, and other resources?[16]

14. Some of the images of involvement shared by consultation participants included ATS as both "host and guest" (hospitality), resource or broker, companion (accompaniment), or dialogue partner.

15. For example, if the Commission were to extend its scope of accreditation to schools outside North America, as some regional accreditors have, could this create a tiered structure of theological education in other parts of the world based on some kind of favored status achieved by schools that would be recognized by the United States Department of Education by virtue of ATS accreditation? Members of the ATS Board of Directors have advised caution, as part of its commitment to an ethics of "global awareness and engagement," if ATS or the Commission were to move in this direction.

16. See Hendrik Pieterse's insightful discussion of what he labels "globalizing theological education: the ATS conversation," in his chapter in this volume. Indeed, Pieterse's challenge to deal explicitly with "internationalization as interpretive construct in (1) illuminating the nature and meaning of the local and the global in internationalizing higher education, and (2) critiquing and reformulating the rationale, aims, and values in educating beyond borders—to wit, contextualization and mission, respectively," are critical for "global awareness and engagement." We wish only to point out, however, that the ATS conversation on the future of theological education is far more extensive, plural, and far-ranging and far-reaching than what Pieterse's chapter might suggest. And while we agree that ATS's experience with WOCATI may have been exacerbated by a failure to learn from the discourses of "internationalization in higher education," a critical question for ATS may be more about why the discussions of "globalization" between say, the 1960s through the 1990s, were not able to keep in step with the wider conversations in international relations, broadly conceived. Perhaps more importantly, why was ATS not able to bring the rich and textured conversations within ATS, post-1996, that included issues of race, gender, ethnicity, as well as contextualization, diversity, inclusion, and hospitality, into direct and explicit conversations with "globalization" as such, especially since these conversations were happening in higher education at that time? That said, we want to suggest that the linguistic move from "globalization" to "global awareness and engagement" is, in fact, a reflection of the fundamental shift among ATS member schools

These difficult questions notwithstanding, the experience of collaboration globally affirmed ATS's "convening capacity," based not only on its long history as a membership organization but also on its commitment to, if not ability for, "big tent" inclusivity in program and accreditation functions. To be sure, ATS is known internationally primarily for its expertise as an accrediting body—an expertise it has quietly shared with partners in Asia and Africa over a long period of time. However, extending the binational reach of its programs and services to a more multilateral, if not more global level, could certainly serve as yet another contribution to the vitality of theological education in many parts of the world. For example, participants in the consultations mentioned above noted that ATS programs like the Presidents' Intensives, the meetings of the Chief Academic Officers (CAOS), and meetings of other specific groups of administrators and faculty that are offered to member schools might be made available to interested institutions outside North America (the external gaze noted earlier). At the same time, such programming could be developed to have a more "global" content, e.g., the consequences of the presence of visa students in ATS member schools for theological education in North America (the internal gaze). ATS could also (as it has in the past) serve as a resource broker for its international partners, recommending or connecting individuals with ATS-related program or accreditation-related expertise.

Various consultation participants also acknowledged that many of the programs of ATS member schools, whether educational, denominational, or missional, already have some kind of global reach. While there is no pressing need for ATS to provide a coordinating function, still it could serve as a clearing house or informational connectional center for these programs. The ATS database, for example, could be utilized to organize information provided by its member schools related to areas of international interest, and made more available or accessible to partners outside North America, as it now does for its member schools.[17]

---

from a more siloed understanding of "globalization" to a more nuanced, expansive one—granted however, such an integrated approach is still in the "morning of its life."

17. Daniel Aleshire's plenary address at the 2013 ATESEA General Assembly in Silang, Cavite, Philippines—as well as David Esterline's and Lester Edwin J. Ruiz's presentations at the 2011 WOCATI meeting in Johannesburg, South Africa—are illustrative of this transborder information sharing. See Aleshire, "Proceedings and Minutes"; Esterline, "North American Quality"; Ruiz, "Question Concerning Quality." The point, of course, is how ATS can make this valuable information and insight more readily available or accessible in ways that affirm both the importance of "high touch" engagement and the need for more sustainable, efficient, and less labor-intensive methods of dissemination.

Consultation participants also acknowledged that the global reach of ATS needs to be deeply attentive not only to the diversities of mission, theology, polity, and identity both within and without North America, but also that its "global awareness and engagement" must be disciplined by a commitment to mutuality, respect, and care. For example, attentiveness to the unevenness of resources and interpretation of "good theological education" could express itself programmatically in the principled sharing of accreditation expertise, but without extending ATS or Commission membership to schools outside the US and Canada. Or such attentiveness to the importance of mutuality, respect, and care could be expressed by ATS opening its programs to interested theological institutions outside the US and Canada, while ensuring that its modes of delivery do not violate the ecologies of local theological education, including the rights of theological self-determination. ATS could also convene presidents of its member schools together with the presidents of theological schools from outside the US and Canada to discuss what partnership in a global context might mean and offer it as an ongoing resource. In this context, it is clear that ATS engagement recognizes the constitutive necessity for diversity and mutuality, as well as the programmatic implications of equity.

"GLOBALIZATION" AND THEOLOGICAL EDUCATION: BROADER DILEMMAS, CHALLENGES, AND PERSPECTIVES

One could argue that the Global Awareness and Engagement initiative is only about organizational programming, planning, and policy. Happily, it is not. There are a number of broader issues that require attention, even as they exemplify the challenges that theological education has always faced.[18] First, there are definitional and substantive challenges, including: (1) how globalization and theological education are to be understood and linked given the contested and uneven experiences of globalization arising not only out of different, if asymmetrical, institutional and educational resources, priorities, preferences, and commitments, but also the fact that (north Atlantic) globalization, which in its multiple expressions have both

---

See WOCATI, *Challenges and Promises*.

18. The issues discussed in this section have been drawn from the consultations with ATS constituencies (Mainline, Evangelical, and Roman Catholic) held between 2010 and 2013. Funding for these consultations was provided by the Henry Luce Foundation.

constructive and destructive effects on life more generally, is only one among many globalizations alongside Chinese, Islamic, Iberian; (2) what constitutes an adequate theology and ministry for a globalizing world, particularly in relation to historic faith and practice;[19] and (3) how "effective global partnerships" should be defined and by what measures and criteria they are to be assessed.[20]

Second, there are political and institutional push-and-pull challenges, including: (1) "brain drain" (for the global South) vis-à-vis "brain gain" (for the global North); (2) the need to develop self-reliant, self-sufficient, indigenous leadership vis-à-vis mission-driven commitments for resource sharing in a world of declining resources; (3) strong denominational missionary commitments vis-à-vis a recognition of the need for the affirmation of the non-Christian "Other"; (4) the perception of North American power and privilege and their accompanying agenda-setting prerogatives vis-à-vis the ethical and moral imperative for hospitality and mutual accountability in an asymmetrical world; and (5) the singular though not exclusive accountability of US theological education vis-à-vis the rest of theological education elsewhere in the world.

Third, there are educational and pedagogical challenges including: (1) the perceived (often assumed) normativity of English in terms of learning, teaching, and research; (2) the very real differences between and among cultures leading to different understandings of theology and pedagogy (for example, the differences between oral and reading/writing cultures), of rote and constructivist learning, and of egalitarian and authoritarian pedagogies; and (3) the growth of new delivery systems and models of education and mission (including distance/online, extension, and competency-based education) that are based on infrastructural asymmetries in technology and resources, as well as the dominance of an academic and curricular structure and culture that tend to privilege the global North at the expense of the global South.[21]

---

19. This appears to be the burden of E. Byron Anderson's chapter in this volume. We find his taxonomy of educational institutions helpful to understand the intersections of institutional identity, missional identity, and educational identity.

20. An insightful example of the need to explore particular definitions of "globalization" and its consequences, on the one hand for identity, mobility, and theology/ecclesiology, and on the other hand for pedagogy, workforce, and finances, as well as innovation and change, is the chapter by Brent Waters in this volume.

21. In this regard, see the chapter by K. K. Yeo in this volume. See also Ruiz, "Revisiting Question," 1–25.

Fourth, there are programmatic challenges related to educational initiatives (whether degree-granting or not) among ATS member schools. Consider, for example, initiatives that involve international extension sites. Issues like the following arise: (1) the viability, sustainability, and desirability of such programs; the role of partner institutions in the implementation of these programs; the effects of global North-run programs on the ecology of theological education in the global South; (2) the role of North American educational institutions, including theological ones, in the credentialing needs and desires of individuals and institutions outside the US and Canada; for example, direct accreditation or assistance in the development, implementation, or improvement of their own practices of accreditation.

EFFECTIVE PARTNERSHIPS: THE RELIGIO-MORAL DIMENSION OF GLOBAL AWARENESS AND ENGAGEMENT

These challenges are illustrative of the complexity of "global awareness and engagement" and instructive for understanding the deeper, perhaps less visible, religio-moral character of global awareness and engagement. By definition, the religio-moral is fundamentally about "what we can and need to do together in the light of what is deemed as 'the good, the true, and the beautiful.'" One way to interpret the work both of ATS member schools and the Association's own initiatives is as a reflection of, and a desire to, engage with Others. What is notable in this regard are the religio-moral assumptions they share, namely, that global awareness and engagement are fundamentally about the practice of effective partnerships. Such partnerships include those institutional, educational, and personal practices that are animated by and enhanced at the broadest levels: mutuality and collegiality, shared responsibility, accountability, transparency, and decision-making between and among the partners at whatever level or kind, with clearly agreed upon purposes that empower and transform those in the partnerships, and that are contextualized, sustainable, useful, and attainable. In short, effective partnerships are normative, value-explicit human activity.

Effective partnerships further illustrate the religio-moral, especially when they include those practices that emphasize the desirability of multilateral, multilayered, and multi-perspectival strategies and voices that (1) seriously attend to the intersectionality of the issues related to "global awareness and engagement," including issues around the dialogical, ecumenical, evangelistic, and justice efforts of faith-based communities (including churches); (2) broaden and deepen collaborations, particularly in terms of inclusion, plurality, and difference; and (3) are intentionally sensitive to the nuances and specificities of asymmetrical space, time, and place. The religio-moral is articulated even more fully in those initiatives that encourage interdependence and relative autonomy in global North-South and South-South relationships, that empower those involved in the partnership, that flatten power differentials that arise out of the unevenness of human, financial, and physical resources, and of history and location. A more intentional multidirectional flow of resources between the global North and the global South, where the notion of resources is redefined in more comprehensive terms than just human, financial, or physical, is illustrative.

Effective partnering as religio-moral practice also includes the formation of a spirituality that is articulated in: (1) the enhancement and improvement of individual and institutional capacities and skillsets for cross-cultural, contextual, interfaith, and multifaith competencies for institutional and educational innovation and change; (2) the knowledge of, sensitivity to, and respect for economic, cultural, and religious differences that shape theological education and practice worldwide; (3) the development and nurture of shared ideals, values, and principles among and between the partnering individuals and institutions; (4) the constitutive and regulative practice of active, empathic, principled, and humble listening, as well as translation and appropriation; and (5) the sobering fact that partnerships take a long time to develop and require trust for their full flowering. The importance of such a spirituality cannot be underestimated, because our generation is heir to an insidious, subterranean spirit of indifference, not only to others but also to the excluded Others, which if left unchecked will compromise the possibility of any kind of partnership—if it has not done so already.

In sum, "global awareness and engagement" cannot be understood apart from the kind of institutional, educational, and personal relationships that characterize such awareness and engagement. Moreover, effective partnerships constitute the meaning, significance, and definition of "global awareness and engagement" itself. Such partnerships are clearly normative and value-explicit: they articulate what communities of faith deem to be of value to their mission and identity. Furthermore, they are fundamentally performative. They come into being as they are lived out and have no meaning apart from this enactment—which means they belong in the public arena and ought to be accountable to the *res publica*. Finally, they are intentionally and unavoidably formative. They are about the creation, nurture, and living out of character, virtue, and skills (what one might also call "embodied spirituality"). Whether this trajectory—the location, embodiment, and definition of the shift from "globalization" to "global awareness and engagement" in "effective global partnerships"—will prove to be the right path for theological education in North America remains to be seen. But in our view, it is clear that this is probably the way to live into the full meaning of "global awareness and engagement," without which theological education in North America is unlikely to flourish.

CONCLUSION: A DIFFERENT KIND OF "GLOBAL AWARENESS AND ENGAGEMENT"?

If nothing else, this chapter has sought to demonstrate that "globalization" and its shift to "global awareness and engagement" can historically, existentially, and even theologically be comprehended as being about effective, loving, embodied partnerships. Such partnerships, in the context of ATS, are foregrounded as "big tent ecumenicity" that includes theological/ecclesial diversity in addition to the more conventionally accepted racial/ethnic, gender, and missional diversities long recognized by member schools. And where these reach to "the global," they have included, based on shared values, constituencies and publics that involve Mainline, Evangelical, and Roman Catholic/Orthodox individuals and groups—a practice for which ATS is known in its work among its member schools. The diverse gifts and virtues that these communities of faith bring to the table, when taken together and bound by love, will not only inspire but also fundamentally shape what ATS calls the "improvement and enhancement of [both] theological schools [and theological education] to the benefit of communities of faith and the broader public."[22]

We suggest, therefore, that the future of theological education in North America, particularly in the setting of ATS, will depend largely on how ATS lives out its commitments to "global awareness and engagement." Moreover, at least in the ATS context, we believe that the kind of engagement exemplified in the work of the Global Forum of Theological Educators (GFTE), a

22. See ATS, "About ATS."

relatively new organization which ATS has helped to bring into being as part of its Global Awareness and Engagement initiative, is how ATS can live fully into its future as a theological institution. We conclude this chapter by telling the GFTE story, while underscoring important lessons learned.

GFTE (http://gfte.org) was designed to provide an opportunity for leaders in theological education from every Christian tradition to meet and learn from those doing similar work but whose faith tradition might be different from their own. The purpose of GFTE is primarily to provide a common platform for theological educators to share experiences and explore commitments and areas for potential collaboration. GFTE is not controlled by or aligned with any one group but provides an opportunity for mutual learning from each of the six Christian ecclesial families: Orthodox, Roman Catholic, Historical Protestant, Evangelical, Pentecostal, and Independent (primarily from Africa and China). Participants engage in the GFTE as individuals (and may be faculty members, leaders of institutions or denominations, or otherwise responsible for or engaged in theological education) rather than as formal representatives of particular groups or associations—a clear contrast, for example, to the organizational structure of WOCATI and its relationship with ATS. *In other words, personal engagement free from the obligations of formally representing an historic organization is a critical part of engagement at a global level.*

The vision for the GFTE comes from the long-recognized need for a place for theological educators from different denominations and Christian traditions to get to know one another, share experiences and commitments, and develop trust across the traditional boundaries. In North America, of course, this opportunity is provided by ATS at its biennial and other meetings. But such opportunities have not regularly existed in other parts of the world. Outside of North America, global gatherings are usually limited to particular groups, and are often few and far between. Conversations take place among ecumenical Protestants, among evangelicals, among Roman Catholics, among Orthodox—but with only occasional crossing of the long-established boundaries between groups. *In other words, the basis of engagement is not necessarily a shared framework but, rather, a shared space where each one feels he or she can belong, even if only temporarily, and where faith and not belief is foundational.*

After a number of years of planning meetings in different parts of the world (going back to 2013)—meetings that intentionally included fellowship and sharing in the midst of business agendas—GFTE held its inaugural meeting on May 16–20, 2016, at *Familienferienstätte Dorfweil* near Frankfurt, Germany, with 86 participants from 37 countries. The three-and-a-half-day agenda included Bible study, worship, and table conversations. These conversations took place at round tables, with individuals from each of the six ecclesial families at each table. These table conversations were the primary agenda for the meeting. Rather than focus on the presentation of papers, in the usual tradition of academic meetings, participants focused on conversations with one another, intentionally across the usual boundaries. The goal was that everyone would become better acquainted, share thoughts and experiences related to the education of pastors and Christian leaders, and better understand one another's work and contexts. To begin the conversation, brief presentations were given on six broad topics related to theological education. Then participants turned to the others at their tables to pick up the conversation themselves. The six major themes were (1) the unique gifts each ecclesial family brings to the common table; (2) how theological education forms people for ministry; (3) integrity and leadership; (4) what geographical and ecclesial contexts offer to theological education; (5) the role of theological education in God's mission in the world; and (6) the role of theological education for the future of global Christianity. In addition to these six sessions, one session brought participants together in geographical groups and another in ecclesial family groups. Each day began with worship (led by a different tradition) and Bible study, again followed by table conversation. *In other words, the preferred modality of engagement is dialogue and conversation, where I and Thou can meet in the context of shared difference and "a deep sense of humility and of mutual openness in prayer."*

The role of ATS in the development of GFTE has been significant, primarily due to ATS's reputation as inclusive and not privileging one group or ecclesial family over another. Since a primary objective of GFTE is to develop trust among theological educators across the long-established boundaries, ATS's well-known commitment to maintaining a "big tent" in which everyone is welcome and no particular agenda is allowed to take precedence over others has been particularly important. The longstanding mistrust between ecclesial families (as, for instance, is often the case between those aligned with the World Council of Churches and those in the World Evangelical Alliance) often means that individuals in one group are unwilling to accept an invitation to a gathering hosted by a different group. When ATS serves as the inviting agency, there is much greater readiness to participate. The funding and administrative support provided by ATS has also been very helpful. However, GFTE should not become identified solely as an ATS entity. Part of the success thus far has to do with GFTE's independence. Several participants indicated that the success of the first global meeting was due in part to the fact that participants were responsible for their own travel and contributed to the cost of the meeting as a whole. It should also be recognized that GFTE is valuable in a number of ways to ATS member schools, including the way it provides opportunities for individual relationships and the development of institutional partnerships and modeling the trust between ecclesial families that is a central ATS commitment. *In other words, mutuality and reciprocity within a shared understanding of self-determination and equality is a crucial assumption for engagement where resources do not become a condition for participation.*

As described by one participant, "People talked across boundaries—both ecclesial and geographical—that many participants had not crossed previously. Perhaps more importantly, people listened to commitments of persons from Christian families that they had not heard before." The second GFTE meeting took place on May 20-24, 2019, at the Orthodox Academy of Crete in Kolympari, Crete, with the theme "Vision and Viability in Contexts: Theological Learning and Formation."

We close with excerpts from the concluding message of the first Global Forum of Theological Educators. They are as instructive as they are prophetic.

> We are living in a critical stage of World Christianity. The landscapes of Christian traditions are changing dramatically—in some countries the existence of Christianity is under threat and Christian minorities are challenged to remain steadfast in hostile environments; there are institutional frameworks of theological education that are crumbling; there is growing religious illiteracy and ignorance that help foster prejudice and extremism; theological institutions are often under pressure to conform to government or other external forms of accreditation requirements. In our many contexts we realize again that unity and cooperation in theological education beyond the traditional divides are not a luxury or mere specialized vocation for some but are essential to the future of theological education. Cooperation and dialogue in theological formation are required for the majority of settings in which the church finds itself in the twenty-first century.
>
> We are aware that we can complement each other and need each other with the different gifts we bring to the common table

in the area of theological education. The need to overcome stereotypes and caricatures of each other is crucial not just for theological education but also for our witness in a world that is torn apart by wars, violence and so many types of injustice. We have been made aware of the need to continue conversations started in this first gathering, to foster friendships and collaboration birthed from our dialogue, and to seek together, as educators, to work toward transformative theological education that serves the churches and God's kingdom.[23]

BIBLIOGRAPHY

Aleshire, Daniel. "Community and Diversity." Plenary address at the ATS Biennial Meeting, Minneapolis, MN, June 20–22, 2012.

———. "Proceedings and Minutes of the Association for Theological Education in South East Asia." General Assembly, Adventist International Institute of Advanced Studies, Silang, Cavite, Philippines, March 25–27, 2013.

American Association of Theological Schools (AATS). *Bulletin* 9 (1934) 15.

Association of Theological Schools (ATS). "About ATS." https://www.ats.edu/about.

———. *Commission on Accrediting: General Institutional Standards*. Pittsburgh: ATS, 2015. https://www.ats.edu/uploads/accrediting/documents/general-institutional-standards.pdf#pagemode=bookmarks.

———. *Educational Models and Practices Peer Group Final Reports*. Pittsburgh: ATS, 2017. https://www.ats.edu/uploads/resources/current-initiatives/educational-models/publications-and-presentations/peer-group-final-reports/peer-group-final-report-book.pdf.

———. *Guidelines on Global Awareness and Engagement from ATS Board of Directors*. Pittsburgh: ATS, 2013. https://www.ats.edu/uploads/accrediting/documents/guidelines-on-global-awareness-and-engagement-from-ats-board%20%282013%29.pdf.

———. *Theological Education* 9.4.S (1973).
———. *Theological Education* 11.1 (1984).
———. *Theological Education* 22.2 (1986).
———. *Theological Education* 26.1.S (1990).
———. *Theological Education* 27.1 (1990).
———. *Theological Education* 27.2 (1991).
———. *Theological Education* 29.2 (1993).
———. *Theological Education* 30.1 (1993).
———. *Theological Education* 35.2 (1999).
———. *Theological Education* 47.1 (2012).

Cox, Harvey. "The Significance of the Church-World Dialogue for Theological Education." *Theological Education* 3.2 (1967) 270–79.

---

23. GFTE, "Concluding Message."

Esterline, David. "North American Quality Standards in Theological Education." Paper presented at the 2011 WOCATI Consultation, Johannesburg, South Africa, July 6, 2011.

Global Forum of Theological Educators (GFTE). "Concluding Message of the Global Forum of Theological Educators." *Asia Theological Association*, June 30, 2016. http://www.ataasia.com/concluding-message-of-the-global-forum-of-theological-educators-gfte.

Kassis, Riad. "Rome Roadmap." Facebook. November 15, 2017. https://www.facebook.com/groups/1241553362592175.

Nancy, Jean-Luc. *The Creation of the World or Globalization*. Translated by Francois Raffoul and David Pettigrew. Albany: State University of New York, 2007.

Roudometof, Victor. *Glocalization: A Critical Introduction*. New York: Routledge, 2016.

Ruiz, Lester Edwin J. "The Question Concerning Quality in Theological Education." Paper presented at the 2011 WOCATI Consultation, Johannesburg, South Africa, July 5, 2011.

———. "Revisiting the Question Concerning (Theological) Contextualization." *Journal of Race, Ethnicity, and Religion* 3.2.4 (2012) 1–25.

World Conference of Associations of Theological Institutions (WOCATI). *Challenges and Promises of Quality Assurance in Theological Education: Multicontextual and Ecumenical Inquiries*. Geneva: WOCATI, 2013. https://www.oikoumene.org/en/resources/documents/wcc-programmes/education-and-ecumenical-formation/ete/wocati/challenges-and-promises-of-quality-assurance-in-theological-education/@@download/file/WOCATI_quality_assurance_%20theological_education2013.pdf.

www.ingramcontent.com/pod-product-compliance
Lightning Source LLC
Chambersburg PA
CBHW051742230426
43670CB00012B/2130